Compassion and Community

Compassion and Community:

AN APPRAISAL OF THE CHURCH'S CHANGING ROLE IN SOCIAL WELFARE

By Haskell M. Miller

ASSOCIATION PRESS • NEW YORK

6|20|85

COMPASSION AND COMMUNITY

Copyright © 1961 by National Board
of Young Men's Christian Associations

Association Press, 291 Broadway, New York 7, N.Y.

Library of Congress catalog card number: 61–7465

Printed in the United States of America

To Ada, among whose many talents is the ability
to endure a husband who writes books

Foreword

There is a need for a book which depicts clearly the relationship of the church to social welfare and to the social welfare agencies working in the community. The historical role of the church in social welfare has been clear for many centuries. Sometimes it has been seen through direct almsgiving, but increasingly in modern times through institutions such as hospitals and homes. However, this role has been changing as non-church private agencies and government agencies have become involved substantially in rendering welfare services.

Some of the questions that need examination are: What is the historical role of the churches and how does it relate to the new and changing social welfare needs of people in a complex and urbanized society? What should be the relationship of the church to the professional social worker? What new and pioneer services should the church offer? How can the church encourage its members to enter social welfare professions? What is the responsibility of the local church for social welfare in its community? How should the local church be related to the many agencies of social welfare which are now in the community?

The Board of Social and Economic Relations of The Methodist Church decided to launch a project to attempt to answer these and other questions. The result is this book.

The Board gave responsibility to a subcommittee. The members of the Committee are:

CIVIC AND SOCIAL WELFARE COMMITTEE
Mrs. James Oldshue, *Chairman*

The Rev. W. Henry Goodloe, *Vice-Chairman*
Mrs. R. G. Pullen, *Vice-Chairman*
The Rev. Monroe J. Wilcox, *Secretary*
Mrs. Edward R. Bartlett
Dr. James P. Brawley
The Rev. James W. Bristah
Dr. Georgia Harkness
Bishop Bachman G. Hodge
Miss Sue Hudson
The Hon. Daniel C. Jenkins
Mrs. John Paul Odom
Mr. D. Stewart Patterson
Bishop Hazen G. Werner

This Committee engaged Dr. Haskell M. Miller, Professor of Social Ethics at Wesley Theological Seminary, Washington, D.C. to be
their author. Deep appreciation is due to the work of the Committee,
under Mrs. Oldshue, and to the author for dedicated, intensive, and
highly competent work.

In addition to the Committee, the entire Board of Social and
Economic Relations spent many hours in reviewing the plans and
the manuscript. Many other persons in other agencies of The
Methodist Church, such as the Board of Education, the Woman's
Division, the Board of Missions, and agencies outside of the church,
were invaluable as critics of the manuscript.

Association Press agreed to publish the book and engaged, as
consultant, Dr. William J. Villaume, the Executive Director of the
Department of Social Welfare of the National Council of Churches,
who acted as a most valuable critic and who supplied data to update
the material at every point, and was thus instrumental in bringing
the book to its final form.

The National Council of Churches is sponsoring the Second
National Conference on the Churches and Social Welfare in October
1961. The book is offered with pleasure to the National Council
and to those who will attend the Conference.

The Board of Social and Economic Relations of The Methodist
Church is delighted also to make this book available to the Division
of Temperance and General Welfare of the new Board of Christian
Social Concerns of The Methodist Church, which will assume re-

sponsibility for most of the areas of social welfare dealt with in the book.

Thus, many people have been involved in the development of the project, and many will be involved in its utilization. And to all we express the hope that this book will be an honor to the Lord whom we serve and be one of His instruments to sharpen the social witness of His church in the world as it attempts to meet the welfare and health needs of people.

ALFRED DUDLEY WARD, *General Secretary*
Board of Social and Economic Relations
The Methodist Church

Table of Contents

Introduction

Of all the phenomenal developments of modern times, none are more significant in the Western World than those that go under the heading of "social welfare." These are the developments to which the sensitivity of spirit nurtured in the Christian tradition and the dedicated genius represented in science and technology have steadfastly pointed. They are the logical fruit for which the tree of Western culture has been pruned and tended. In their proliferating expression at the middle of the twentieth century they are but the "first fruits," full of promise of richer blessings to come.

Men are finding ways of living together in mutual helpfulness in the great organizational structures of modern corporate life. They are discovering how to make the corporate process serve the needs of all the individuals of whom the society is composed. Slowly and clumsily, but nonetheless surely, they are accepting the fact that the highest welfare of each individual is embraced in maximum provision for the welfare of all.

The Christian Church is the mother of these insights in Western society. Science and technology are maximizing opportunities for demonstrating their validity.

The situation as it relates to social welfare in the United States is especially dynamic. Social services of all kinds are rapidly expanding. At the same time considerable confusion is being generated. While little debate exists concerning the importance of making the total social order serve the best interests of all the people, there is much uncertainty as to how it may best be made to do so.

In the meantime, social work is becoming a highly skilled profession, and vast secular programs of social security and social service, supported principally by government, are assuming impressive dimensions.

The Protestant Church in America, engulfed in what appears to be almost a tidal wave of these developments, is in a peculiarly significant position. In a very real sense it is experiencing a crisis with respect to its relationship to social welfare—a crisis on the outcome of which the quality of the church's future relationship to the whole of American culture may largely depend.

While there is danger in crisis, let it be noted that there is also opportunity. This book is written to help the Protestant churches of America assess the nature of the crisis with which welfare developments are confronting them. Though a part of the intention is to point to the dangers against which the churches must be on guard, the larger purpose is to underscore the unparalleled opportunity which the Protestant Church as a whole has in America at the present time in connection with what is happening in social welfare. The book makes an unabashed plea for a vigorous, intelligent, and enthusiastic appropriation of this opportunity. At the same time it recognizes the practical hazards and serious adjustment difficulties that are involved in such an appropriation.

Actually, the book is addressed to two audiences. Primarily it attempts to speak to thoughtful Protestant churchmen who are concerned with the tide of events, and who are seeking understanding of the role the church should continue to take in social welfare. Secondarily, but hopefully, it invites consideration by the dedicated professional people in all branches of social work and welfare administration who are seeking ways of maintaining maximum value-relatedness in what they are doing, and who are anxious to keep social work and social welfare programs positively affiliated with the validities of the Christian faith.

Frank recognition is given to the fact that there is confusion in the minds of churchmen over how to react to the secularization and professionalization of social work, and in the minds of social workers over what place religion and co-operation with the church should have in the practice of their profession. Some of the reasons for such consequent estrangement as exists between the church and social work are explored. Churchmen are importuned to take the initiative in eliminating this estrangement.

The writer would hardly have had the temerity to undertake so large a task as the theme of the book represents if he had not been requested to do so by the Committee on Civic and Social Welfare of the Board of Social and Economic Relations of The Methodist Church. To this Committee and each of its members he is deeply indebted for encouragement, inspiration, and practical guidance. Back of the Committee, furthermore, and of the project from its inception, was the keen perception and invaluable guiding genius of the Reverend A. Dudley Ward, Executive Secretary of the Board.

A special word of appreciation is due several other agencies of The Methodist Church also, for providing consultants to help plan, review, and edit the manuscript in its first revisions. These agencies include the Editorial Division of the General Board of Education, the Woman's Division of Christian Service, the Board of Hospitals and Homes, and the Board of Temperance.

In the final stages of revision, Dr. William J. Villaume and his staff of the Department of Social Welfare of the National Council of the Churches of Christ in the U.S.A. were of immeasurable assistance in correcting and supplementing data, and in suggesting many important changes and additions. Dr. Villaume graciously permitted extensive borrowing from unpublished manuscripts of several of his recent speeches for the composition of the section in Chapter III which has to do with church and state relations. To him also is due credit for securing permission to use the notes prepared by Miss Inez M. Cavert, which form the basis for the discussion in Chapter II of the role of the Protestant churches in the history of welfare developments in the United States.

The writer is also indebted to Professors John B. Howes and Clifford Ham, his colleagues in the Department of Social Ethics at Wesley Theological Seminary, for their help and encouragement. Professor Howes read the manuscript in its entirety and commented insightfully on it. Professor Ham wrote the section in Chapter VI on the subject of housing and urban renewal.

Since the writer can make little claim to originality in what is presented here, he wishes to underscore his great indebtedness to the many persons whose ideas, both in and out of print, have helped to focus and sharpen his thinking. Though he has tried faithfully to give footnote credit where credit is due, he is fully aware that so large a debt cannot be adequately discharged in so casual a manner.

HASKELL M. MILLER

Wesley Theological Seminary
Washington, D.C.

Compassion and Community

I: The Church in the Historic Background

Throughout its history the Christian Church has been deeply involved in the concerns and activities which are usually classified under the heading of social welfare.[1] In some respects it has added new dimensions to the human impulse to charity. As Professor Latourette has pointed out, its ideal requiring not only charitable contributions but also actual self-giving of the rich and the poor through personal ministrations to the needs of the unfortunate seems to have been, in its emphasis, "new, not only in the

---

[1] The term "social welfare" is somewhat ambiguous. Among the most noteworthy attempts to define it are the following: "the state of well-being of all people" (*Policy and Strategy in Social Welfare: Report to the Churches*. N.Y.: National Council of the Churches of Christ in the U.S.A., 1957, pp. 18f); "the organized system of social services and institutions, designed to aid individuals and groups to attain satisfying standards of life and health" (Walter A. Friedlander, *Introduction to Social Welfare*. Englewood: Prentice-Hall, Inc., 1955, p. 4); "an organized concern of all people for all people" Gertrude Wilson and Gladys Ryland, *Social Group Work Practice*. Boston: Houghton-Mifflin Co., 1949, p. 16). The term, which has evolved in comparatively recent times, not only covers conventional provisions for charity but also embraces a vast assortment of protective and helpful arrangements for all members of society made necessary (and possible) by conditions of modern life with which traditional social institutions were not adequately prepared to cope. Along with such terms as "social services" and "social agencies," it is used to indicate the specialized agencies and programs which are being provided to assure that the basic economic, health, educational, and life-adjustment needs of all persons will be cared for to at least a minimal degree.

Graeco-Roman world, but among the rest of the human race."[2]

It must not be assumed, however, that charity began with or has ever been an exclusive monopoly of the Christian Church. Though the church's teachings and works in this field have had great influence on social welfare, particularly in the Western world, it must be noted that motivations to aid the weak and to provide for the common welfare did not originate with the church. Furthermore, they have not necessarily always been best expressed in practice by the church during the period of its history.

For this reason it seems desirable to begin this discussion of the relationship of the church to social welfare with a review of some of the more salient points in the historical background. In so doing, (1) the part which the church has played and the role which it should continue to play in social welfare may be made more understandable; (2) a perspective may be developed for interpreting the consequences of the church's shrinking proportion of services in the welfare field; and (3) a foundation may be laid for bringing the church and other agencies laboring for social welfare into a more appreciative relationship with one another.

The Earliest Beginnings

As anthropology and sociology have been making clear, human society is itself witness to the fact that men have always been at least as interested in helping each other as they have been in taking destructive advantage of one another. Within their own limited, intimate groups the principle of mutual assistance and of the responsibility of the strong to protect and provide for the weak has been clearly established from the most ancient times. Despite such occasional exceptions as those represented in infanticide, abandoning or killing the aged, sick, or handicapped, and cruelty to the insane and the criminal, which were usually induced by hard living conditions or by errors of interpretation, this principle has provided the basis for family life, for government, for community, and for most, if not all, the major social institutions.

Though there has always been competition, there has also always

---

[2] Kenneth Scott Latourette, *A History of the Expansion of Christianity*, Vol. I, "The First Five Centuries" (N.Y.: Harper & Brothers, 1937), p. 268.

been co-operation. In fact, such values as those which competition has produced seem generally to have been dependent in one way or another upon a framework of co-operation. Society could never have existed without mutual aid and sensitive responsiveness to the needs of the weak and helpless. The dependency of the mother and infant during the long period of human maturation is commonly cited as a focal point of societal development.

Because charity and mutual helpfulness were so practical and apparently carried something of a natural appeal to human conscience they were early identified as positive virtues and embraced, in one fashion or another, as ideals by practically all religions. To be sure, the atomized kinship, tribal, racial, political, and other arrangements of society have often imposed serious restrictions upon the interpretation and expression of these virtues, as well as upon religious ideals generally. But within these restrictions, and often transcending them, the ideals of charity and mutual aid have almost universally been upheld as valid.

As society has advanced, however, from simple kinship groupings into larger and more highly organized patterns the arrangements for assuring the expression of these virtues have had to be altered from time to time in the direction of more formal and comprehensive organization. The first steps toward formal benevolent arrangements apparently involved formal religion, and there seems ever since to have been a complementary relationship between the development of organized charity and that of organized religion. It remains to be seen whether or not that relationship is being seriously altered in the modern era.

The Shaman, or medicine-man priest, seems to have been one of the first specialists to emerge as food-gathering kinship groups grew into larger and larger tribes. He was a result of his group's sense of weakness and need, but was also a symbol of its unity and fellowship. His activities were defined largely by the group's concern for its most unfortunate members. Around him organized religion developed. Upon him gradually devolved responsibility for leadership in the care of the sick, the helpless, and the otherwise unfortunate. Thus, in time, benevolence and charity naturally became major emphases in organized religion and were interpreted

as being among the loftiest expressions of religious devotion.]
These emphases are evident, in varying form and degree, in almost
all known religions, whether ancient or modern; and rendering aid
to one's fellows, particularly to the helpless, is almost everywhere
a primary religious duty.[3]

The Old Testament

There can be little denying, however, that the religion of the Hebrews
as reflected in the Old Testament represented a more highly and
consistently ethical emphasis than any of the religions which had
preceded it. The Hebrews, better than any other people, came to
understand God as an absolutely ethical being who always dealt
with men in terms of fairness, justice, and compassion. From this
understanding of Him they were led into an exceptional awareness
of their own ethical responsibility in their relationships with one
another. This awareness is expressed again and again in the law,
the history, the messages of the prophets, and the devotional literature which became their sacred scriptures.

The codes of law, developed around 621 B.C. and laid down in
Deuteronomy and Leviticus, dealt with such matters as freedom,
equality, relief of debtors, redistribution of the land, and the care
of widows, orphans, and the destitute. The tithe of produce each
third year was to be stored up in the towns for the support of the
Levite, "the sojourner, the fatherless, and the widow" (Deut.
14:28–29). It was commanded that "you shall not harden your
heart or shut your hand against your poor brother, but you shall
open your hand to him, and lend him sufficient for his need, whatever it may be" (Deut. 15:7–8). In order that no man's poverty
would become a condition of permanent embarrassment, all debtors
were to be released from their obligations every seven years. Prosti-
tution and slavery were outlawed; it was required that runaway
slaves be given refuge and not returned to their masters (Deut.
23:15). It was permissible for a hungry person to eat grain or fruit
in any man's field or vineyard at any time (Deut. 23:24–25). Forgotten sheaves and second-round gleanings of olive trees, vineyards,

---

[3] Friedlander, *op. cit.*, p. 9.

and grain fields were to be left for "the sojourner, the fatherless, and the widow" (Deut. 24:19–22). The land was to rest each seventh year and such harvests as grew of themselves on it were to be available for food to anyone who had need of them. Each fiftieth year was to be a year of jubilee when all individual titles to land were surrendered, and the propertyless, as well as the propertied, returned to a basis of equality on the land of their fathers (Lev. 25). Poor and needy hired servants, whether brethren or strangers, were not to be oppressed, and must be given their pay on the day they earned it (Deut. 24:14).

Though many of these laws, and numerous others similar to them, were probably never faithfully kept, they reflect a quality of ethical sensitivity which continued to be dynamic through all of subsequent Hebrew history. The prophets in particular articulated and enlarged upon the spirit expressed in them.

Among the evils which Amos, the shepherd of Tekoa, denounced were failing to remember the "covenant of brotherhood," casting off "all pity," ripping up women with child in order to enlarge borders, selling "the righteous for silver, and the needy for a pair of shoes," trampling "the head of the poor into the dust of the earth," and turning aside "the way of the afflicted" (Amos 1, 2). His vehemence was focused especially upon the rich, including the society women ("cows of Bashan"), "who oppress the poor, who crush the needy" (Amos 4:1), and upon the judges, "who afflict the righteous, who take a bribe, and who turn aside the needy in the gate" (Amos 5:12).

Micah cries out against the callousness of oppressors "who hate the good and love the evil, who tear the skin from off my people, and their flesh from off their bones; who eat the flesh of my people, and flay their skin from off them, and break their bones in pieces, and chop them up like meat in a kettle, like flesh in a caldron" (Mic. 3:2–3). "What," he asks, "does the Lord require of you but to do justice, and to love kindness, and to walk humbly with your God?" (Mic. 6:8).

While space does not permit a summary of the messages of all the prophets, it would be unpardonable not to mention Isaiah, in whom these sentiments and sensitivities came to their loftiest expression.[4] He preached against injustice, greed, and corruption, deploring the exploitation and oppression of the poor, the widow, and the orphan. He admonished the people of Israel to "cease to do evil, learn to do good; seek justice, correct oppression; defend the fatherless, plead for the widow" (Isa. 1:16–17). In a burst of great inspiration he proclaimed: "The spirit of the Lord God is upon me, because the Lord has anointed me to bring good tidings to the afflicted; he has sent me to bind up the broken-hearted, to proclaim liberty to the captives, and the opening of the prison to those who are bound" (Isa. 61:1).

Similar themes are repeated many times, also, in the Psalms. "The needy shall not always be forgotten, and the hope of the poor shall not perish for ever" (Ps. 9:18), declared the Psalmist, enjoining God to place a curse upon the man who "did not remember to show kindness, but pursued the poor and needy and the broken-hearted to their death" (Ps. 109:16). "Blessed," he sang, "is he who considers the poor!" (Ps. 41:1).

Jesus

The prophetic message of Isaiah 61:1 became a central theme of Jesus' ministry. The story of the wilderness temptation reflects his commitment to the role of a "suffering servant," and the scripture he chose for his homecoming message to the people of Nazareth began with: "The Spirit of the Lord God is upon me, because the Lord has anointed me to bring good tidings to the afflicted." His comment, upon finishing the reading of this passage, was, quite significantly: "Today this scripture has been fulfilled in your hearing" (Luke 4:21).[5]

Jesus taught that God is a loving Father who is deeply concerned

---

[4] Though some biblical scholars seem to feel that there was more than one Isaiah, the Book of the "second Isaiah" beginning with Chapter 40, this point is not material to our discussion.

[5] It may be, of course, that, as the rest of this account suggests, Jesus was on this occasion interpreting the reference to apply more to the affliction of his neighbors' prejudice and bigotry than to that of their physical need. In either case, his concern was essentially the same.

for all persons, from the smallest and most innocent child to the worst adult sinner, and that the only proper basis for men's relationships to one another, as well as for their relationship to God, is that of sincere love. The law of obedient love, he declared, which takes its cue from the nature of God rather than from worthiness in any other object of love, is supreme, even as Moses and the prophets had pointed out, and must take precedence over every other consideration. His Good Samaritan parable, given in support of this emphasis, has probably done more to encourage humanitarianism and social welfare than any other single influence in all of religion, literature, or history.

His ministry was consciously directed to the poor (Matt. 11:5; Luke 4:18). In more than one instance he laid down a requirement of response to the needs of the poor as a prerequisite to entrance into the Kingdom of God (Matt. 19:21; Luke 19:8).

Jesus did not, however, so much advocate simple almsgiving as he did an overflowing generosity of spirit that led the giver to a deeply personal identification with the person in need. "As you wish that men would do to you, do so to them," he said; "give to every one who begs from you"; and "from him who takes away your cloak do not withhold your coat as well." "Be merciful, even as your Father is merciful" (Luke 6:29, 30, 31, 36).

His instructions to those who were in position to play the role of hosts were not to invite friends or kinsmen or rich neighbors to their banquets, but to "invite the poor, the maimed, the lame, the blind." "You will be blessed" for inviting these, he declared, "because they cannot repay you," but "you will be repaid at the resurrection of the just" (Luke 14:12, 13, 14).

So completely did Jesus himself identify with the needs of the unfortunate that he made it clear that humanitarianism in meeting the needs of "the least of these my brethren" is the yardstick by which service to God is measured. In the final judgment, as he described it, the righteous will be separated from the unrighteous on the basis of whether or not their lives have manifested true responsiveness to God in the feeding of the hungry, the giving of drink to the thirsty, the clothing of the naked, the visiting of the sick and imprisoned, and the extending of hospitality to strangers (Matt. 25:31–46).

Moreover, in numerous practical ways Jesus practiced what he preached. He was deeply and primarily interested in the inner spiritual life of the individual; and this interest was entirely in harmony with, if not more comprehensive than, what is in today's social work practice referred to as mental health, emotional health, personality integration, life adjustment, and the like. Above all, however, he was interested in people as persons and was unreservedly responsive to them in all their needs. The record of his ministry is replete with accounts of his healing the sick, feeding the hungry, opening the eyes of the blind, encouraging the discouraged, unburdening the guilty, instructing the ignorant, and performing similar acts of love and mercy. In fact, one student of the gospels concludes that, from what appears in the record, "two-thirds of His work was what we call social work, caring for the physical needs and comforts of men."[6]

The Early Church

In simple sincerity the early Christians took Jesus seriously. They tried to carry out the expression of love upon which he had insisted. They were handicapped, however, by the fact that they were a very small minority struggling for survival in a hostile environment. This made it difficult for them to get beyond their own critical needs to the assumption of responsibility for meeting needs in the whole of society.

Enthusiastic "love of the brethren," coupled with anticipation of Jesus' early return, led the original group in Jerusalem to form a close-knit community which held "all things in common." "There was not a needy person among them, for as many as were possessors of land or houses sold them, and brought the proceeds of what was sold and laid it at the apostles' feet; and distribution was made to each as any had need" (Acts 4:34–35). This was not, let it be noted, as Dean Inge has pointed out, an experiment in ideological communism but "a voluntary sharing of goods by a

---

[6] David Watson, *Social Problems and the Church's Duty* (London: A. & C. Black, 1908), p. 185.

band of enthusiasts."[7] Problems of fairness in distribution, ticularly in the care of widows, soon arose, however, and led necessity of organizing the "serving of tables" under the sup- vision of specially appointed deacons (Acts 6:1–6). Thus, at its very beginning, the church found it necessary to organize itself for its social welfare responsibilities, and consequently the office of deacon became a permanent part of its structure.

As time elapsed and the church grew, this original simple com- munal arrangement was gradually abandoned. The apostle Paul, who apparently did not especially favor such a communal pattern of interdependence, continued, nevertheless, to stress the doctrine of solidarity—that all were members one of another, that if one suffered all suffered, and that therefore the strong ought to bear the infirmities of the weak.[8] Though wealth was not unanimously condemned, there was apparently a universal conviction that property must be used freely to assist the needy, particularly those of the "household of faith" (Gal. 6:10). This resulted in a unique emphasis on benevolence and charity by voluntary con- tributions, a concept which has distinguished the church through all its subsequent history.

Latourette says that this emphasis differed from the charity traditions of the Graeco-Roman world in at least three significant ways: (1) It increased the number of givers; (2) it modified the motive; and (3) it altered the form of beneficence. Whereas non- Christians had held gifts to the public welfare to be a duty of the rich, Christians taught that rich and poor alike should give, each according to his ability, and that giving should be made a part of the ritual of public worship. Where the motive had been public duty, political expediency, or desire for renown, Christians added the dimension of love and the hope of an eternal reward in the future. Where giving had been very impersonal, Christians made it quite personal. Instead of building schools, libraries, temples, baths, theaters, arenas, markets, monuments, and other public buildings, or throwing grain in the streets to quiet starving rioters, Christians

---

[7] W. R. Inge, *The Social Teaching of the Church* (New York: Abingdon Press, 1930), p. 50.

[8] Watson, *op. cit.*, p. 187.

supported their unemployed, their orphans, their widows, their injured, and their sick. They also entertained Christian travelers, provided burial for their dead, ransomed their members from servitude and prison, and sent relief to other churches in time of famine or calamity.[9]

Eventually, of course, Christians too built temples and public institutions, and were affected in their motivations by the patterns of the culture which surrounded them. Even so, they made voluntary philanthropy—involving love and self-giving as well as the giving of means for strictly humanitarian purposes—a more deeply personal obligation of every individual than had been the case in the Graeco-Roman world before their time.

They tended, also, to overcome in time their narrowly restricted interest in their own group. Though this limitation was real and may never have been completely removed, the fact is that it was probably never quite so narrow a concern as it gives the impression of having been. There was always, it must be remembered, an emphasis on evangelism, which kept the door to the bosom of the fellowship open to "whosoever will." Early provision for those of "the household of faith" undoubtedly stemmed more from the pressure of circumstances than from callousness to the fate of unbelievers. Indeed, there were many spectacular instances in which Christians demonstrated that their compassion extended far beyond their own circle. Even during the periods of persecution they often so distinguished themselves by acts of charity toward their pagan neighbors that great sympathy, acclaim, and strength for their cause was aroused thereby. In particular, they became known for their courageous and sacrificial relief work, administered to all alike, in times of plague or public calamity. In Alexandria and Carthage, for example, through a series of terrible epidemics they stayed on and ministered to the sick and dying after able-bodied pagans had fled in panic. Furthermore, Christian missionaries, who went everywhere preaching the "good news," always concentrated on such works of love as healing the sick and "casting out demons," even as they welcomed opportunities to share their

---

9 Latourette, *op. cit.*, pp. 265–266.

fellowship and hope with slaves, prisoners, the outcast, and the poor wherever they found them.[10]

It is to the early church's compassion for humanity that much of the credit is to be given for Christianity's rapid spread under the conditions of oppression, insecurity, and abject poverty which prevailed in so much of the Roman Empire at the time. The masses of slaves, exploited, and impoverished, saw the tender care which Christians gave to children, widows, the sick, and the disabled. They were impressed by the Christian community's concern to give burial to the poor and to provide work or relief to those who could not find jobs. They witnessed the persistence of Christians' attention to prisoners condemned to work in the mines, even after the enactment of such laws as that passed by Licinius forbidding anyone to supply food or "to show mercy to those who were starving in prison"—so that a visit to prisoners entailed the risk of becoming a prisoner. They saw all this and more, and out of the depths of their misery they responded. Christianity appealed to them as a religion of bread, and sympathy, and hope.[11]

After Constantine made Christianity the official religion of Rome, the charitable activities of the church were, of course, greatly broadened to meet the larger social needs and opportunities. Under Christian influence the state took active interest in organized charity. Laws were passed by Constantine and later emperors abolishing crucifixion, encouraging the liberation of slaves, discouraging infanticide and divorce, prohibiting gladiatorial shows and games, and in many other ways revealing increasing sympathy for the weak and the unfortunate.

As early as the first century, schools had been established by Christian communities for the instruction of children in the faith. This was the beginning of many formal programs and services, some of which became institutionalized as the movement grew and

---

[10] *Ibid.*, p. 266; also, Adolph von Harnack, *The Mission and Expansion of Christianity* as reported by James Myers in *Social Progress and Christian Ideals*, edited by William P. King (Nashville: Cokesbury Press, 1931), p. 47.

[11] *Ibid.* (King), pp. 48–49; Inge, *op. cit.*, pp. 50–51, says that during the persecutions the church on the social side resembled a benefit society with very liberal management.

strong churches were established. Employment services, hospitals, orphanages, and many other forms of charity gradually came into distinct focus. Before Constantine the church in Rome is said to have been supporting as many as fifteen hundred widows and other persons in distress. The church in Antioch, some time after Constantine, is reported to have been providing for three thousand widows and virgins, many persons ill in inns, many prisoners, and many poor. Hospitals, in particular, became a favored institutional arrangement, not only providing care for the sick but also giving food, lodging, and other forms of hospitality to travelers, widows, orphans, and the destitute. Some hospitals were supported entirely by the church. Others were founded by rich Christians. At least a few were endowed by the emperor through gifts of land to the church. Eventually monasteries were erected and endowed, and took on many of the responsibilities for Christian charity.

Much more could be said about this tremendously interesting and important formative period in the life of the church. But this limited summary will suffice to indicate that works of charity were an integral part of the Christian movement from its inception. It will also serve to point out that one of the distinctive contributions of Christianity to the pagan society in which it took root was in the direction of a broadened and refined humanitarianism expressed in many practical arrangements for the personalized relief of distress.

Before the early period ended, it should be added, a few tendencies of far-reaching significance were beginning to be evident. Among these were the following:

1. Christianity represented no broad revolutionary program for social reform. It was seeking no radical organic change in the structure of society. It sought rather to show love and to arouse the response of love. Charity was for this purpose rather than for the healing or correcting of social wrongs. Love, operating through persons in their relationships with one another, would effect all necessary changes. Keeping this emphasis dynamic was a relatively simple matter within the small intimate groups in which it originated. It became much more of a problem, however, as Christian communities grew large—and was difficult, indeed, after Christi-

anity was made the official state religion of Rome. In any case, the main social sources of most of the major social problems remained relatively unaffected by the impact of Christianity.[12]

2. A distinction between the "sacred" and the "secular," the church and "the world," developed rapidly. Jesus apparently had been inclined to view the ordinary life of humanity as, despite its sin, full of traces of divine goodness. The Christian movement, the more it "closed its ranks and became an organized and unified body . . . tended to regard the rest of life as the 'world.' " This made for denial or depreciation of all the forces for good that might exist in the world outside the church. The tendency toward such denial or depreciation has been a problem ever since.[13]

3. Conflicting motives for charity sometimes clouded the Christian witness. Genuine sympathy for persons in distress did not always coincide with desire for the favor of the Almighty and for eternal rewards in the future. It did not always resist the "worldly" desire for recognition and acclaim. Consequently, from the beginning, difficulty was associated with the matter of keeping love for persons uppermost in the performance of charitable acts.

4. As Christianity changed from small, intimate groups to a great organized movement, direct personal charity steadily gave way to formal programs of assistance administered under the direction of bishops or other officials. The result was depersonalized charity from which the average Christian's only recourse became indiscriminate almsgiving.[14]

5. As the Christian movement gained prestige, and Christians began to enjoy increased opportunities and improved social status, class differences began to appear in their ranks. The spirit of brotherliness began to decline, and a subtle shift of emphasis away from the earlier notions of the virtues of poverty to the virtues of almsgiving out of relative abundance took place.[15]

---

[12] Ernst Troeltsch, *The Social Teaching of the Christian Church,* Vol. I (New York: The Macmillan Co., 1931), pp. 88, 134.

[13] *Ibid.,* pp. 100, 101.

[14] *Ibid.,* p. 136.

[15] M. Beer, *The General History of Socialism and Social Struggles* (New York: Russell & Russell, Inc., 1957), pp. 195–197.

The Church in the Middle Ages

There was no sharp break between the early period and the Middle Ages in so far as the work of charity in the life of the church was concerned. Under the Roman Empire, philanthropic administration increasingly had been concentrated in the hands of the church, and as chaos slowly descended upon the empire this aspect of the church's program became ever greater.

The final era of the Roman Empire saw territorial revenue decline, production fall off, feudal patterns of landlordism cover the countryside, and unemployment and poverty rise in the cities. Many traditionally free peasants, seeking to escape oppressive rural landlordism, crowded into the cities to compete for jobs that were constantly getting scarcer. The church, which had always cared for its own sick, poor, widows, orphans, and other distressed, and which was now charged with practically all social work obligations of the state, found itself with a very large responsibility.

Wealth and power, however, had already begun to flow into the control of the church. Consequently, it was able to care for a sizeable portion of the need. In fact, its resources and organization were such that even after the Roman state disappeared ecclesiastical organizations continued to carry great social work responsibility. Among other things, they provided most of the services which were available for poor relief, and for the care of widows, the orphaned, the aged, and the sick.[16]

Selfless devotion to prisoners, the poor, the sick, and other unfortunates continued throughout the Middle Ages to be considered the mark of an ideal Christian. St. Francis and his friars went so far as to renounce all their worldly possessions and take the vow of poverty in order to share the suffering of the poor and impart to them the gospel of love.[17] While private property and wealth were condoned—the church itself and many members of its ecclesiastical hierarchy becoming extremely rich—the duty of possessors of this world's goods to relieve the distress of the destitute was greatly emphasized.[18] Several heresies and most of the monastic movement

---

[16] Latourette, *op. cit.,* Vol. II, p. 363.

[17] King, *op. cit.,* p. 60.

[18] Latourette, *op. cit.,* Vol. II, p. 363.

represented a continuing strong undercurrent of sympathy for the communal living and renunciation of private property which characterized the early Christians.[19]

Unfortunately, the giving of alms, and even the begging for alms, came to be considered acts so meritorious within themselves that they led to an exaggerated emphasis on the merit of external good works—a distortion which helped to spark the Protestant Reformation.[20] The church contributed to this exaggeration through efforts to increase its revenues by means of tithes and offerings. So did monasteries and fraternal orders in their quest for funds for charity work. At the same time, a correlated influence which contributed to over-emphasis on the merits of such good works as almsgiving was the great amount of mendicancy associated both with the crusades and with the rootlessness and suffering of the peasantry as feudalism began to break up toward the end of the era.

The church's increasingly deep involvement in works of social welfare developed in several ways. Its traditional concerns evolved into more and more widespread programs of poor relief, hospital and orphanage development, and the like. Its growing position as wealthy landlord of great feudal estates put it under the social obligation of prevailing practice in the matter of providing for the security and welfare of its tenants and serfs. Its close identity with the state thrust it into a role of great political responsibility for the total social welfare. Great welfare responsibilities were also acquired by the church through missionary conquests. The monasteries and fraternal orders, which sprang up somewhat independently but which were eventually made an integral part of the church's program, expanded its ministry in numerous specialized directions.

Bishops and abbots used vast amounts of church funds for welfare purposes. It was often necessary for them to appoint special agents to direct this phase of their administration.

Penance performed through acts of charity became customary. Monasteries looked to the needs of the poor, the sick, and travelers. Hospitals were established by cathedrals, parish churches, and monasteries. Many brotherhoods and orders arose to serve in

---

[19] Beer, *op. cit.,* Part 2, pp. 11–14.
[20] King, *op. cit.,* p. 61.

hospitals. Homes were established for widows and unmarried women, who earned their living by working, and who often did additional work without pay in the care of the sick. Extensive provision was made for the care of persons afflicted with leprosy. Numerous efforts were made to rescue prostitutes. Likewise, measures were taken to extend protection to pilgrims and the ship-wrecked.[21]

Among the multitude of special charitable religious orders which arose were: (1) the Cellites or Alexians, in the fourteenth century, among uneducated artisans who lived in groups of four or six and devoted themselves to the care of the sick and the burial of the dead; (2) the Brethren of the Common Life (date of organization uncertain), who conducted schools and ministered to the poor; (3) the Order of St. Mary Magdalene, in the thirteenth century, to rescue prostitutes; (4) the Crucigeri, in the thirteenth century, to operate leper asylums; and (5) the Knights Templar, the Johannites, and the Lazarites, during the time of the crusades, for such purposes as serving the sick, protecting pilgrims, and ransoming Christians taken captive by Moslems.[22] These and many other orders founded on religion and chivalry placed at the disposal of Christendom special organs for social purposes of all kinds.[23]

The church was neither adequate nor above reproach, however, in the welfare field during these long, varied, and complicated Middle Ages. One might well ask how it could have been. These were the centuries, let it be remembered, which stretched from the collapse of Rome to the Protestant Reformation and the rise of new, powerful nation states. They were centuries of slavery and serfdom; of invasion by the Germanic hordes and invasion by the Moslems; of incessant wars between feudal estates and rival political factions; of the almost complete cessation and painful re-establishment of trade and commerce; of great contention and corruption within the church; and of terrific struggle for supremacy between the church and civil authorities. They were centuries of crisis upon crisis, in which the movement was: (1) from stagnation under rural

---

[21] Latourette, *op. cit.*, Vol. II, pp. 363–366.
[22] *Ibid.*
[23] Troeltsch, *op. cit.*, p. 223.

patterns of feudalism and isolation, in which the masses of people lived in mud huts with dirt floors, were bound to the land and to the service of the landlord, and enjoyed very few comforts or privileges; (2) through a chaos of insecurity when the feudal patterns began to break up and the masses of rural people lost the little security with which feudalism had provided them; (3) to the rise of cities where the uprooted congregated in quest of employment and new opportunities, but instead often found themselves helpless victims of poverty, vice, disease, and exploitation. They were centuries without sanitation, without significant medical science, without economic or political stability—centuries of plague, death, and brutality, intermixed with chivalry, humanitarianism, and Christian idealism.

The welfare needs were, of course, overwhelming, and the response of the church to them sometimes took on heroic proportions. Still, the pittance of what the church did was by no means comparable to its vast holdings of land, wealth, and political power. Whereas almost all offerings in the early centuries had gone to charitable purposes, most of them during this period were diverted to the support of ecclesiastical structure. The upper levels of the ecclesiastical hierarchy were so identified with the privileged upper classes that they seldom challenged the terribly inequitable social conditions which caused many of the needs. Indeed, they were often inclined to the same patronizing attitudes toward the poor and afflicted that characterized other wealthy, powerful, and self-indulgent members of society. Church offices, which came to be also offices of political power, were sometimes sold at very high prices. The cost was eventually extracted from the common people, whose existence was marginal at best, in the form of higher charges for the everyday ministrations of the church.

As the administered programs of the church's organized charity expanded, the element of personal concern on the part of the giver for the person receiving his gift was increasingly diluted. Even the widespread practice of almsgiving was perverted into an almost callous expression of selfishness and indifference. Almsgivers tended to be more interested in heavenly rewards than in the welfare of the persons in need.

It must be recognized, however, that this is not the whole story, for there were at least two main currents of welfare concern flowing through sometimes separate and sometimes united channels in the Christian movement of these centuries. One was that of the organized and officially administered welfare program of the church. The other was the spontaneous and highly personal expression of love and compassion which had characterized Christianity from its beginning. This latter current repeatedly broke through the institutional impedimenta of the church to find fresh expression in individuals, in small groups, in the special orders, and in the monastic movement.

It should be said, too, that despite all its faults and failures the church nurtured in this era the ideal of a Christian civilization in which the total social process would be devoted to the expression of God's will for mankind. Instead of maintaining an antagonism toward "the world" of political and social institutions, as the early Christian movement had been inclined to do, the church of the Middle Ages sought to become a comprehensive, unifying whole, embracing political and social institutions along with religion.[24] Though it did not completely or permanently succeed in this effort, and often seemed to compromise Christianity in the process of trying, it did at least succeed in establishing the idea that organized society has a responsibility for the total social welfare; and it crystallized the conviction that the discharge of this responsibility in humanitarian concern is an obligation of political and social institutions as well as of the church, whether or not these institutions are under the control of the church.

A final notation must be added in this summary to the effect that though most charity and welfare work in the Middle Ages was done either directly or indirectly under the sponsorship of the church there were several significant minor provisions not under its auspices. Many of the feudal estates made their own provisions for certain basic welfare needs of their people. When Charlemagne came to power there were so many of these provisions that he attempted to standardize and regulate them. Many of the cities, as they began to grow, built and maintained their own hospitals and established other charity programs. The craft guilds made numerous provisions for

---

[24] *Ibid.*, pp. 202–203.

the welfare of their members. How many of these and other similar services should be credited to the church or Christianity and how many of them should be assigned to distinctly different sources would be difficult to determine.

To say the least, the church during the Middle Ages popularized and universalized the ideals of humanitarianism. While it encased many of the dynamic impulses of original Christianity in rigid institutional encrustations, and failed to make a frontal attack on many evils and injustices of the social order, it managed to evoke within itself a sense of relevance to the whole of society, and within society at large a sensitivity to human need and a sense of responsibility for trying to meet need. To be sure, much of the warm spirit of brotherliness had gone out of the church. It had identified itself with the secular order and busied itself with brutally doing to death its "heretic" members who dared to criticize its official dogmas and policies. Still, it had managed, even through its institutional formality and clumsiness, to infuse into the disparate elements of European culture the rudiments of humanitarian concern which were eventually to rescue European society from total depravity in the era of industrial and colonial exploitation.

The Protestant Era

The sixteenth century was a time of general social upheaval and revolt in Europe. Feudalism, holding the peasants in bondage on the soil, had collapsed. The Holy Roman Empire, through which the church had attempted to exercise control over political life, was breaking up. A commercial revolution was under way. Cities were growing rapidly, and powerful independent nation states were taking shape.

Corruption had penetrated the clergy all the way to the office of the pope, and the affairs of the church were in a bad state on many counts. So much mismanagement of hospitals, endowments, poor relief, and other programs of charity under the church's control was in evidence that civil authorities, armed with increasing power and independence, had begun to step in with considerable frequency to force reforms.

Actually, not one but two reformations were generated. One, the

Protestant Reformation, of which Luther became the first outstanding leader, represented a revolt against the old church and a complete break with it. The other, the Catholic Reformation, sometimes called the Counter Reformation, spearheaded by Ignatius Loyola, occurred within the Roman Catholic Church and worked to correct its weaknesses and abuses. Both reformations strove "to lift the level of the masses of Christians more nearly to New Testament standards."[25]

The Protestant Reformation developed among the proletarian masses who had accumulated in the cities and were inclined to be critical of many things associated with the old feudal order from which they were attempting to escape. Luther, Calvin, and Zwingli, the leading Protestant reformers, were all of peasant stock.[26] The Reformation was not a purely religious revolt, but was an integral part of the general social revolution. In particular, it was a revolt against the imperiousness of ecclesiastical autocracy in the Roman Church, associated with moral corruption of the clergy. This revolt coincided with and complemented the rising tide of nationalism which was breaking the church's dominance in the political field.[27]

Most of the early Protestant bodies immediately became state churches. This meant not only that they placed themselves under a large measure of control by secular authorities,[28] but also that they now looked upon the relationship of the church to the social order in a somewhat different light. Luther set the pattern for this with his contention that the dominance of the church should be solely in the spiritual spheres of edification and instruction and that all other matters of a political and social nature should be entirely in the hands of the government.[29] He expected, of course, that the government would be Christian and ruled by a Christian conscience.

The Protestant influence on social work and social welfare is somewhat difficult to assess. Perhaps its greatest immediate impact was in the direction of placing the responsibility for social welfare

---

25 Latourette, *op. cit.*, Vol. III, pp. 12–17.
26 *Ibid.*, p. 16.
27 *Ibid.*, p. 13; King, *op. cit.*, p. 73.
28 Latourette, *op. cit.*, Vol. III, p. 26.
29 Troeltsch, *op. cit.*, Vol. II, p. 565.

squarely on the shoulders of government. This, for the first time, clearly defined welfare as a public responsibility, distinct from the work of the church as such. Protestant churches nevertheless continued many of the traditional charity programs and emphases which had always been a part of the work of the church. They served, too, as the chief agents of the state in administering welfare services which were undertaken by the government.

In many respects Protestantism represented, as Latourette points out, a fresh, vigorous impulse "to recapture the spirit of the religion of Jesus and re-establish its spontaneity in the heart and life of the individual believer."[30] This led to renewed emphasis on voluntarism in response to the needy and to a more sympathetic identification with them in their plight. Luther denounced the selfish reward and punishment motives in almsgiving which had been appealed to so frequently in the Middle Ages. He insisted that almsgiving should be a voluntary response to God's love arising out of a spirit of gratitude.[31]

It may be added, however, that this shift away from ecclesiastical authoritarianism, with its promises of heavenly rewards, forgiveness of sins, and release from suffering in purgatory, as a basis for almsgiving resulted, at least for a while, in a reduction in giving. Benefactions fell off to a rather marked degree. Luther, however, combined voluntarism with a new and important basis of authority. He appealed to the princes to forbid begging entirely and to organize a "common chest" in every parish to receive "regular contributions" and "voluntary gifts" of money, food, and clothing for the assistance of the needy.[32] "Regular contributions" hinted strongly at the principle of general taxation.

Protestantism's impulse "to recapture the spirit of the religion of Jesus" was not expressed, however, in the pattern of monasticism, which had represented something of the same impulse at an earlier date. Where monasticism was inclined to withdraw from society, Protestantism tended toward activistic involvement in society. Monasticism had ministered to many victims of social evils; Protestant-

---

[30] Latourette, *op. cit.*, Vol. III, p. 26.
[31] *Ibid.*, p. 405.
[32] Friedlander, *op. cit.*, p. 11.

ism, while not refraining entirely from such work, exerted an influence more in the direction of engendering widespread attack on
social ills through reform movements aimed at making alterations in
social institutions and social patterns to relieve distress. While
Protestantism thus did much that monasticism and earlier Christianity had failed to do, it deprived itself, in its rejection of monasticism, of the monastic-type organizational arrangements through
which most Christian philanthropy had long been expressed. From
this loss Protestantism was slow to recover, though in time it did
develop its own charity agencies and organizations.[33]

It must be acknowledged, however, that Protestantism never gave
rise to hospitals and other charitable institutions and agencies under
direct control of ecclesiastical organizations to an extent comparable
to that of the Roman Catholic Church. It never had the same purpose to do so. Instead, Protestantism's compensating achievements
were: state charities were encouraged; social reforms, correcting
many of the causes of destitution and suffering, were accomplished;
and great emphasis on thrift and industry helped move many persons
beyond the need of relief.[34]

Protestantism's emphasis on thrift, industry, and the requirement
and dignity of work was in keeping with the expanding economic
opportunities of the times. Though it was a necessary emphasis, if
emancipated peasants, who had long depended on the paternalism
of feudal landlords, were to learn to care for themselves, it laid the
foundation for an extremely troublesome attitude toward destitution. Because it embraced little or no comprehension of social
causes of destitution which lie beyond the control of the individual,
it provided grounds for the assumption that economic destitution
on the part of an able-bodied person is always evidence of sinful
laziness or carelessness—a mark of inferiority and divine disfavor
meriting social stigmatization. At the same time, it provided a
basis for believing that economic success and prosperity justify all
the opposite assumptions.

On such premises a tenacious set of vicious attitudes, which
reached a climax during the terrible exploitations in the early years

---

[33] Latourette, *op. cit.*, Vol. III, pp. 403, 405.
[34] *Ibid.*, p. 405.

of the Industrial Revolution, was established. Many of these attitudes have persisted to the present time. For example, there have been occasions when churchmen have argued that a widow should not be given assistance because she had a part in her husband's thriftlessness, which brought on her destitution. Such attitudes seem strange and incongruous in Protestantism, which has always embraced so many social reform movements, and which has been more aware than Christianity had ever been before of the broad implications of social evils. It may be well to remember, however, that this overemphasis on the religious value of thrift and industry evolved before there was a consistent scientific awareness of social, particularly economic, processes. There have been many religiously inspired social reform movements aimed at correcting the emphasis since scientific awareness has enlarged understanding of the possible social causes of destitution.

Though Protestantism did not do so much as Roman Catholicism had done, and continued to do, in the direct sponsorship of organized charities, it certainly did a great deal. Apparently it never developed any significant awareness of desire to remove itself entirely from the main stream of church tradition in this respect. Even Luther, who at first suggested the state should take over charity responsibilities, expected only that the state would provide the authority, collect the funds, and have general administrative oversight. His obvious assumption was that the state would work hand-in-glove with the church and use church channels and agencies in its welfare distributions. Moreover, Luther and his followers quickly developed impatience with what the government did in this field and were soon involved in promoting charity directly through the church in many of the old traditional ways. Since that time Protestantism seems to have supported a dual emphasis to the effect that the state must assume responsibility for social welfare, but that since the state will never meet all the need, the church—as well as private individuals with resources and Christian motivations —must continue to do as much as possible. Church, private, and public philanthropy have therefore received encouragement in practically all Protestant lands.

While Protestantism has been referred to in this discussion as though it were a unity, it must be remembered that it was never one movement, but has always been a number of more or less distinct movements. In some respects the Anabaptists, whose origins reach far back into the Middle Ages, with their extreme emphasis on personal religious commitment and complete surrender of life, were more closely related to the monastic movement than to Luther. The Methodists, under John Wesley, probably had much more in common with the Anabaptists, Quakers, and Moravians than they did with the Church of England, despite the fact that Wesley was a priest in the Church of England. Presbyterianism under John Knox in Scotland was quite different from Lutheranism in Germany. Yet all these, and many other Protestant groups, while drawing characteristic peculiarities from their leaders and social environments, were part of a great Protestant complex, and merit consideration as a unit.

Understandably, not all the Protestant groups made the same approaches to social welfare. The Methodists in England, for instance, did not stress the state's responsibility to the same degree that the Lutherans of Germany or the Calvinists of Geneva had emphasized it. Instead, with great zeal, they threw themselves into evangelism, especially among the working classes, and gave spontaneous response to needs as they found them through the organization of numerous benevolent and mutual aid programs. John Wesley himself took part in helping the Methodist societies organize a Benevolent Loan Fund, the Strangers' Friend Society, the first free medical dispensary in England, book rooms, a program to give shelter and employment to unemployed women in textiles, and many similar services. Methodism also played a large part in social reforms associated with purification of morals, revision of penal laws, abolition of slavery, establishment of popular education, and guidance of the labor movement.[35]

While no thorough history of Protestant social work has ever been written, a voluminous amount of fragmentary evidence indicates that welfare activity has always been a highly significant part

---

[35] Walter G. Muelder, "Methodism's Contribution to Social Reform," in *Methodism,* edited by William K. Anderson (Nashville: The Methodist Publishing House, 1947), pp. 192, 197.

of Protestant concern and enterprise. Only a few among the many additional examples can be cited.

The Religious Society of Friends engaged in relief work in England, to persons outside the Society, as early as 1690, during the Irish War.[36] Friends in England also established, in York, the first hospital for the mentally ill that treated the patients as anything other than prisoners.[37]

One of the most important Continental developments resulted from the work of Dr. Theodor Fliedner, a Lutheran pastor. He began at Kaiserswerth, Germany, a refuge for discharged women convicts, and soon expanded it into a hospital to care for the sick. Several other institutions were added later. He is credited with being the first in the Protestant tradition to bring together and train church women as deaconesses who were pledged to give their lives to nursing or social work. It was from his program that Florence Nightingale drew inspiration for her work. He thus influenced the beginnings of modern trained nursing service, and the establishing of the order of deaconesses which is found in many denominations in many lands.[38]

Calvin sought to eliminate social problems through regulation of all phases of the life of Geneva, and John Knox, his disciple in Scotland, did not overlook the point of this concern. In his *Book of Discipline* Knox stressed the ideal that in every parish all persons unable to work should be supported out of public funds, that all persons able to work should be compelled to do so, that an opportunity for education should be given every child, and that the way to the universities should be open to all youth of promise.[39]

On the whole, Protestantism's contribution to social welfare—a contribution made up of varying emphases by many groups at different times and in many places—may be summarized as having

---

[36] Howard Brinton, *Friends for 300 Years* (New York: Harper and Brothers, 1952), p. 170.

[37] Albert Deutsch, *The Mentally Ill in America* (New York: Doubleday, Doran and Company, 1937), pp. 93–96.

[38] Inez M. Cavert, *Notes on the History of Protestant Social Work* (Unpublished manuscript held in the files of the National Council of the Churches of Christ in the U.S.A.).

[39] Latourette, *op. cit.*, Vol. III, p. 399.

been toward: (1) assumption of responsibility by the general public through agencies of government, (2) private and church philanthropy based on voluntarism and sincere response to the love of God, (3) emphasis on thrift and industry as a means of gaining God's favor and being able to provide for oneself, and (4) limited social reform designed to correct some of the more glaring social evils. Certainly Protestantism did much to make awareness of and concern for humanitarianism and general welfare needs a possession not only of the church's conscience but also of the conscience of all persons and agencies in the whole of secular society beyond the church.

During the Protestant era, the Catholic Reformation also accomplished many reforms both within the Catholic Church and outside it. Many of the moral abuses which gave excuse to the Protestant revolt were corrected, and many new and wonderful programs of charitable services were initiated. In general, however, there were no major alterations of the basic welfare patterns which had been traditional in the church; and since the Protestant influence came to predominate on the American scene, which is the primary concern of this study, further consideration of the Catholic Reformation will not be undertaken here.

Summary

This sketchy review of the church's historic role in social welfare has pointed out the following facts: The impulse to humanitarianism and mutual assistance is older than organized religion. Organized religion from its earliest beginnings related itself to expressions of welfare concern. The ethical orientation in the religion of the Hebrews placed outstanding emphasis on welfare considerations. Jesus accepted and enlarged upon the social sensitivities and welfare emphases in his Hebrew background, making them major foci of his Gospel. The early church, taking its cue directly from Jesus, spontaneously devoted itself to a program of compassionate sharing and mutual aid. As the church grew older and stronger it assumed increasing responsibilities in the welfare field. The impulse to implement the charity emphases of the Christian gospel took the church beyond its early, almost exclusive focus on the needs of its own members to an effort to assume responsibility for the whole society in the Middle Ages, and a determination to motivate government to assume the major portion of the burden as a public responsibility in the Protestant era.

It has also been pointed out that, while secular welfare arrangements and expressions of humanitarianism have always been in evidence in society, what the church has done has been far superior and more consistent in both ideal and practice. It is obvious that the church has had to carry the major responsibility, almost to the point of dominating the field, and that it has succeeded in making welfare philosophy and motivations conform, by and large, to the Christian frame of reference.

That the church has had difficulty in clarifying and implementing its concern for social welfare is more than evident. The Christian social ethic was apparently far more readily adaptable to small, informal, intimate groups than to large, complex, formal organizations. The church has made many embarrassing mistakes and has been often at a loss to know how to proceed in attempting to apply its ethic in the increasingly complex massive structural arrangements of whole societies. Especially difficult, too, has been the task of keeping the charitable impulse true to the spirit of Jesus—free of maudlin sentimentality, on the one hand, and of the calculating self-interest of persons and institutions, on the other. The Good Samaritan pattern of sincere and unqualified response to the person in distress has not been easy to maintain. It seems to become more difficult as social complexity increases. Carrying the element of personal concern over into organized programs of philanthropy has been especially difficult.

Still, individual problems and personal relationships have been more readily perceived and made amenable to Christian definitions than have most of the more involved social relationships. The church has been far more inclined to respond sensitively to individual problems and to condemn personal practices of injustice than it has to see clearly how broad social conditions incorporate responsibility for personal casualties.

Though the universal element in the Christian gospel has always been at least vaguely sensed, the charitable impulses of the Christian social ethic have always been seriously circumscribed by limitations imposed upon them by narrow groupism. The early Christians' difficulty in identifying with needy persons outside their own group was prophetic of the Inquisition's torture of heretics and infidels and of later European Christians' indifference to the plight of exploited colonial peoples. All partook of the same myopic social and spiritual essence.

Nevertheless, it is to Christianity, expressed and maintained, however imperfectly, through the church, that most of the credit must be given for the growing spirit of humanitarianism, the increasing conviction of the dignity and worth of the individual, and the deepening sense of social responsibility which have characterized the development of Western culture.

The centuries of struggle to articulate the spirit of Christianity were not in vain. By the time the modern era dawned, the church, Catholic and Protestant, had laid the foundations for the development of those concepts of social welfare which have evolved, in modern times, into the elaborate welfare programs which characterize all nations of the Western World. It had finally established the value perspectives which undergird today's professional discipline of social work.

QUESTIONS FOR DISCUSSION

1. What, if any, have been Christianity's unique contributions to the concepts and practice of charity?

2. How can we account for the fact that human societies have tended to develop so much interest in their weak and unfortunate members?

3. Does the New Testament reflect more or less social sensitivity than the Old Testament? What differences in emphasis are identifiable?

4. Do the differences between the early church and the church of the Middle Ages suggest that Christian charity emphases are more appropriate for small groups than for large, complex societies?

5. What present-day practices seem best to represent the original Christian charity emphases? What perversions of these early emphases are evident today?

6. Has Protestantism's effect been to strengthen or to weaken the expression of Christian charity? In what respects?

FOLLOW-UP SUGGESTIONS

Individual

Review the New Testament, making note of all expressions of concern for the types of needs that are usually classified under the heading of "welfare." Compare the attitudes and practices of Jesus with those of the disciples, the Apostle Paul, and the early church.

Group

Have a committee consult references on church history and compile a report citing as many examples as possible of outstanding works of charity performed by Christians during the first 500 or 1,000 years of the life of the church. Use this report as the basis for a discussion of the differences between the church of those early centuries and the church of today in the expression of Christian charity.

II: Perspective on Modern Social Welfare

As this account is being written from an office on the new campus of Wesley Theological Seminary, Washington, D.C., workmen are busy completing installation of three huge, oddly shaped blocks of stone, weighing approximately forty tons, on the front of the beautiful seminary chapel facing Massachusetts Avenue's hurrying traffic. Inside the chapel on a framework of wood and wire is a sculptor's plaster model of an original and sensitively imagined full-length figure of Christ posed as He may have appeared when welcoming the multitudes. The stone on the chapel's face bears little resemblance to this figure of Christ; yet the blocks were cut at the quarry to cubical dimensions appropriate for accommodating its ultimate expression. The task still remaining is for skilled carvers to bring from the cubes of stone, which have in them only the promising contours of potentialities, the finished form of the warmly expressive figure for which the model, shaped by the master artist's hand, waits within the chapel.

Somehow, this seems analogous to the situation which had developed in the relationship of the church to social welfare by the time the modern era dawned. The church contained an image and an ideal of Jesus and his spirit which it had not yet been able to make clearly visible to the restless multitudes in the society around it. It had succeeded, however, in giving crude form and dimension to possibilities for the expression of Christ's spirit in enlightened

50

humanitarianism and had enlisted society's interest in them. Many skilled carvers, not all necessarily its own devoted members, would be required to bring these promising possibilities into warmly expressive reality. Though the job might never be done to absolute or enduring perfection, it offered an inspiring hope and a stimulating challenge. What is more, there were good reasons for confidence that the multitudes' capacities for appreciation were such as would make their response favorable as the finished likeness became more and more visible.

It is, of course, difficult to say when the modern period began. The term is relative and does not necessarily require dating, as long as it gives adequate form and substance to the present. In so far as the relationship of the church to social welfare is concerned, one could argue that the period began with the Protestant Reformation in the sixteenth century; or that it emerged with the Industrial Revolution in the eighteenth century; or that it awaited the advent of the "social gospel" in the last half of the nineteenth century; or that it dawned with the development of government programs of "social security" in the first half of the twentieth century.

In any case, it is appropriate to say that when the modern period began, such Christian ideals as those of mercy, love, justice, sharing, the worth of persons, and the responsibility of all to be compassionate and helpful to the weak and distressed, were beginning to take root in the general social consciousness. It is also appropriate to say that the principle of state (public or government) responsibility for social welfare was beginning to be accepted. The church was not withdrawing from its interest in welfare. Rather, it was defining its sphere as that of teacher, conscience, inspirer, and supporter of the state. It was increasingly viewing its responsibility as being that of setting an example for the state in matters pertaining to welfare, rather than as that of serving as chief administrator of welfare programs.

The transition from church dominance to state dominance was not smooth, easy, or immediate. The state took over reluctantly and quite clumsily. But it had to take over, because welfare needs and problems were expanding, social sensitivities demanded that more and more be done about them, and the church no longer com-

manded material resources sufficient for the task. The process was
not so much one of the church's giving up services it had been rendering as it was one of calling upon the state to do what the church
could no longer do adequately or what it was unable to undertake
in the way of additional responsibilities. In many respects church
programs of charity continued to grow and expand, though they
were generally considered to be supplementary to the services of
the state.

No clear-cut division of labor between the church and the state
was ever established, however, and one of the continuing problems
has been that of determining what boundaries belong to the respective spheres of responsibility. This problem has become especially
acute for the church in its attempt to define its welfare duties and
responsibilities as state services have gradually expanded in almost
all directions.

As the state took over, the prevailing tendency was for it to make
each local community responsible for the welfare needs within its
own bounds. Since the conception of welfare was largely in terms of
the relief of the poor, this made vagrancy a serious problem. Few
communities were able or willing to assume responsibility for the
destitute who might wander in from other areas. Repressive measures against vagrancy have, therefore, been characteristic, even to
the present time, and it is still common practice to discriminate
against the non-resident or "drifter" in the administration of welfare
services.

Charity continued to be almost the sole emphasis for a long
while. But since about the middle of the nineteenth century, there
has been a significant expansion of emphases in the direction of
providing public health services, unemployment protection, expansion of medical facilities, preventive and therapeutic social services, various forms of insurance for social security, and the like. In
other words, practical programs of public services to meet the needs
and provide for the welfare of all the people have emerged. These
programs appear more and more to be taking precedence over the
old, strictly charitable concerns.

It is not easy to account for the revolutions which have occurred
in the social welfare field in modern times, although each develop-

ment has been logical in terms of the social context in which it occurred. As has been pointed out, there were plenty of reasons why the main burden of responsibility was shifted to the shoulders of the state. A detailed look at records of the many crises in the history of the industrial revolution and the evolution of complex society based on technological processes would no doubt make equally clear the logic of step-by-step moves in the direction of organized provisions for the general public welfare. Beyond the specific situational logic, however, there are the broad general influences, which are not so easily appraised.

Humanism and science certainly made significant contributions. From them sprang fresh approaches to social problems and new insights into human nature and human behavior. From them also came the great technology which has yielded so large a measure of relief from drudgery and, despite its liabilities, so much more comfort and security for life. To humanism and science, moreover, must be given much, possibly most, of the credit for the philosophy and political institutions of democracy. They are responsible, too, for the data and motivations upon which most of the "helping" professional services are based. They are the foundations upon which the great secular structures of modern society have been erected.

Humanism and science are not, however, so far removed from the influence of Christianity as they have sometimes been made to appear. Though they deserve credit for having produced secularism, the distinction between "secular" and "sacred" has never been so valid nor so absolute as some definitions would have it. While it has been common practice to contrast the "sacred" and the "secular" in society as though "sacred" meant what was Christian and "secular" meant what was irreligious or anti-Christian, the truth is that many of the impulses in modern secularism have been far truer to the real spirit of Christianity than many of the "sacred" emphases which bore the official Christian label. The church's weaknesses and perversions in the past stimulated many men, imbued with ideals and motives which flowed from the original sources of Christianity, to seek ways of expressing their concerns outside the institutional framework of the church. It would be unfair and untrue to say that what they did was not Christian simply because it did not develop under the formal auspices of the church or did not coincide with fleeting definitions of orthodoxy. It would be a misinterpretation of fact to assume that their action did not actually stem from the fact that the church had been operating in the world. Not all secular developments merit such defense, of course, but many, especially in the field of social work and social welfare, unquestionably do.

The Industrial Revolution, regardless of its causes, which were many, gave great impetus to the expansion of organized welfare services. Beginning near the middle of the eighteenth century with the introduction of power machinery and factory processes in the weaving of textiles, it rapidly grew into a dominating economic influence. It drew people into the crowded environment of cities, made them dependent on economic processes they could not individually control, and subjected them to great hazards and merciless exploitation. Though many benefits, including a much higher general standard of living, have flowed from it, the problems of suffering, need, and dependency generated by this great revolution in economic life created unprecedented requirements for general welfare arrangements.

On the background of these limited observations, it will be the purpose of the remainder of this chapter to interpret the present status of social welfare in the United States as it has developed through English and American history and as it relates to the conditions of contemporary life.

Developments in England[1]

Philanthropic developments in England during the Middle Ages were not strikingly different from the trends which were general

---

[1] The standard reference on the development of social welfare in England is *England's Road to Social Security, 1349 to 1947,* by Karl de Schweinitz (Philadelphia: University of Pennsylvania Press, 1949). For the summary given here special indebtedness is also expressed to: Walter A. Friedlander, *op. cit.;* Dorothy Zietz, *Social Welfare Principles and Methods* (New York: John Wiley & Sons, 1959); Arthur E. Fink, Everett E. Wilson, and Merrill B. Conover, *The Field of Social Work* (3rd ed.; New York: Henry Holt and Co., 1955).

throughout most of Europe. Feudalism, the church, and various guilds and fraternities functioned there much as they did elsewhere. Such marginal adaptations as were necessary to adjust the processes of change to the English situation, however, established patterns and pointed directions which have had great bearing on social welfare developments in America. In a sense they are a very real part of the history of public welfare in the United States.

Early Developments

A few of the early developments of special significance may be summarized as follows:

1. The priority of state sovereignty and responsibility was established.

In the eleventh century William the Conqueror set up a special Court of Chancery to deal with matters involving the proprietary rights of the Crown. This court gradually expanded its functions to include many matters not covered by the common law, which was based on statutes and earlier court decisions, and to provide protection for persons who could not obtain justice in local or feudal courts. Its efforts to define the proprietary rights of the Crown led eventually (in 1722) to enunciation of the principle that, since every loyal subject had a right to the King's protections, such persons as idiots, lunatics, and infants were entitled to the protective jurisdiction of the Chancery Court. In the case of infants this was especially significant, since English common law had always been inclined previously to give the father priority in the custody and control of his children. The principle of the Crown's priority, even over the claims of parents, in matters affecting the welfare of children has had far-reaching consequences.[2]

2. Discriminatory classification of the destitute was begun.

A distinction began to be made as early as the fourteenth century between the able-bodied poor, who were capable of earning their own living, and the impotent poor, who could not be expected to work. Feudalism was disappearing, serfs were free, agricultural laborers for wages were in great demand, and there was much

---

[2] Helen I. Clarke, *Social Legislation* (New York: D. Appleton-Century Co., 1940), pp. 16, 206, 207; Zietz, *op. cit.*, p. 30.

migrancy, rootlessness, and vagrancy. The King and Parliament began to be concerned about how to keep laborers on the job and how to preserve order among them. As it had elsewhere in Europe, this concern led to the intrusion of governmental authority into those realms of charity which had previously been left almost exclusively to the discretion of individuals, the guilds, and the church.

Following the "Black Death" plague of 1348, which is estimated to have killed possibly two-thirds of the English population in two years, and which created a tremendous labor shortage on the manors, the *Statute of Laborers* was issued by Edward III in 1349. This was the first of many repressive measures aimed at curbing begging, preventing vagrancy on the part of the able-bodied poor, and forcing rural workers to stay on the land. It prescribed that able-bodied beggars should not be given alms, that able-bodied persons who were destitute must accept employment from anyone willing to hire them, and that all laborers must stay within their own parish. The penalties were quite severe, ranging from whipping, or confinement in the stocks, to branding, mutilation, condemnation to the galleys, and hanging.

3. Poor relief, which had been a voluntary and unrestricted activity, primarily of the church, was brought under state regulation.

As already noted, the 1349 *Statute of Laborers* had forbidden the giving of alms to able-bodied beggars. Later, Henry VIII confiscated church property, the guilds lost their strength and influence, monasteries were crippled or put out of action altogether, hospitals had to find secular support, and unemployment increased. A 1531 statute issued by Henry VIII required mayors and justices of the peace to investigate applications for assistance on the part of all persons maintained by the parish. Only those unable to work were to be given assistance; such as were deemed worthy were to be registered and licensed to beg in an assigned area.

A law passed in 1536 prescribed that alms were to be collected by the churches each Sunday, that local authorities were to help relieve the impotent destitute, and that any individual giving alms to a beggar could be fined ten times the amount he had given. This law, establishing the first plan of public relief under the auspices of the government, also required paupers to register in their parishes,.

prescribed three years' residence in the parish as an eligibility requirement for assistance, stated that able-bodied beggars should be forced to work, and provided that idle children between five and fourteen years of age of destitute families should be taken from their parents and placed in the care of masters who would work them and give them training.

4. Compulsory measures became necessary as a substitute for voluntary financing of poor relief.

The first step in this direction was in the 1536 requirement that alms be collected by the churches each Sunday. This and other similar semivoluntary arrangements proved inadequate, however, in meeting the increasing volume of critical need; and in 1572 the law which established overseers of the poor imposed a general tax to provide the funds necessary for poor relief.

5. The need to systematize the state's participation in charity work was recognized.

The burden of responsibility for charity work among the poor and helpless had been so gradually and grudgingly accepted by the state that in the course of a few centuries a great hodgepodge of laws and regulations had accumulated. So fragmentary, duplicating, contradictory, and confusing were these jumbled statutes, most of which had been passed from time to time as emergency measures, that the need to systematize or codify them so as to weld them into an organic unity eventually became obvious. This was done in 1601, near the end of the reign of Queen Elizabeth, and the resultant act, sometimes referred to as "43 Elizabeth," is commonly known as the Elizabethan Poor Law.

This code merits special attention, since it set the pattern for government participation in public relief in Great Britain and the United States for the next three hundred years. Many of its main features are still recognizable in present-day concepts and practices.

To begin with, the code divided persons eligible for public assistance into three categories: the able-bodied poor, the impotent poor, and dependent children. It stipulated that the able-bodied poor should be provided work and forced to work; that the unemployable impotent poor should be given care in almshouses; and that children whose families could not care for them be apprenticed or placed as indentured servants with other families or individuals who would care for them free or take them at the lowest bid. It provided that there should be "overseers of the poor" in each parish with responsibility to investigate all applicants for relief, make proper assignment of the applicants, maintain an almshouse and a workhouse, and otherwise administer the Poor Law within the parish.

The Poor Law also continued the requirement that a person must have been born in the parish or have resided in it for three years to be eligible for relief. Furthermore, it strongly affirmed the principle of "family responsibility," making any person ineligible who had a husband, wife, parent, or child able to support him. Lists of relief recipients and their grants were to be publicized so as to discourage as many persons as possible.

6. The principle of local responsibility under state regulation was firmly established.

The local community had, of course, carried responsibility for poor relief from the earliest times. The Elizabethan Poor Law did not alter this arrangement, except that it outlined general principles and imposed requirements to govern relief. The entire administrative responsibility, however, was left in the hands of the local parish. This arrangement was continued for over two hundred years with no major alteration. Not until the Poor Law Revision of 1834 were changes made in the direction of providing a measure of centralized administrative control.

7. Repressive and punitive approaches to the problem of poverty, though they prevailed for a long while, gradually gave way to more constructive approaches.

Most of the government measures for over two centuries were frankly repressive. It was felt that the able-bodied poor especially should be able to look after themselves and should be punished if they failed to do so. Poverty was a form of crime for which no one but the individual and his family were responsible. By 1601, however, there were glimmerings of a more positive attitude. At least a modest awareness of conditions of poverty that punishment could not correct was beginning to be evident. Some recognition was being given, too, to the idea that government had an obligation to use public resources to help individuals who were unable to provide for themselves.

Developments after the Industrial Revolution

The foregoing are some of the highlights of developments in England prior to the beginning of the Industrial Revolution, near the middle of the eighteenth century. Welfare problems, which, as these references indicate, were obviously becoming increasingly acute before that time, were rapidly and enormously exaggerated by the Industrial Revolution's impact.

The ranks of the poor and unemployed had been greatly swollen by (1) changing agricultural conditions which substituted the low manpower requirements of wool production for the much greater labor requirements of crop cultivation, (2) the break-up of monasteries and convents, (3) the periodic release from the army of great numbers of soldiers, and by numerous other conditions. This provided a situation ripe for all manner of exploitation when factory processes of manufacturing were introduced. The masses of poor quickly congregated around the factories, where they lived in squalor and competed with one another for the jobs which were available. Wages were depressed, conditions of housing and sanitation were deplorable, health and accident hazards knew practically no limits, and ignorance, immorality, and crime were almost the common denominator of existence.

Employers were quick to take advantage of opportunities available to them through the provisions of the old Poor Law. Many built workhouses in connection with their factories and contracted with overseers of the poor for the cheap forced labor of paupers. The apprenticeship, indenture, and low-bidding arrangements for the care of dependent children proved especially profitable. An employer could get practically free labor by agreeing to assume responsibility for the care of a number of small children. These he could treat in almost any way he wished, and could sometimes work until they were twenty-one years of age. The competition for dependent children, even infants, became so great that manufacturers were known to stretch their magnanimity to the point of agreeing to accept one idiot with every twenty sound children allotted them.

The threat of the workhouse also enabled manufacturers to hire the women and children of poor families at extremely low wages. When the allowance system for partial relief, through supplementing wages judged to be below subsistence level, was introduced in 1795 employers immediately took advantage of it by deliberately depressing wages to substandard levels and referring their workers to the guardians of the poor.

The prevailing laissez faire economic philosophy argued that no relief should be given the poor, since any amount would interfere with the law of supply and demand in the labor market and would tend to keep down production and profits.

Nevertheless, reform of the Poor Law and its attendant philosophy was an inevitability. It came slowly, and was resisted at every point, but the imperative for it was so great that it progressed with dogged persistence.

The first reform measures were aimed at relieving the plight of children. As early as 1759 public concern had been expressed over the terrible conditions under which children worked in cotton mills. At about the same time, a committee investigating mining operations found girls seven to twenty-one years of age working naked to the waist alongside completely naked adult colliers, and was further appalled at discovering a twelve-year-old girl making twenty-five or thirty trips a day from the pit carrying a hundred pounds of coal each trip.

The Health and Morals of Apprentices Act, passed in 1802, limited pauper apprentices' work in cotton and woolen mills to no more than twelve hours daily, and forbade that they be worked at night. It also required the mills to give their pauper apprentices instruction during some part of each day, and to provide them adequate clothing and adequate ventilation. Because mill operators tended to evade provisions of this act by employing free children rather than pauper apprentices, an amendment was added in 1819 to cover all children.

The Mines' Regulation Act was passed in 1842. It came after another investigation had discovered children four years of age in the pits and had uncovered the fact that the age at which colliers were initially hired tended to be between eight and nine years. This act forbade the employment underground of women and girls and of boys under ten years of age.

Education of children up to the age of ten was made compulsory in 1876.

Among the numerous changes which took place in the Poor Law between 1834 and 1909, the main trends were toward: (1) the development of specialized services for such groups as dependent children, the sick, the insane, the feeble-minded, the blind, and the deaf; and (2) a reversal of the repressive and punitive philosophy which was so strongly reasserted in the 1834 revision.

Despite everything that was done, however, the pressure of need for public relief continued to build up in England, and discontent with lingering tendencies toward repressive measures continued to rise. The threat of mass unemployment at the beginning of the twentieth century brought the matter to a climax. It was obvious that whole communities could not be forced into workhouses. Clearly, too, poverty and unemployment could no longer be defined as crimes for which the individual should be held entirely responsible.

Consequently, the Liberal Party, immediately upon succeeding the Tories to power in 1905, appointed a "Royal Commission on the Poor Laws and Relief of Distress." This commission launched itself upon a critical analysis of the philosophy and results of the Poor Law, and was so impressed with its shocking discoveries that it recommended sweeping changes. Among these were: (1) changing the punitive character of poor relief to a humane public assistance program; (2) consolidating local relief administrations into county councils; (3) abolishing mixed almshouses and giving special care to people in the various categories of need; and (4) the introduction of free employment services, free hospital treatment for the poor, pensions for the aged, and a program of unemployment insurance.

The report of the commission, in 1909, marked a significant turning point in British social welfare policy. Though not all the commission's recommendations were at once adopted or translated into legislative action, the report marked the end of the era of poorhouses, workhouses, indenture, "contract" exploitation of destitute laborers, and the treatment of poverty as though it were a crime. It clearly identified the national government's responsibility for public relief, in contrast with the old notions of local community responsibility under a modicum of government regulation; and it shifted the emphasis from a grudging dispensation of charity to positive concern for conservation of the nation's human resources.

The story in England since that time has been one of an almost steadily expanding program of social security designed for the protection and benefit of every citizen. An Unemployment Insurance Act was passed, followed by a National Health and Contributory Pension Act, and by a Workmen's Compensation Act. In 1948 a comprehensive program of National Insurance, embracing and expanding upon these provisions, was inaugurated.

The National Insurance program classifies all persons above school age as (1) employed, (2) self-employed, or (3) nonemployed; and it requires that they make payments accordingly. It is based on the philosophy that the individual is important to the community, that by his work and social conduct he helps the community, and that in return the community should help him when he is in need of help. The program divides responsibility between the central government, the local community, and the individual himself. Its benefits, which are available to everyone, cover maternity, sickness, unemployment, industrial injury, retirement, widows' pensions, guardianship grants for dependent children, and funeral expenses.

A system of family allowances, public assistance, institutional care, and welfare services not involving financial aid parallels and supplements the National Insurance program.

Despite the comprehensiveness of the government's social security program, however, private social services still have an important place. British public authorities encourage them, and many private agencies continue in operation. One of their major traditional functions, that of collecting and distributing alms, is, of course, no longer of great importance. There are, however, many other helping services of a personal assistance, counseling, educational, and organizational nature for which they seem uniquely equipped and are greatly needed.

Included among the services which private agencies are still rendering are: the operation of maternity homes and homes for the aged, as well as clinics, sanitariums, nurseries, hostels for defectives, social clubs, marriage councils, and adult education centers; the provision of nursing and aftercare services for the sick, midwives' services, ambulance and transportation services, and a variety of visitation services; the conduct of probation, parole, and rehabilitative work among juvenile and adult offenders; and the relief of suffering in the wake of disaster.

The functions of these remaining private agencies may be summarized in terms of (1) experimentation to develop new methods and patterns of social work, (2) organization of private resources to supplement public social services, (3) interpretation of social work and of social needs to keep the public and public agencies better informed, and (4) action to determine needs, arouse response, and secure better legislation and public services.

The contribution of Protestantism to all these developments in England is difficult to assess. The Evangelical revival of the late eighteenth and early nineteenth centuries "created a moral sentiment that permanently changed England's attitude to distant and defenseless peoples, and to her own brutal and degraded masses at home." Consequently, from the Evangelical movement, it has frequently been pointed out, came the abolition of the slave trade and of slavery in the British colonies, a movement for popular education exemplified in the Sunday schools established by Robert Raikes for "ragged children," a new concern for child welfare, the beginning of industrial reform, and increased participation in many types of philanthropic work.[3]

Developments in the United States

The philosophy of the English Poor Law dominated the thirteen colonies in North America, and dictated the pattern of social services which emerged in the new nation. Poverty and dependency were looked upon as disgraceful, almost a crime, repressive measures were adopted, and provisions for relief were kept to an extreme minimum in the firm conviction that relief in any amount constituted an encouragement to moral turpitude.

Nearly all provisions were local. Great restrictions were placed

---

[3] Ernest Marshall Howse, *Saints in Politics* (Toronto: University of Toronto Press), pp. 6, 8, 128.

on "outsiders." Indenture, apprenticeship, "contract" labor of the able-bodied poor, and sale of the care of the invalid destitute to the lowest bidder were common. Poorhouses eventually became almost universal and served as general dumping grounds for all manner of destitute, degenerate, and afflicted. As changes took place in English thought or practice, they tended to be reflected on the American scene after an interval of a few decades.

The General Picture[4]

The American situation was different, however, and Poor Law philosophy and practice had to be altered accordingly. Among the more important differences it should be worthwhile to note the following:

1. Sovereignty was more divided, making it more difficult to achieve uniformity of standards or administration.

Geographic isolation, the manner in which the colonies were separately chartered, the fact that some of the colonies gave minority groups with deviant views semi-autonomous power that they could not have exercised in England, and many other conditions made co-ordination of procedure a practical impossibility. Many dual sovereignty questions relating to the authority and responsibility of the states versus the federal government, remaining unsettled, still seriously hinder welfare efforts.

2. The traditional services of strong, stable institutions were largely lacking.

Even the church, which tended to be extremely weak and disjointed, was stripped of capacity to render many of the welfare services it normally provided in older countries. Consequently, welfare from the start was largely a public responsibility of the township or local unit of government. In fact, gold rush conditions in the settlement of California made even the local community so impotent to handle needs that provisions at the state level almost immediately became necessary.

3. Greater cultural and racial diversity among the people produced varied and sometimes conflicting emphases.

---

[4] Indebtedness is acknowledged to Friedlander, *op. cit.*, for much of the factual material included in this section

Almost every major racial, cultural, and national group on earth managed to get at least a few of its representatives established fairly early in this new land of opportunity.

This made it extremely difficult for any unanimity of thought or uniformity of practice to develop. The tendency was for each group to look after its own members in its own way. Practically no group, individual, or agency of government was able to give comprehensive and unbiased consideration to the needs of all persons in all groups. Reluctance to make welfare services equally generous and equally available to Indians, Negroes, and members of other less powerful and less favored groups has been a persistent tendency which has seriously retarded the development of practically all public welfare programs.

This diversity in welfare programs, however, has greatly stimulated experimentation and general efforts to increase the adequacy of services provided under private and local auspices.

4. Unique aspects of the physical environment, especially the fact of limitless opportunity on a vast, expanding frontier, greatly affected welfare policy.

In the early period, population was sparse, land was cheap, and the opportunities for successful individual enterprise were exceptional. Naturally, labor was in great demand. For these reasons, few able-bodied people were inclined to seek alms, and those who did were usually confronted with radical forms of discouragement.

The conditions of life in small, isolated settlements encouraged patterns of informal, unorganized mutual aid in preference to the more stilted and formal arrangements which were developing in the older societies of England and Europe. The frontier was a great leveling influence, and such help as Americans gave one another tended to be in the spirit of assistance rendered between social equals. Even the man who was temporarily disadvantaged might soon recoup his fortune and stand on a parity with his benefactor. Since there were few people of outstanding wealth and social status for others to lean upon, and since hardship and deprivation were the lot of all, regardless of wealth and status, the need for formal welfare arrangements was not readily identified.

Through all the nation's history, at least until the twentieth century, the beckoning frontier, ready to receive the hardy individual with courage enough to venture upon it, continuously siphoned off the major portion of need which might have created demand for extensive welfare services in the older communities.

Immigration, the expanding frontier, rapidly changing social and economic patterns, and numerous other conditions have also put a greater premium on mobility in American society than was the case in England and most of Europe. It has been both necessary and desirable for Americans to move about a great deal more than could have been easily tolerated in most older and more stable societies. Excessive mobility, however, combined with fragmented sovereignty and atomized local arrangements, has been a serious discouragement to the development of adequate welfare services. Each step in the evolution of more adequate services has been handicapped by the conflict between a mind-set against mobility, largely imported from the English and European background, and the facts of an American situation which demanded a high degree of mobility. Even today, when probably a fifth of the American people find it necessary to change their residence every year, social agencies find it difficult not to penalize the needy person who is a newcomer to the local community.

The many unusual hazards involving dependency risk in the American situation constitute another very influential factor which must not be overlooked. Conditions of life were hard in the early settlements and on the frontier. Adults were frequently crippled or killed, children were orphaned, and whole communities were victimized by numerous forms of disaster. Indian wars, in particular, caused great suffering and often filled local areas with suddenly impoverished masses of refugees for whom local resources were not adequate to provide. Such conditions, while stimulating concern for welfare arrangements, tended in the main further to aggravate and confuse an already difficult situation. The refugees from Indian wars, however, did at least force early recognition of the fact that on some occasions the local community could not handle the burden of need forced upon it. It soon became customary, therefore, for colonial or state governments to lend a helping hand in such emergencies.

5. The social and psychological "climate" contained significant elements of difference.

Many of the immigrants who came to the North American shores were imbued with great religious or political idealism, or both. Within their limited group identities they were deeply motivated to set up as ideal societies as they could conceive. At the same time, they tended to be greatly influenced in matters pertaining to charity and social welfare by attitudes which were current in the homelands from which they came. Such notions as those that poverty was a crime, a sin, or a mark of divine disfavor, that welfare assistance should always be given in a punitive way, that the individual and his family were alone responsible for his plight, that there should be no interference with the operation of natural laws in the social process, and the like, were, in consequence, often greatly exaggerated on the American scene. Passionate idealism teamed with conviction to give them a momentum sometimes much greater and more lasting than they had achieved in the old country.

In truth, many influences combined to cause a form of utopian idealism, centered on individual responsibility, to become institutionalized in American life. Not the least of these influences was Protestant Christianity's emphasis on the priesthood of the individual believer. This, together with Christianity's traditional emphasis on individual almsgiving and works of charity, helped to set the stage for a remarkable willingness of Americans to give generous support to a multitude of private charities.

Recognition of the differences in the American situation should not obscure the more central fact, however, that the philosophy of the English Poor Law tended to dominate American thought and practice.

Although England was already placing most of her paupers in poorhouses and workhouses in the seventeenth and eighteenth centuries, only a few of the larger cities in the Colonies were using such establishments at that time. Moreover, whereas England had many privately endowed hospitals, asylums, and orphanages, few private charities of any consequence existed in the Colonies by the end of the eighteenth century. Even the limited number under the auspices of the churches and fraternal orders were extremely weak and insignificant.

By the beginning of the nineteenth century, the increasing numbers of the destitute (due in part to the growth in population), the rising cost of poor relief, and the obvious neglect and mistreatment of persons being farmed out to the lowest bidder led to widespread adoption of the county almshouse, which was usually referred to as the "poorhouse." By 1830 practically all the states had authorized the establishment of such institutions in every county.

The "poorhouse" was usually a farm with a few nondescript buildings, or a dilapidated city property acquired at little cost, which served both as a shelter for the invalid indigent and as a workhouse for the able-bodied poor. It quickly became a disgraceful "human scrap heap," where poor families who had previously been given assistance in their own homes, and individuals who had been boarded out with private families, were forced to accept care along with prostitutes, criminals, idiots, epileptics, the insane, and whatever other variety of persons might happen to fall to the county's responsibility. Few provisions were made for the separation of the sick from the well, the old from the young, the criminal from the merely dependent, or even of the males from the females. Cots and straw usually served for beds, sanitary facilities were almost entirely lacking, and other provisions were of a comparably crude and depressing caliber.

Before the nineteenth century ended, the poorhouse, which had been adopted on grounds of humanitarianism as well as of economy, had produced so many obviously bad conditions of its own that public conscience saw the need for additional provisions for poor relief. Numerous private relief societies arose to rescue children, invalids, and old people from the demoralizing influence of the mixed almshouses. Churches, along with fraternal orders and benevolent associations, were quite prominent in establishing orphanages and various types of homes and asylums for these invalid "worthy poor." In addition, the states were prodded into assuming responsibility for the care of such groups as serious criminals, the insane, and the feeble-minded.

The county poorhouse continued in operation, however, and is still used in some sections of the nation, often under a more euphonious name, as an unspecialized catch-all institution for the varied assortment of adults who become public charges and for whom a place in other more specialized institutions is not available.

From colonial days, paupers had been subjected to great public humiliation. Though most of them were widows, orphans, invalids, crippled, and aged, all were subjected to shame, punishment, and public disgrace as though they were guilty of crimes. It was customary to force them to take the "pauper's oath"; they automatically lost the right to vote; and their names and the amount of their relief were published in the newspapers and posted in public places. Before the nineteenth century ended, this punitive, deterrent attitude toward poor relief was, however, being seriously challenged.

As a matter of fact, the last half of the nineteenth century, particularly the period following the close of the Civil War, was marked by many changes in the social welfare field which indicated increasing alienation from the old English Poor Law tradition. Conspicuous among the new developments were a greater idealism, an enlarged humanitarianism, and an increasing awareness of the necessity of a more centralized and co-ordinated organization of social services.

After it was finally recognized that the crude local and county arrangements were not adequate for the care of the rising tide of need, state services proliferated with amazing rapidity. Hospitals, penitentiaries, schools, reform schools, asylums, and numerous other institutions sprang up in every state. The development was piecemeal, however, requiring a special legislative act for each new service and putting each new agency under a separate governing board. So much administrative chaos resulted that by 1870 a trend was under way toward establishing state Boards of Charities to give centralized administration to the growing program of charity work within each state.

Private charities, which were also multiplying at an extremely rapid rate, soon came to face a similar need. Operating in isolation from one another, they soon were involved in so much competition and duplication of services that they were seriously handicapped in carrying out their purposes. Before long it became obvious, too, that not all relief needs were being equally well met and that there was a great amount of waste in the use of such private relief resources as were available. Partly out of their own sense of need and partly as a result of public pressure, the private charities began in the 1870's to turn to the Charity Organization Society pattern which had been developed in England a few years earlier. This was the beginning, in most of the major urban communities, of what have later come to be known as councils of social agencies. It was the purpose of the Charity Organization Society in each community to effect co-operation of all local charity agencies through a board made up of representatives from each agency. It became standard procedure also to maintain a confidential central register on all relief recipients and to have "friendly visitors" to investigate all applicants for agency services.

Community welfare councils, or councils of social agencies, have greatly expanded since the beginning of the Charity Organization Society. Their governing boards have become more independent and more representative of the whole communities in which they serve, and they function in terms of greatly enlarged objectives. In addition to the original purpose of co-ordinating welfare activities, the councils now aim at (1) the promotion of co-operation between public and private social agencies, (2) the achievement and maintenance of higher standards of service, (3) the recruitment and training of community leadership, and (4) comprehensive planning for the welfare needs of the whole community.

In 1913 the first "Community Chest" was founded (largely as a result of the efforts of clergymen) as an adjunct to the welfare council. Its purpose was to combine the various agencies' public appeals for funds in one large asking. By 1960 the national federation known as United Community Funds and Councils of America included 484 members.

Another development of significance near the close of the nineteenth century was the beginning of the settlement house movement. This was a sympathetic response of certain socially minded idealists from backgrounds of culture and privilege to the plight of the depressed masses in the slum areas of the great cities. In settlement houses educated persons from good backgrounds devoted themselves to living among and sharing the life of the poor families of slum neighborhoods in order to help them combat demoralizing influences and develop the social and spiritual qualities which make for good citizenship. Chicago's Hull House, founded in 1889 by Jane Addams and Ellen Gates Starr, is one of the best known examples of such an agency.

In order to understand how strong were the pressures for expansion of services and change in poor relief policy in the period following the close of the Civil War it is necessary to remember what great upheavals were taking place in American society. Industrialization began almost suddenly and on a massive scale. The movement of population, which had been almost exclusively toward the rural frontier, now turned primarily toward the urban industrial centers. Immigrants by the millions were imported from the impoverished rural areas of southern and central Europe and concentrated in the cities to help man the factories and mills. Freed slaves and casualties of the war were everywhere. "Robber barons" were amassing fortunes through almost unrestricted exploitation of workers and natural resources. Amazing wealth and colossal wretchedness were growing side by side. Cities mushroomed without planning or direction. Economic panics and crises recurrently precipitated mass suffering on an unprecedented scale.

Yet this was the era of ebullient optimism. Progress was in the air; utopia, or the kingdom of God, was just around the corner. Consciences were made uneasy by the obvious inconsistency between the American ideal and the disparities which were becoming so evident in the American social scene. Robber barons sought to salve their consciences by means of great philanthropies, and social reform movements became the order of the day. The social gospel began to take shape in the minds of churchmen in a way that led to the adoption by the Federal Council of Churches of the "Social Creed of the Churches," modeled after an earlier creed adopted by the Methodist Episcopal Church. These creedal statements were formulated in the first decade of the new century, and the churches proceeded to busy themselves with works of charity on a scale which had never been possible to them before.

Welfare needs had so outrun local and private resources, however, that when the twentieth century dawned, the stage was set for it to become the century of the development of welfare services administered on a national scale.

Five classes of "Federal Wards" had already been identified before the twentieth century. These were war veterans, violators of federal laws, immigrants, passengers and crews of ocean-going vessels, and Indians. Under the influence of a lobby led by Dorothea Dix, Congress had passed a bill in 1854 authorizing a land grant of 12,250,000 acres to the states to be used for the care of the insane, the blind, and the deaf. President Pierce had vetoed this bill, however, on the grounds that the constitution did not confer upon the federal government power to provide such relief to the needy and unfortunate members of society. Not until after the stock market crash of 1929 was another such proposal made for direct federal participation in public relief.

Nevertheless, as the twentieth century began there was growing awareness that welfare problems were of a magnitude which demanded that they be considered on a national scale. Many private welfare agencies were forming national organizations, and despite the fear of federal interference with state and local interests, sentiment was shaping up toward greater involvement of the national government in welfare concerns.

One of the first major developments was the calling of the first White House "Conference on the Care of Dependent Children" by President Theodore Roosevelt in 1909. From this conference—to which were invited leaders of child welfare services from all over the country—came recommendations which resulted in enactment of state laws providing pensions or allowances to widowed or deserted mothers for the care of dependent children, and in the establishment of the Children's Bureau as an agency of the federal government in 1912.

The Children's Bureau, which may be said to have initiated the federal government's active participation in social welfare, was charged with responsibility for gathering and disseminating information on conditions affecting the welfare of children throughout the nation. With the passage of time and the enactment of federal legislation pertaining to children, its duties have been expanded, and it is now one of the most important bureaus of the Social Security Administration in the United States Department of Health, Education, and Welfare.

Subsequent White House Conferences, planned with the assistance of the Children's Bureau, were held in 1919, 1930, 1940, 1950, and 1960.

When the depression struck, following the 1929 crash, local and private welfare agencies were almost immediately swamped with relief needs stemming from unemployment. Reaction to this situation was in terms of renewed efforts to secure increased voluntary support of private relief services. Hope was expressed that this would meet the need and that the crisis would soon pass. As the depression continued, however, and the rolls of the unemployed steadily increased, voluntary contributions fell off, and city, county, and state governments found themselves approaching bankruptcy in the effort to provide needed relief funds. The demands for federal aid increased. Congress passed several bills authorizing funds for relief. President Hoover felt constrained, however, to veto all the bills until finally, in 1932, he decided to sign the Emergency Relief and Construction Act authorizing $300,000,000 for loans to states, counties, and cities, on an emergency basis. This proved to be so tantalizingly inadequate that the new administration which began a few months later, under President Franklin D. Roosevelt, was confronted with the urgent necessity of far more drastic measures.

Unemployment had jumped from 2,860,000 in the spring of 1929 to more than 15,000,000 in late 1932. Many previously independent families were destitute. Relief rolls included as high as 40 per cent of the population in some states, and up to 90 per cent in some counties.

The Federal Emergency Relief Act was passed on May 12, 1933. It repudiated the old poor relief philosophy and frankly recognized that in a complex society the individual was no longer in complete control of his economic destiny. It faced and accepted, also, the federal government's involvement in responsibility for the welfare of its citizens. It cancelled the emergency loans and substituted a system of direct grants to the states for relief purposes.

Other programs came in rapid succession: the Civilian Conservation Corps in 1933; the Works Progress Administration in 1935; the National Youth Administration in 1935; the Farm Security Administration in 1937; and the Works Projects Administration in 1939. Most important of all, however, was the Social Security Act passed on August 14, 1935, for the purpose of providing for the general security of the population against such major risks as those represented in unemployment and old age.

The main provisions of the Social Security Act were for (1) social insurance covering old age retirement and unemployment, (2) public assistance grants to help the states provide old age assistance, aid to the blind, and aid to dependent children, and (3) health and welfare services of several types. Subsequent legislation has added several minor features to the original provisions of the Act, but they have tended to be more in the nature of expanding its coverage than of altering its basic structure.

Dimensions to which the program has grown may be indicated by the fact that in the year ending June 30, 1959, federal grants to the states to assist in financing the approved categories of public assistance amounted to $1,966,400,000. Aproximately 40,000,000 persons were covered by unemployment insurance, and 58,200,000 were included in the public retirement programs. The Old Age and Survivors Insurance Trust Fund had accumulated assets aggregating nearly $20,141,000,000, and it paid benefits in 1959 amounting to $10,116,000,000.[5]

So far all efforts to enact legislation providing general health insurance and medical care have been unsuccessful. Moreover, very little interest has been shown in such programs as the system of family allowances by which England puts a financial floor under all its families on the basis of the number of children in them.

It is obvious, therefore, that the American program of social security is not so comprehensive or integrated as that of England. While the federal government has assumed considerable responsibility, it is a limited and restricted responsibility. Many needs are not covered; responsibility is still divided between local communities,

---

[5] U.S. Department of Health, Education, and Welfare, *Health, Education, and Welfare Trends* (*1960 Edition*) (Washington: United States Government Printing Office, 1960), pp. 28, 73, 76.

counties, states, and the federal government; and the undergirding philosophy, while leaning toward maximum provision for the security and welfare of all citizens, is still somewhat hyphenated with the reluctance and negativism which characterized earlier poor relief traditions. To put the matter another way, it appears that Americans still feel that the individual should assume a large measure of responsibility for his own welfare, that it is better to avoid too much centralization of power by preserving as much local autonomy as possible, and that the danger of demoralization requires that welfare provisions be kept on something of a minimal basis.

In the meantime, a multitude of private charities, both sectarian and non-sectarian, flourish, and Americans in all walks of life make generous voluntary contributions to their support. Competition, confusion, duplication, and spotty coverage still characterize them to some extent, and they are increasingly affected by the encroachments of public services, but they are still a very vital part of the social welfare structure.

The Role of the Protestant Churches

The manner in which the stage was set by Protestant influences for the broad patterns of American welfare developments is a long and complicated story which has never been fully told.[6] Social welfare was a necessary concern of every Protestant group from the time the group established itself on American soil. Life was hard, and stable social patterns were few. Each one of the myriad Protestant sects and denominations, indeed each local segment of most of them, was almost inevitably drawn into one or another expression of Christian compassion for unfortunate persons in community life, as well as for the welfare of the religious group or the community as a whole.

In early New England, "the town looked upon the church as part

---

[6] The most serious effort to tell this story is represented in the unpublished manuscript by Inez M. Cavert entitled *Notes on the History of Protestant Social Work,* to which reference has already been made. Grateful acknowledgment is made of the fact that most of the comments included here on Protestant social work in American history came from this manuscript, through the courtesy of the National Council of the Churches of Christ in the U.S.A.

of itself . . . [and] the church naturally felt its responsibility for the well-being of the town," say the authors of a history of Congregationalism in America. "There have," they add, "scarcely ever been communities where the poor and needy were more carefully, though frugally, looked after than obtained in the New England towns under the rule of the democratic town meetings. In these town meetings church people have always taken an active part in behalf of justice and well-being." Indeed, according to these authors, the fellowship of the churches "had for its mission the cure of injustice and the lifting of the level of the whole of life."[7]

The Society of Friends became widely known for its devotion to works of charity. The Acadians, banished from Canada in 1755, were helped by Friends in Philadelphia.[8] When Boston was under siege during the American Revolution, Friends in New England, Pennsylvania, and New Jersey raised 1,968 pounds sterling for relief work in that city. General Washington and General Howe would not allow the Friends bearing this gift to pass through the lines into the city of Boston even though these persons explained that "their mission was visiting the fatherless and widows, feeding the hungry, clothing the naked, without distinction of sects or parties." Arrangements were made, however, to send their funds to be distributed by Friends in the city. The members of the gift-bearing committee then set about helping the towns around the city "where multitudes of people 'were in want of victual, wood, and clothing.' " The records of the town of Salem, Massachusetts, where Friends once at an earlier date had been whipped through the streets, carry "a vote of thanks" to the Friends for this help in 1775–76.[9]

From such a background it is not unusual to find Friends Meetings in this country today that have a proud record of nearly three hundred years of continuous social service. Only a few other of the many landmarks along the way in the development of the Friends' record as a whole can be mentioned here.

In 1795 Philadelphia Friends provided relief and employment

[7] Gaius Glenn Atkins and Frederick L. Fagley, *History of American Congregationalism* (Boston: Pilgrim Press, 1942), p. 248.

[8] Brinton, *op. cit.*, p. 170.

[9] Rufus Jones, *The Quakers in the American Colonies* (London: Macmillan Company, 1911), pp. 151–152.

for women left destitute because of a yellow fever epidemic. In 1814 the same group organized a Shelter for Colored Children which is still in existence.[10] The first private institution, and the second one of any kind, for the mentally ill in the United States was the Friends' Asylum, opened in Frankford, Pennsylvania, in 1817. It, too, is still in existence, though it is now located in Philadelphia. While it was originally designated for the care of such Friends "as may be deprived of their reason," it was opened to others in 1834.[11]

Many important works which Friends helped to organize, and which were conducted according to Friends' methods, were never under the control of a Meeting. The Women's Prison Association, for instance, was organized in New York in 1844 by Abigail Hopper Gibbons to help women released from prison. Now, as then, those in charge of it, including a majority of the Board of Directors, are Friends.[12]

The American Friends Service Committee was organized in 1917 "to assist conscientious objectors and send relief workers abroad." Much relief and reconstruction work was done in France, Russia, and Germany during and just after World War I. At one time a million children were being fed in Germany alone. Work in the United States was begun in 1920, and China and India were added to the list of countries receiving service during World War II. The program of the Committee has gradually been expanded to include such a wide variety of undertakings as internes in industry, work camps, community integration of minorities, adult education, housing, neighborhood houses, social and technical assistance in many lands, and work with refugees here and abroad. In all this work the Friends have been supported and assisted by a much larger group of like-minded persons outside their membership "for whom they have acted as instruments and with whom they have collaborated."[13]

Methodists in America were as quick to engage in charitable enterprises as were those in England. John and Charles Wesley embarked for Savannah, Georgia, on October 14, 1735, to serve in the

---

[10] *Handbook of Friends' Agencies* (Philadelphia: Philadelphia Yearly Meeting of Friends, Social Service Committee, 1946).

[11] Deutsch, *op. cit.*, pp. 93–96.

[12] *New York Times*, June 23, 1955.

[13] Brinton, *op. cit.*, pp. 170–172.

colony established by Oglethorpe "in trust for the poor" and holding as one among the many aims of its association "the conversion of
negro slaves."[14] George Whitefield, who succeeded them there in
1738, established two years later near Savannah an orphan asylum,
which he named Bethesda. To this orphanage Whitefield contributed
3,000 pounds of his own money. In addition, he raised some 15,000
pounds for it in England, Scotland, and the American colonies. The
orphanage lasted for 30 years until it was destroyed by fire.[15]

Methodist "circuit riders," as Methodist ministers, who usually
traveled on horseback over a wide area, were called, soon came to
play an important part in welfare work throughout the colonies,
especially in the frontier areas. In the recurring periods of economic
depression, when "extensive destitution" was created, and when
churches in the larger cities were opening soup kitchens for the feeding of hungry and starving people, the circuit riders busied themselves with seeking out "old and young who were in trouble and in
physical distress, offering counsel and providing relief." In fact, it
is said to be "scarcely possible to explain the regard and affection
in which they were held by the common people" without a realization of the extent of destitution, and of the ways in which the
circuit riders entered into fellowship with the people in the hardships they endured, as well as of the practical methods they found
of extending aid. Many of them, for instance, learned much of the
simpler medical practices of their day and helped people when professional medical service was not available. As more settled pastor-
ates became available, the circuit riders "gradually increased intensive social work." An example of this is in the case of a Methodist
minister assigned to the Seamen's Chapel in New Bedford, Massachusetts, who provided a reading room for the sailors, became their
counselor, and served as "the guardian of their families in their
absence."[16]

Many Methodist schools, hospitals, orphanages, homes for the

---

[14] Holland N. McTyeire, *A History of Methodism* (Nashville: Publishing House of the Methodist Episcopal Church, South, 1904), p. 72.

[15] Eric McCoy North, *Early Methodist Philanthropy* (New York:
Methodist Book Concern, 1914), p. 89.

[16] Wade Crawford Barclay, *Early American Methodism, 1769–1844*
(Vol. 2), p. 9.

aged, and other institutions were established. The oldest of these institutions still in existence is Warren A. Candler Memorial Hospital in Savannah, Georgia, which was founded in 1830. The New York Methodist Church Home for the aged dates from 1850. Eventually a Board of Hospitals and Homes was set up to give guidance to these institutions engaged in welfare services. At least as early as 1912 the General Conference of the Methodist Episcopal Church called upon quarterly conferences of local churches to set up hospital committees, and urged area annual conferences to support "at least one of our hospitals."

In a projected program of "City Evangelism" outlined in the *Discipline* of the Methodist Episcopal Church for 1904, attention is called to the fact that evangelistic effort in the large cities might properly include the maintenance of kindergartens and industrial schools, the promotion of social and settlement work, and the support of institutions for the relief of the sick and the destitute and for the recovery of the outcast.

Presbyterian and Baptist denominations also have a long and honorable history of contributions to welfare work in the nation. Since many of their efforts and emphases paralleled those among the Congregationalists and Methodists, however, and because of limitations of space, details of their story will not be included here.

Organized Lutheran work apparently developed somewhat more slowly than did welfare work in some of the other denominations. The first Lutheran institution of mercy was a hospital in Pittsburgh established in 1849 by Dr. W. A. Passavant. Within a few years there were, as a result of his efforts, three other hospitals and four orphanages. Altogether, he secured more than $1 million for these Lutheran "institutions of mercy." It was he, also, who introduced the Protestant order of deaconesses into this country by bringing a group of Lutheran sisters from Kaiserswerth. The almost immediate appeal which this order made to women in other denominations became very significant. Deaconesses were soon extensively organized in Lutheran, Methodist, Evangelical and Reformed, and other bodies. Several denominations still maintain active orders.[17]

---

[17] Abdel Wentz, *The Lutheran Church in American History* (2nd ed. rev.).

The Evangelical and Reformed Church, which resulted from
the merger in 1934 of the Evangelical Synod and the Reformed
Church in the United States, both largely of German background,
was also early concerned with charity. The Reformed Church in
the United States, with congregations mainly in the Middle Atlantic
states and the Middle West, was for a long time rather loosely
organized. The first members came to this country in the eighteenth
century. The first formal proposal for denominational action in
regard to charity was for the establishment of a Widows' Fund in
1755. In 1773 the synod at Lancaster decided to establish such a
fund, and a state charter was eventually secured for it in 1810.[18]

For a long while this German Reformed Church in the United
States of America, as it was then called, functioned in two separate
synods. One was in the East and the other in the Middle West. At
the first General Synod, held in Pittsburgh in 1863, a report was
received from a Committee on Orphan Asylums. The following
resolution, contained in the report, was adopted: "That the General
Synod of the Reformed Church . . . hereby solemnly engages to
enter upon the duty of more systematically providing Christian
Homes, for the poor orphan children that may be left . . . to our
care." A General Board of Directors, consisting of two ministers
and three laymen, was elected to carry on this work. It was directed
that any local homes that might be established by the churches of a
city or by an association of individual members should be under
the control of their local boards but that these boards should submit
annual reports to the General Board. The report to the second
General Synod, in 1866, stated that the Orphans' Home at Brides-
burg had "about 100 orphans" under its care.[19]

The Evangelical Synod of North America, which brought together
German migrants and Lutherans from the Eastern United States,
in the setting of Missouri, was equally involved in works of charity
from an early date. Beginning about the 1830's the first efforts were
by sewing societies and ladies' aids in local churches "to care for the

---

[18] Census of Religious Bodies, 1926, Vol. 2.

[19] Acts and Proceedings of the First General Synod of the German Reformed Church in the United States of America, held in Pittsburgh, Pa.,
1863; also of the Second Triennial Session, held at Dayton, Ohio, 1866.

poor and the sick, the widows and the orphans within their midst." The fact that there were already several non-church charitable organizations at work in St. Louis greatly stimulated this church's concern for social welfare. Conscious fear was expressed that secular fraternalism, with its philanthropic interests, "might be considered an adequate substitute for the church." A series of articles written in 1853 urged that parochial school teachers be used also as social workers, and that in larger cities nurses be employed "at the expense of the congregation."

Various types of organizations were formed in local churches. Most numerous were the "indigent societies." There were also *Sterbekassen* to secure an honorable burial to the church members, and *Sparkassen* for the encouragement of small savings by the poor. Local situations determined the extent to which such activities were carried on. "There was hardly a German congregation, however, which was not confronted by the problem of serving its poverty-stricken members. In girding to meet these needs the *Kirchenverien* (as the Evangelical Synod was then known) was not far from what later was heralded as the social gospel."

The congregation was urged to care for its poor. The poor who were outside the church were to be helped by individuals.

In 1857, after several years of discussion, the Pastors' Widows' Pension Fund was organized.

The first Evangelical Hospital was begun by Louis Nollau, one of the pioneer Evangelical missionaries. Including orphanage facilities as well as care of the sick, it was started as a personal enterprise in 1857, and was never officially a synodical institution. Nevertheless, it was supported by the church paper and was generally regarded as an Evangelical institution. Its first report declared "no distinction of creed, race, nationality, or color would be made in the acceptance and treatment of patients."[20]

The Protestant Episcopal Church seems to have been comparatively slower in getting its work started, though it was early on the scene. This may have been in part because it was a state church in some colonies and in part because of its disorganization after the

---

[20] Carl E. Schneider, *The German Church on the American Frontier* (St. Louis, Mo.: Eden Publishing House, 1939), pp. 334–348.

Revolution, which left most of its clergy in the position of being generally regarded as Tories. The Protestant Episcopal City Mission Society was organized in about 1824. When the Episcopal Church Congress, composed of clergy and laity, first met in 1874, it immediately manifested concern with social questions, and by the late seventies was struggling with such problems as civil service reform, the tariff, charity organization, and social service. Seth Low, William Graham Sumner, and other prominent laymen led these discussions.[21]

A significant early development which must not be overlooked was the formation of Women's Cent Societies. During the Revolutionary War churchwomen had sewed and knitted for the soldiers and had devoted themselves to caring for the widows and orphans. Soon the need for more than interested individuals could do was recognized. The women in "all denominations" began to organize in "Cent Societies," which raised funds for missions and for relief of the poor. Friends led the way in this, also, but others were equally involved. The Baptist Female Cent Society of Boston was organized in 1800. In 1803 the Presbyterian "Female Society for the Relief of the Poor and Distressed Persons in the Village of Newark," New Jersey, was organized. The first independent women's work in the Dutch Reformed Church was a female Cent Society in Brooklyn, of which there is record as early as 1815.

The causes supported by these societies varied. Some were strictly charitable societies "instituted for benevolent purposes in their own community." Some contributed to day schools for poor children. Others supported a variety of causes. Presbyterian societies around Buffalo were said to have "given to missions, helped in local charities, sewed for institutions, and to have met in prayer circles." A Philadelphia society organized to support a missionary "to preach in the almshouse, hospital, and prison in the vicinity." Women of other denominations, it may be assumed, carried on similar activities.[22]

It must be remembered, too, that the social gospel movement,

---

[21] Charles Howard Hopkins, *The Rise of the Social Gospel* (New Haven: Yale University Press, 1940), pp. 37–38.

[22] Florence Hayes, *Daughters of Dorcas* (New York: Presbyterian Board of National Missions, 1952), pp. 7–16.

which arose in the churches toward the end of the nineteenth century, exerted a profound influence on social welfare. Spokesmen for this movement became keenly aware of the great "social inertia" which had developed in the churches during the first two or three decades following the Civil War. While they were not unappreciative of the churches' traditional concern for the evangelization and social welfare of Indians, and of Negro slaves and freedmen, they insisted that there must be a fresh and vital expression of concern for the welfare of society as a whole and for all the people in it who were being afflicted by the multitude of social problems so glaringly in evidence.

Washington Gladden, one of the Congregational pioneers in social reform, upon becoming editor of *Sunday Afternoon, A Magazine for the Household* in 1878, proposed to include "questions of social life and of national well-being" within an inclusive aim of providing "wholesome and entertaining Sunday reading." Subjects subsequently discussed included pauperism, poor relief, children's aid, destitute and delinquent children, women in prison, tenements, and financial ethics. Contributors included Charles Loring Brace, founder of the New York Children's Aid Society, William Graham Sumner, pioneer American sociologist, and Edward Bellamy.[23]

Much talk of social problems occurred in practically all national church meetings in the last two decades of the nineteenth century. Baptist churches were stimulated for many years by Walter Rauschenbusch, Shailer Mathews, W. H. P. Faunce, and Samuel Zane Batten (who later became Baptist director of service work). Josiah Strong, pastor of a church in Cincinnati, and later general secretary of the Evangelical Alliance (one of the forerunners of the Federal Council of Churches), called an interdenominational congress to meet in his church in 1885 to discuss current issues.

So-called institutional churches evolved during this era in an effort to provide a program to meet the needs of people in the immediate neighborhoods of the churches in the crowded, changing urban centers. The pioneer in this work, though the term was not used until later, was William S. Rainsford. When he was rector of

---

[23] Hopkins, *op. cit.*, p. 37.

St. George's (Episcopal) Church in New York City in 1882, he began continuous weekday use of the church plant. In 1894 the interdenominational Open and Institutional Church League was organized. Among its founders were Josiah Strong, Frank Mason North, Gaylord S. White, Elias B. Sanford and others who a few years later worked for the organization of the Federal Council of Churches. The platform of the League declared: "The open and institutional church aims to save all men and all of the men by abolishing so far as possible the distinction between the religious and the secular, and sanctifying all days and all means to the great end of saving the world for Christ."[24]

Thus by the last decade of the nineteenth century the churches in America were taking steps toward becoming more specifically effective agencies in meeting social needs. The "most significant early socio-religious survey" was made in Hartford, Connecticut, in 1889 under the direction of Graham Taylor. It found that Hartford's greatest need was an "associated charities organization." An even more famous survey was that made in New York City in 1897 by the newly organized Federation of Churches and Christian Workers in New York City, the organization which eventually evolved into the present-day Protestant Council of the City of New York.

Such developments justify the statement that in this era "the churches were recognized as significant social service agencies." There was good reason for the fact that *The Annals* of the American Academy of Political and Social Science devoted an entire issue in 1907 to "The Social Work of the Churches." There was unique significance, also, in the discussion held at the National Conference of Charities and Corrections in 1911 on the question of whether the church ought to inspire, interpret, guide, or administer social work.[25]

As social work began to be professionalized, the church contributed much to the profession and received much help in return from social workers, despite the fact that "in the main" the social service movement "developed outside and apart from religious

---

[24] Josiah Strong, *Religious Movements for Social Betterment* (New York: Baker and Taylor Company, 1900), p. 44.
[25] Hopkins, *op. cit.*, pp. 275–278.

bodies" and represented something of a "break with the church" because of what was interpreted as the church's seeming indifference to the obvious calls to serve suffering people.[26]

Much of the secular social work that took shape around the turn of the century was begun by deeply religious people who were inspired to express their concern on a community level. Charles Loring Brace, for example, of the New York Children's Aid Society, was one of the pioneers in developing new methods for working with needy children. Octavia Hill, English pioneer in housing reform and in London Charity Organization Society, and partner of Canon Barnett in founding Toynbee Hall, exerted very great influence on American social work. The first Charity Organization Society in the United States was established at Buffalo, New York, by an Episcopal rector, the Rev. S. Humphreys Guryeen, who had become interested in the work of the London society while on a visit there. As a matter of fact, many of the early professional workers were individuals who came into social work from the active ministry.[27]

Many persons prominent in the social service and social work field were actively engaged in the early efforts to make the Federal Council of Churches a success. For example, John M. Gleen, organizer and general director of the Russell Sage Foundation, and Edward T. Devine, writer, social worker, and teacher of social work, served on important committees of the Federal Council of Churches during its first quadrennium of existence. Moreover, they continued this relationship as long as their health permitted, and were joined and succeeded by many other persons of equal prominence with social work orientations.

Still, there were real and significant bases for a certain amount of estrangement and alienation between the churches and the people who were struggling in the emerging social work movement. Not all the churches, by any means, were as liberal as the social gospel leaders had sought to make them, and not all were in full and effec-

[26] Shelby M. Harrison, *Religion and Social Work: Perspectives and Common Denominators* (New York: Federal Council of the Churches of Christ in America, Department of Christian Social Relations, 1950), pp. 6–7.

[27] *Ibid.*, p. 7; see also, Arthur Miles, *American Social Work Theory*, p. 93.

tive accord with the "modernism" of the Federal Council of Churches. "Christianity was," according to the writings of John R. Commons, based on his conversations with social workers and labor leaders in several states in 1894, "strong in promoting charity but weak in promoting justice."[28]

International Developments

Mention, at least, must be made of the fact that concern for social welfare has been increasingly spilling over national boundary lines during the last century. Before that time, the missionary activity of the church represented about the only expression of such concern. Near the middle of the nineteenth century, however, representatives of charity and welfare services began coming together in a series of significant international conferences. These conferences greatly facilitated sharing of experiences, problems, and insights. As a result, in due time numerous international organizations were created.

When the League of Nations was formed it placed international concern for social welfare on a more solidly official basis. Its Health Organization and standing committee on social welfare came to be recognized as among the most valuable features of its program. Still, social welfare was a relatively minor concern of the League of Nations as compared with the emphasis placed upon it in the United Nations, which has a permanent Economic and Social Council with a vast program embracing more than two dozen commissions and specialized agencies. Its Commission on Human Rights has been of tremendous influence, and a new dimension has been added to the alphabet through the addition of such words as WHO (World Health Organization), UNESCO (United Nations Educational, Scientific, and Cultural Organization), UNICEF (United Nations International Children's Emergency Fund), ILO (International Labor Organization), IRO (International Refugee Organization), and FAO (Food and Agricultural Organization), which represent some of its better known agencies.

In addition to the agencies under international governmental

---

[28] James Dombrowski, *The Early Days of Christian Socialism in America* (New York: Columbia University Press, 1936), p. 8.

auspices, and the numerous international private organizations, considerable social welfare work is also being done across national boundaries by agencies of national governments, and by many private agencies of a national character.[29]

The World Council of Churches, at its first meeting, in 1948, gave much attention to the subject of the church's responsibilty to the needs of society, and one of its major continuing organizational departments has been devoted to the study of church and community. Many churches have also co-operated in a program of Interchurch Aid and Service to Refugees, to which American churches have given liberal support and with which Church World Service, a department of the National Council of Churches, has closely co-operated.

The Professionalization of Social Work

Social work, which ostensibly began originally as a spontaneous expression of concern on the part of members of society for one another, and which for many centuries was defined primarily in terms of its being a voluntary obligation assumed by anyone who saw it as his religious duty, has become a highly specialized secular profession in modern times.

There are many reasons for this. With the increasing complexity of society, and the increasing burden of need, it became necessary to provide ever more carefully organized social services. Organized programs involved the appointment of individuals to the special responsibility of administering them, as was the case when the leaders of the first century Christian Church found it expedient to appoint Stephen and others as deacons. As more and more people became involved in full-time work of a similar nature, and responded to the challenge of the baffling problems and complexities with which their jobs confronted them, they naturally began to develop a common interest in sharpening their skills and improving their methods.

For a very long while after organized social work began, however, it was primarily an occupation engaged in by a miscellany of

---

[29] For a helpful comprehensive discussion of international social welfare work, see Friedlander, *op. cit.*, Chapter 19.

persons without particular skills, who came into their positions in
a great variety of ways, and who functioned in relative isolation
from one another. Social work was largely local, parochial, and
inadequately supported. Jobs were either voluntarily assumed, without pay, or were very low-paid and insecure. Some individuals did
their work with more skill and understanding than others, but
practically all fell either judgmentally or sentimentally into the
same pattern of "doing for" the needy.

A number of circumstances began to converge toward the close
of the nineteenth century in ways destined to produce a radical alteration in this picture. For one thing, social work programs were
greatly expanded and given a broader base of assured support.
Moreover, improved communication media and the fact that governmental sponsorship was heavily involved brought them under
more careful scrutiny by a public being conditioned to demand
professional competence. Science was developing emphasis on research and verifiable knowledge, and important new methods and
insights were being revealed, especially in medicine, psychology,
and the social sciences. Education was demonstrating the importance of refined knowledge and skill, and raising the level of
public awareness and expectation. Religion was daring to become
introspectively objective through embracing the "higher criticism,"
and to seek a greater practical relevance through the "social gospel." Technology had replaced scarcity with at least relative abundance. More people, with better general educational backgrounds,
greater job security, and a broader perspective on their tasks, were
being drawn into the field in programs of unprecedented breadth
and complexity.

Dissatisfaction with the damage done by carelessness and lack
of skill, and with the apprenticeship system, which had been the
only method of training, finally led in 1898 to the organization
of the first school for the training of social workers. It was founded
by the Charity Organization Society of New York, and immediately
demonstrated its practical worth. Today there are sixty-three (including seven Canadian) professional schools of social work accredited by the Council on Social Work Education. All are affiliated with recognized institutions of higher education; all operate on

the graduate level; and all require at least two years of graduate study, in a combination of class work and agency internship, for the professional master's degree. Only holders of this degree from one of these schools are eligible for membership in the National Association of Social Workers.

Because social work programs are expanding more rapidly than trained workers can be produced, however, many people without special training are still being employed in social work practice. Add to this the fact that there are so many agencies with such a variety of standards and of administrative control, and that the profession is so new, and it is easy to understand why social work is not yet so fully standardized and carefully disciplined as some other professions of greater maturity and status. Nevertheless, it is rapidly achieving professionalization at a very commendable level of competence.

The discipline, which is now engaged in by more than 125,000 professional social workers in the United States, is currently organized in six divisions, which may be designated as follows: social casework, social group work, community organization, social welfare administration, social welfare research, and social action. The new methods which have been worked out, and the professional convictions which support them, go far beyond the old sentimental dispensations of charity in programs of "doing for" needy people. These new methods constitute a carefully skilled and disciplined process of "working with" people in ways designed to help them live their own lives more effectively. From a somewhat accidental occupation, social work has become a profession based on "competence."[30] From limited absorption in the relief of physical distress, it has vastly broadened itself to embrace concern for (1) improving social arrangements, (2) helping persons achieve inner adequacy, and (3) helping persons make satisfying adjustments to life and the world around them.

Should it not be added that while these developments have occurred in a so-called secular setting, they are eminently compatible with some of the most sincere and vital concerns of the Christian

---

[30] Wilson and Ryland, *op. cit.*, p. 15.

Church? That they were not directly produced under the overt leadership of the church through its traditional charity programs, may seem a matter for regret to some churchmen, but that they partake of the essence which Christianity has distilled in society and merit the wholehearted approval of the churches can hardly be questioned.

The Mounting Welfare Crisis

That there is a welfare crisis which is growing in dimension and intensity, has been apparent for some time. Evidence of it exists on every hand. The vastly expanded welfare programs of the governments of Britain and the United States, as well as of many other nations and of the United Nations, are good barometers of the situation. Only enormous pressures could have produced developments such as these. Furthermore, they are programs which undoubtedly will have to be expanded further rather than diminished in the future.

Within American society the crisis is reflected in increasing distress in family life, increasing juvenile delinquency and crime, increasing mental illness, increasing welfare legislation, increasing tensions over income, employment, housing, retirement, and the like, increasing demand for helping services of all kinds, increasing strain due to continuous overloading of all services available, and in many other similar conditions. The amount of money alone involved is staggering, though everyone acquainted with the needs is well aware that many times what is currently available would be required to make even modestly adequate provision for all the legitimate need which actually exists. Nevertheless, in the fiscal year 1958 the United States spent more than $20 billion of public funds for social insurance, public aid, and other welfare services ranging from vocational rehabilitation to school lunch programs. However, $16 billion of the total represented payments of social insurance benefits.[31] Expenditures of voluntary agencies amounted

---

[31] U.S. Department of Health, Education, and Welfare, *Health, Welfare, and Education Trends* (Washington, D.C.: U.S. Government Printing Office, 1960), p. 26.

to something more than $2 billion, almost wholly in the field of welfare services as contrasted with financial aid.

Although it is never easy to establish causation of complicated social problems, a number of fairly obvious conditions which may help to account for this mounting crisis in social welfare can be identified.

For one thing, there is a much higher level of social awareness, expectancy, and demand than ever existed before. New methods of communication have penetrated the barriers of ignorance and isolation everywhere, and people with serious unmet needs in any place on earth know better than to submit to their suffering in fatalistic acceptance of its necessity.

Technology, too, must bear much of the blame. It has kept more people alive to older ages, and has bound them together in great, complex, interdependent units. In consequence, they not only no longer think of themselves in terms of looking after their own needs in lonely solitude, but would actually be unable to do so even if they were inclined to such independence. The old framework of a "household economy" involving the family in co-operative labor to produce directly most of the goods it requires for survival no longer exists to any significant extent. Instead, the security of American families normally depends upon the availability of jobs and adequate, dependable incomes, derived through participation by employable members in corporate economic processes over which the individual and the family have almost no immediate control. Where persons are not employable or cannot secure employment, society must either come to their rescue or leave them to perish. Moreover, as complexity increases, even the employable with low intelligence, inadequate education, or crippled characters find it ever more difficult to manage their affairs in such ways as to provide minimum satisfaction for all their basic needs. In the complexity, too, are great psychological and emotional hazards which often create problems quite overshadowing physical needs.

Great human displacement is also occurring in the economic process. Not only has technology made people increasingly interdependent economically; it is now making them increasingly unnecessary in the productive processes. If automation is not accompanied by the utmost of careful attention to the needs of displaced workers and their families, welfare problems will surely rise to an intensity to which nothing in society's previous experience can be considered comparable.

It should be added, of course, that scientific knowledge and technological developments have provided, and are providing, the foundations on which the hopes and the realities of greater social security are based. The needs represented in the mounting welfare crisis are not driving society hopelessly into a dead-end street, but are, instead, merely prodding it into more diligent labor on a highway which can quite feasibly be constructed through the tangled social wilderness. Christians and other religious persons may well be inclined to feel that now, for the first time, men have available, at least potentially, the resources for implementing the religious ideals of humanitarianism in a reasonably adequate manner.

Many continuing handicaps remain to be dealt with, however, in the dynamic process of working out ways of making the best use of social resources for the general social welfare. Great value conflicts and philosophical inconsistencies must be ironed out; new knowledge must be gained; new skills and methods must be achieved; new organizational and administrative patterns must be evolved; and the hierarchy of social motives and purposes may have to be rearranged.

Summary of Conditions and Trends

This sketchy review of developments in modern social welfare should be helpful in establishing a perspective for the more detailed consideration of the church's continuing role and responsibility in American society, which is to be the burden of the chapters which follow.

The following are among the more important observations which have been made or implied concerning conditions and trends relating to the development of modern social welfare:

1. Social welfare is being moved almost entirely out of the earlier informal, natural-group process, and away from the almost exclusive responsibility of local political units and community

groups, to formal, corporate-group processes and highly centralized organizational administration.

The situation is still more mixed and fluid on this point in America than in England, but the tendency is marked and unmistakable in both places.

2. Government is increasingly taking over responsibility for welfare needs, but there is still an important place for private agencies.

Enlarged governmental provisions are primarily in the areas of physical and material needs, making such concerns increasingly of less importance to the private agencies. In the realm of the intangibles, however, private agencies still retain a major proportion of responsibility. To minister to the intangible needs of the human personality and spirit, in both individual and group settings, through psychological, sociological, and religious channels, appears to be their increasing opportunity.

3. Social welfare emphasis is changing from minimum relief reluctantly provided for the needy few to maximum provision wholeheartedly sought for the security and welfare of all.

Poor relief as a temporary palliative administered more or less punitively is being displaced by programs broadly aimed at the prevention of demoralizing need and insecurity and at curative therapy for the afflicted.

4. A marked tendency is in evidence toward viewing welfare problems and needs in terms of the functioning of the whole society as a unit.

This view is replacing the more traditional atomistic one which focused on the individual as though he existed in a social vacuum, apart from broad social processes and the organization of community life.

Social thought in America still vascillates somewhat between these two points of view, but there is every indication that the old aggressive philosophy of individualism is yielding ground in the movement of American life. There is too much scientific knowledge concerning the dynamics of sociology and social psychology, and too much obvious dependency involvement of everyone in the complex social order, for the arguments of absolute individual responsibility to be any longer tenable.

5. Social welfare value-objectives, which originally were formulated mainly in informal social relationships and within the loosely structured program of the church, have been largely taken over and are being organized into an integrated and consistent discipline by the profession of social work.

This was needed, and is an over-all gain of considerable magnitude for human welfare. While it is doubtful that professional social work has invented value-goals that the Christian gospel has not long embraced, there is no doubt that it has effected significant improvement in the methods which the church and society have traditionally employed in their pursuit. It may be, also, that within the limited range of its disciplined concern the profession of social work is clarifying values and objectives which the church has had difficulty in bringing into focus as clearly as it should have.

6. The development of social welfare concern in the modern period is toward giving increasing attention to man's spiritual welfare, though this is occurring within a secular frame of reference.

Whereas in time past attention was given almost wholly to the meeting of physical needs essential to survival, the focus now embraces the added dimension of a great and growing concern for mental and emotional health, personality development, and the achieving of a degree of adequacy in social relationships which will undergird the individual's self-respect and happiness. This means that the old careless ways of meeting physical needs are being revamped so as to avoid damage to personal integrity, and that therapy and rehabilitation are taking places of equal importance alongside traditional material "relief."

7. The church's role in social welfare appears to be becoming increasingly vague.

From clear-cut dominance in the field, the church seems to have moved to a relatively minor and somewhat confused position. Though its dominance was never so clear in America as in some other societies, there is little doubt of a relative reduction of its significance even here. What the church can do and should do about this will be the center of attention in the remainder of this discussion.

QUESTIONS FOR DISCUSSION

1. Why has no clear-cut division of labor been established between the church and the state in welfare work?

2. In what respects, if any, are welfare services under church administration better than publicly administered services?

3. Why have welfare services been expanding so rapidly in the modern era?

4. Should the trend toward centralization of welfare services under governmental control be encouraged or resisted?

5. Will it be possible for society ever to make adequate provision for the security and welfare of all its members in ways that neither stigmatize nor demoralize individuals?

6. In what ways are the churches of America today succeeding or failing in their welfare responsibilities?

FOLLOW-UP SUGGESTIONS

Individual

Write the United States Department of Health, Education, and Welfare, Washington 25, D.C., for information concerning the variety of programs and services which it sponsors.

Visit the local public welfare, public health, or vocational rehabilitation office, and make inquiries concerning the services available and the problems being encountered.

Group

Plan a program around the theme of "Social Welfare Trends in the United States." Invite several key persons from the staffs of public and private social agencies to participate in a panel. Include, if possible, a representative from a church agency to comment on what is happening to church-sponsored welfare services.

III: The Church in Modern Social Welfare

Though the church never had a dominant administrative responsibility for social welfare in America, there was little question of its dominance in the realm of philosophy and ideology as long as the social patterns remained those of a relatively simple, homogeneous agricultural economy, carried on primarily in a setting of small neighborhoods. All social work, whether or not directly church-related, was motivated by and under informal compulsion to conform to the standards and perspectives of which the church was the acknowledged guardian.

As American society, under the impact of vast technological and social change, has become more complex and heterogeneous, however, the immediate centrality of the church's influence has been seriously challenged. Church-administered programs of social welfare have continued to expand at a rather remarkable rate, considering the church's limited economic resources, and the dynamic impact of church influence on the welfare field continues to be far greater than the relative proportion which the church is carrying of the total welfare burden. Even so, welfare needs have increased so rapidly that the expansion of church programs has been far outdistanced by secular developments. At the same time, while there probably has been no significant lessening of the church's traditional moral, philosophical, or theological emphases, many other ideological frames of reference have arisen to compete with them and have often led to a bypassing or ignoring of the church's position.

The result in the field of social welfare is that many of the church's traditional interpretations and approaches have been subjected to critical scrutiny and either have been discarded or have fallen into disrepute. The vast body of secular social work is simply no longer consciously dependent upon a church-structured moralistic or theological frame of reference. Moreover, within the church itself there has been considerable shock at discovering that concepts and emphases which evolved in the outside secular society, often in spite of the church's opposition, have in many instances actually become more influential in the church's own welfare activities than are its traditional emphases.

It is useless to try to fix the blame for this condition, or to say that it is an altogether evil development. The church did not consciously weaken its theological teachings or abdicate its responsibility for social welfare, and social work did not deliberately seek estrangement from the church or alienation from a theological context. The exigencies of a crisis situation induced by catastrophic social change imposed unprecedented requirements, for which none of the older patterns or institutions of society were adequate.

It was through an evolutionary process of gradualism that "secularism," based on criteria of usefulness rather than of tradition, developed in the area of social welfare. Its primary stimulus arose from the necessity of shifting the main burden of social welfare from private to public hands. By and large, the American churches encouraged this shift because they recognized that the need required it. Increased assumption of responsibility on the part of the general public seemed to them an altogether desirable development entirely in harmony with their broad social objectives. Most of the churches tended to look upon it as being evidence more of an extension than of a diminution of the church's influence in society. They have been surprised and disturbed to discover that the development appears actually to have resulted in a large measure of alienation from the church.

It must be remembered, of course, that these comments pertain to Protestant churches in the United States, and that they are justified because the Protestant influence has been so dominant on this part of the American scene. Indeed, the very fact of this dominance has contributed to the process of "secularization" in social welfare work. Because Protestantism was solidly established as the dominant religious tradition, it tended to feel "at home" in the society[1] and was under no great compulsion to use social work programs for the preserving or furthering of a unique ethnic or religious way of life. Humanitarianism was a part of its concern. Separation of church and state was one of its most solidly established tenets.

In a situation where the state seemed in full accord on these points, the church was understandably more relaxed than it might have been under other circumstances. Churchmen sensed no great need to be struggling to hold social work and social welfare programs under the control of the church's specifically and consciously articulated doctrinal and ecclesiastical objectives. They might have felt otherwise if Protestantism had been a minority influence in the society. As things were, however, the church and its spokesmen were in agreement with the trend toward public assumption of welfare responsibility. Such criticisms as were offered were against what appeared to be the non-humanitarian aspects of secularism.

So pervasive has been this spirit of relaxed confidence in the general relationship to society that many of the social services conducted under Protestant auspices have never been seriously directed toward specifically Protestant, as distinguished from general social or humanitarian, objectives. Protestant social services today are therefore sometimes spoken of as being more identifiable by their auspices than by any specifically "Protestant" content or practice.[2]

Protestantism is now becoming uncomfortably aware, however, that all is not so well with this relaxed relationship as it has been accustomed to assume. This awareness has been stimulated by a number of factors.

For one thing, the evidence is that American society is drifting

---

[1] F. Ernest Johnson and William J. Villaume, "Protestant Social Services," in *Social Work Year Book, 1960* (New York: National Association of Social Workers, 1960), p. 442.

[2] *Ibid.*, p. 440.

rapidly away from identifiably Protestant philosophical and value orientations. Generalized secular orientations are increasingly displacing specifically Protestant influence. Embraced in this shift has been a change in welfare concern from primary emphasis on traditional works of charity, an emphasis with which the church had long been clearly identified, to the more secularly evolved absorption in programs of social security. Moreover, as public welfare services have rapidly overshadowed church-administered programs, and as the discipline of social work has developed techniques and emphases independent of and sometimes contradictory to long-established church practice, the Protestant churches have begun to feel displaced and insecure.

Added to this general feeling of displacement is the more specific fact that the Jewish and Roman Catholic groups have developed strong, independent programs of welfare services which seem to be quite effective in furthering the sectarian objectives of the sponsoring faiths. By comparison, Protestant programs and agencies often appear to be at a great competitive disadvantage. Much evidence in current reactions to this situation suggests that in the pervasive secularism of present-day society Protestantism sees itself no longer as the firmly entrenched dominant influence but as a minority influence arraigned alongside the Roman Catholic and Jewish minorities in a competitive struggle for status.

It may be something of an understatement, therefore, to say that for reasons such as these the Protestant branches of the church in the United States are experiencing considerable confusion at the present time with respect to the question of what is their proper role and responsibility in social welfare.

Without doubt, much of the difficulty stems from the fact that Protestant churches have never been quite clear as to what are their social welfare objectives. In the main, they appear to have wanted to see what they considered to be Christian welfare ideals permeate the whole society, and to have disclaimed interest in having these ideals embraced exclusively in programs administered under the direct control of the church. At the same time, however, they have busily involved themselves, almost to the limit of their resources, in setting up welfare services which they are sure have a "plus" factor in them which non-church-related services cannot give, and which sometimes compete with services not under church auspices. Such behavior, of course, strongly suggests vascillation between the broad goal of getting human need met and a narrower goal of furthering dogmatic or sectarian purposes. Rationalizations usually offered are to the effect that the church is only calling attention to the necessity of meeting the whole needs of the whole man, or that church-related agencies are especially congenial for the church constituency.

Protestant vascillation is also reflected in other ways. For instance, many social services are Protestant in terms of auspices only, and pursue no specifically Protestant ecclesiastical or sectarian objectives. While these services seek to meet need in a simple spirit of humanitarianism, others bearing the Protestant label have been and are being used as an integral part of missionary and evangelistic work. There seems to be a desire to have Protestant services considered unbiased, undogmatic, and unselfish efforts to minister to the human needs of all persons in community life. At the same time the churches have difficulty in not using these services primarily for their own constituencies or as a means of providing leverage for the furthering of sectarian interests. The evidence is, too, that though on the one hand Protestant churches think of their social services as an expression of disinterested love for humanity, on the other hand they evidently suffer guilt feelings if they permit their welfare activities to be no more than "sub-Christian ethical humanitarianism."[3]

Confusion of objectives is also suggested by the fact that though they stress voluntarism and the responsibility of individual church members to carry their Christian principles with them into the affairs of society outside the church, the Protestant churches seem uncomfortable with the fact that so-called "secular" programs, conceived, developed, and operated, in the main, by people from their constituencies, have evolved outside and beyond the churches' con-

---

[3] Roswell P. Barnes in the "Introduction" to *Churches and Social Welfare,* Vol. I, *The Activating Concern,* by E. Theodore Bachmann, Editor (New York: National Council of the Churches of Christ in the U.S.A., 1955), p. 2.

trol. This, it seems, constitutes further evidence that from broad roles of influence, encouragement, and conscience to society at large, Protestant churches appear to be wavering toward limited, authoritarian programs, possibly affected by considerations of status advantages in the arena of sectarian strife or by a feeling of displacement in the informal channels of social control. In any case, many denominational leaders are currently expressing concern over the fact that in their opinion religion is being too much left out of social work, and are apparently beginning to feel strongly that the church "must reassert itself, and reclaim some of the ground it has lost."[4]

The churches are developing a growing awareness of these conditions and problems, however, and are manifesting a serious determination to come to grips with them in a positive way. In fact, it may be said that a great amount of soul searching is going on at this point throughout American Protestantism. Such a development is probably long overdue and surely portends much good both for the future of the church and for the welfare of society. If the trend signifies that Protestantism in America is at long last moving away from a laissez faire, or line-of-least-resistance, base of operation with respect to social welfare to more carefully conceived and integrated emphases, it will indeed mark the beginning of a new era. Still, there is always the danger that in planning .and integration of purposes and efforts, just as in a laissez faire process, imbalance and distortion may occur and some of the important emphases may be overlooked.

Nevertheless, for better or worse, Protestantism seems to be swinging away from its traditional relaxed reliance upon community-sponsored agencies, and to be stepping up its efforts to establish health and welfare agencies of its own. In fact, it seems anxious and determined to make Protestant social work a far more distinct entity than it has usually been heretofore.

The following, more specific resume of how the church is relating itself to modern social welfare is designed to be helpful to churchmen who seek a broader comprehension of the situation,

---

[4] Bachmann (Ed.), *op. cit.*, Vol. I, p. 120.

who are anxious to see the church improve its ministry in the area of social service, and who must assume responsibility in the decisional processes which will determine the patterns of the churches' relationship to social work and social welfare in the future.

The Quest for New Role Definitions

The quest for new role definitions for the church in social welfare is rapidly gaining momentum, and is moving in several directions.

It is viewed by church spokesmen as a careful, honest effort at self-examination on the part of the churches—an effort arising not out of their frustrations but out of their vitality, strength, and confidence. It is, these spokesmen affirm, expressive only of a commendable desire on the part of the churches for a fresh analysis on which to base a more clearly relevant restatement of their basic purposes and objectives.[5] In any case, it is a quest being almost ardently pursued in both formal and informal, conscious and unconscious, ways.

These are among the more important areas and directions in which the quest is being conducted:

In Terms of Theology

One of the most soul-searching struggles going on in the churches has to do with the basis on which social work must be done. Neo-protestant biblical theology, arising after events in the mid-1930's had chastened the prevailing optimism of social and theological liberalism, has been insisting that all welfare effort must be carefully grounded in a biblically disciplined theology. This theology asserts that there must be recognition of the all-corrupting influence of sin and of the dependence of men on God's forgiveness mediated through Christ the Saviour. According to exponents of this view, it is not enough for humanity to strive toward God, using Christ as teacher, master, and example; rather, men must turn toward God in a far more profound and humbling sense of obedience to his authoritative Word. The simple ethical humanitarianism which undergirds most secular social work and which was so con-

---

[5] *Ibid.*, p. 1.

genial to the earlier theological liberalism is defined in this context as being inadequate, sub-Christian.[6]

Proponents of this drive toward more solidly biblical foundations for social work contend that the churches must definitely anchor their welfare responsibilities in the Word of God, and that they must also articulate the thesis that secular social work is inadequate to whatever extent it varies from this foundation.

While this neo-orthodox biblical emphasis has been gaining increasing recognition for a number of years, it appears to have approached its zenith, and a resurgent liberalism is beginning to challenge the alienating tone of dogmatism which it contains. Encouraged by such theologians as Paul Tillich, who sees the truth of religion which is revealed in the Bible as also expressed in every honest, creative quest for truth and ultimate reality in the total culture,[7] many churchmen are beginning to take a hard second look at the possibility that social work done on a less dogmatic basis of ethical humanitarianism may not be so far afield of Christian concern after all. At least, they are distinguishing between the values of humanitarianism and the evils of God-neglecting humanism.

In Terms of Goals and Purposes

For a number of years the churches have been developing an awareness that their goals and purposes in social welfare need clarification and restatement.

The Department of Christian Social Relations of the Federal Council of Churches brought the subject up from time to time. In a statement issued in 1948, for instance, it spoke strongly of "the increasing secularization of the welfare services," of the fact that religion seemed to be "just about left . . . out," and of the widespread feeling among churchmen that the time may have arrived when the church "must reassert itself."[8]

Finally, the first National Conference on the Churches and So-

---

[6] *Ibid.*, pp. 2, 113–115.

[7] David Wesley Soper, *Major Voices in American Theology* (Philadelphia: The Westminster Press, 1953), p. 124.

[8] Bachmann (ed.), *op. cit.*, Vol. I, pp. 119–120.

cial Welfare was called by the National Council of the Churches
of Christ in the U.S.A. to meet in Cleveland, Ohio, November
1–4, 1955, "to consider the role and function of the churches in
relation to the changing needs in social welfare." Approximately
1,500 churchmen and social workers, representing thirty-one
Protestant and Eastern Orthodox bodies, were in attendance.

Preparatory materials and conference discussions focused upon
such basic questions of principle and policy as: Is social welfare
a marginal and optional field in the life of the churches? Is a
church under any biblical or theological mandate to work in this
field, or is it impelled only by a fading tradition? Should the
churches abandon the field to nonsectarian agencies and concentrate their energies and resources on what is generally described as
their unique spiritual functions? If they should not abandon the
field entirely, should they limit themselves to caring for their own
constituents or for their own professional servants? What consideration should be given to the fact that our Roman Catholic and
Jewish friends maintain very extensive programs and institutions
providing welfare services?[9]

The Conference revealed wide variation in policy and opinion.
It also showed how great was the common ground of problems
and concern. Though it did not evolve a core of common policy,
it did make a beginning toward "a more precise formulation" of
the churches' role and function in social welfare.[10] Above all, it
was emphatic in the unequivocal assertion that social work, far
from being a peripheral concern of the churches, belonging in a
position secondary to missions, evangelism, and Christian education, is on a parity with these other emphases as "a necessary expression of the love of God in which the church must be more
largely involved if it is to be true to its fundamental message to
men."[11]

In "A Message to the Churches," which the Conference adopted,

9 *Ibid.*, p. 1.

10 Bachmann (ed.), *op. cit.*, Vol. III: *The Emerging Perspective*, (New
York: National Council of the Churches of Christ in the U.S.A., 1956),
p. ix.

11 *Ibid.*, p. xiii.

the declaration was made that "we . . . have a profound obligation in social welfare to express our concern for our fellow men,
and to dare to speak afresh of Christian faith in action." The message also called attention to the need for research, study, planning,
education, and the broadest possible base of co-operation. It
stressed the importance of giving attention to public policy, of
supporting "the great human services" of public welfare, and of
correlating church welfare services with those offered by other
agencies. It encouraged church social agencies to make full use
and serve as demonstrations of "the very best standards of professional care and service." It called for greater financial support of
church welfare services, for more serious recruitment of personnel
to social work as a most important Christian vocation, and for a
strengthening of democratic practices as a means of helping the
churches and society deal most effectively with the numerous issues
of social policy which remain to be resolved. Finally, the message
called the church's attention to the importance of serving "the
needs of the whole man" in the confidence that for so great a challenge "Christ is sufficient" even though "we are not sufficient."[12]

In connection with, and as a result of this Conference, the National Council of the Churches of Christ in the U.S.A. published
three significant volumes under the general title of *Churches and
Social Welfare*. Volumes I and II were produced as preparatory
material for the Conference, and Volume III resulted directly from
the Conference as a report of program and findings. Volume I,
carrying the subtitle, *The Activating Concern*,[13] raised the basic
questions and included authorized reports from fifteen denominations which outlined historic development and set forth theological
views in social welfare within these communions. Volume II, sub-
titled *The Changing Scene*,[14] made use of the composite denominational picture to summarize details of development of social welfare
over the preceding fifty years, indicated current trends and issues,
and challenged the churches to re-evaluate procedures. Volume

---

[12] *Ibid.*, pp. 1–7.

[13] Bachmann (ed.), *op. cit.*, Vol. I.

[14] Bachmann (ed.), *op. cit.*, Vol. II: *The Changing Scene*, by Horace R.
Cayton and Setsuko Matsunaga Nishi.

III, appropriately designated as *The Emerging Perspective*,[15] reflecting "the heart and spirit of the Conference," carried the findings of the forty sectional groups which met during the Conference, the "Message to the Churches," and other program materials indicating "response and prospects."

So valuable was this initial Conference that the desirability of further steps in the same direction immediately became apparent. The need for greater consensus on policy and strategy was especially obvious, and the National Council of Churches almost immediately began exploratory work in that direction. A poll of 2,000 church and welfare leaders across the nation was taken to ascertain the questions on which it was felt further clarification of policies was most needed. Over 75 area and regional conferences were held from coast to coast. On May 7–10, 1957, in Atlantic City, New Jersey, 241 voting delegates from twenty-two denominations, 24 voting delegates from local and state councils of churches, and 22 non-voting representatives of other denominations and related organizations which were not members of the National Council of Churches gathered in a second national conference. This was designated a National Conference on Policy and Strategy in Social Welfare.

The purpose of this Conference was narrower and more specific than that of the first. Though it did not seek uniformity of policy, it embraced as a goal "a general agreement that will enable us to understand each other better and to move toward such a measure of consistency as will permit us to exert a more effective influence in the nation and in local communities." The delegates, all of whom were persons of special competence in the area of church tradition and practice in social welfare, reached a remarkable degree of consensus. Of the eight important reports which were adopted, four were by unanimous vote, two received only one dissenting vote each, one received three dissenting votes, and one received five.[16]

---

[15] Bachmann (ed.), *op. cit.*, Vol. III.

[16] *Policy and Strategy in Social Welfare: Report to the Churches* (New York: National Council of the Churches of Christ in the U.S.A., 1957), pp. 3–4.

The results of this eminently successful and significant Conference were published under the title of *Policy and Strategy in Social Welfare: Report to the Churches*.[17] Few documents of such significance have issued from church sources in many years. The statement on motivation, included in the report of the Findings Committee, has been called "the Magna Carta for the churches' activity in social welfare." Among other things, it says: "Social welfare is an integral part of the church, not an optional part of its program"; "In response to the grace of God, the Church is impelled to . . . [serve] the whole man in all his relationships, and all men as children of God"; "the social welfare mission of the Church cannot be evaluated in terms of its success in making Christians out of those whose need is served."[18]

As illustrations of present basic concerns, the Report of the Findings Committee also included these seven specific objectives:

1. The churches through a social ministry should seek ways of bearing their testimony to the community, bringing their influence to bear at every point where human need can be met.

2. The churches should seek through their social welfare activity . . . to receive into their total corporate lives the insights and disciplines emerging from the field of social service.

3. The churches, through their members, must be involved in the totality of life in a ministry to people . . .

4. The churches should assist the parish pastor to minister effectively to the social welfare needs of people in his congregation and community.

5. The churches need to pioneer in new and important services to people . . .

6. The churches ought to seek to assist in the creation of the best possible type of society in which every person has an opportunity to develop to the fullest capacity of his God-given endowment and to make his maximum contribution to the whole community . . .

7. The churches should recruit and train workers for a social ministry . . .[19]

---

[17] *Ibid.*
[18] *Ibid.*, pp. 3, 8–9.
[19] *Ibid.*, p. 10.

While this statement of policy and strategy was greatly needed and is very important as a first attempt at establishing a Protestant definition of functions and responsibilities, it is by no means a final answer for the churches in their quest for clarification of goals and purposes. In the first place, some denominations did not participate in the statement's formulation, and it was not officially adopted either by the National Council of Churches or by the denominations whose officially appointed delegates were involved in formulating it. Instead, it was simply printed and transmitted to the churches and national agencies for "study" and "comments."[20]

It may well be asked, also, if this statement of policy and strategy does not actually represent the discovery of common ground on which the churches were already conducting their welfare programs and doing their thinking concerning social welfare more than it does a pioneering "break-through" on the front where the major policy dilemmas really confront the churches in social welfare.

For instance, the statement can hardly be said to have produced a clear-cut delineation between the church's responsibility in social welfare and the responsibility of government and voluntary secular agencies. Instead, it leaves the matter at about where it has long stood, by asserting that the church "should be vitally related to all aspects of social welfare" by urging efforts toward general social improvement even though "such social improvement does not of itself meet the deepest needs of people"; by recognizing that most social work is done by non-church agencies and that there should be the fullest possible co-operation with these agencies; by affirming that the individual church member may find expression of "the Christian motive for social welfare" in non-church agency settings; by expressing concern over the "dangers in centralized governmental action" but approving "the development of the system of public assistance" by the government; by expressing deep

---

[20] *Ibid.*, p. 6. It was subsequently adopted, however, in 1959, by the General Assembly of the United Presbyterian Church in the U.S.A., and in modified form by the National Lutheran Council Division of Welfare. It will also serve as the basis of discussion in the Second National Conference on the Churches and Social Welfare to be held in Cleveland, October, 1961.

anxiety over the increasingly "serious problems between church and state" which are being created by "the enlarged role of government" in the field of social welfare; and at the same time, by encouraging the churches to "continue to increase the number and improve the quality of their health and welfare agencies to meet the needs of people."[21] Though such statements reflect significant agreement on the importance of strengthening church programs of social welfare, they neither fix boundaries to church responsibilities in the field nor clearly face up to the need for a definition of the spiritual values in secular social work.

It may be accepted, therefore, that as a beginning the statement was extremely valuable and significant. No comparable effort had been made before to define the role and function of the church in social welfare. At the same time, the statement left much to be desired in the way of conclusive answers to many of the most perplexing problems.

That the quest for further clarification of goals and purposes is still, however, a dynamic one in the minds of church leaders is indicated by the fact that a Second National Conference on the Churches and Social Welfare is to be held under the auspices of the National Council of Churches, October 23–26, 1961, in Cleveland, Ohio.

The conclusion seems justified, nevertheless, that, despite commendable effort and encouraging progress, the church is still far from a clear understanding of what exactly is its role and function in social welfare. It is still somewhat confused as to what constitutes proper and adequate social expression of the impulses of Christian affection and brotherly love.

In Terms of Adaptive Techniques

The church's quest for new role definitions is clearly reflected in the vigorous efforts being made to adapt church-related welfare activities to changing needs and circumstances, as well as to the new techniques and emphases which have been evolved in modern social work. While it would be impossible to catalogue all evi-

---

[21] *Ibid.*, pp. 19, 20, 23, 25, 26, 27.

dences of such efforts, the purposes of illustration may be served by a few examples.

In many congested, disorganized urban areas of great change and transition, so-called "institutional churches" have been evolved in response to numerous pressures of unmet need. Such churches began in the 1880's, and have increasingly represented an interesting effort at hybridization of traditional religious emphases and professional social work emphases at the local church level. Along with most of the customary church activities they combine a variety of casework and group work programs as nearly in keeping with standard social work practices as possible. Because most of the people they serve come from low income groups, some type of financial subsidy is usually necessary for the support of the program. Sometimes this subsidy is provided by the denomination at large, or by a group of co-operating churches, but it is often obtained by persuading the Community Chest to underwrite the cost of the social work phases of the program. Experience has shown, however, that to maintain a satisfactory balance between the religious and social work emphases in church agencies receiving Chest subsidies is very difficult. The merit of this type of effort on the church's part is, therefore, often debated.

While the "institutional church" represents a type of ministry the church probably should have been specializing in for a long time in our chaotic urban communities, it has never been taken seriously enough to be given an adequate basis of support, and it has not been guided by enough careful research and study to produce a well-integrated program. Notation should be made, too, that there is now increasingly less need for this type of church, as the growing network of community welfare services achieves more adequate coverage in the transitional areas of the cities.

A somewhat different type of adaptation is represented in the case of a number of strong, prestige churches which have added trained counselors, case workers, or other specialists to their staffs to perform a variety of functions in which religion and social work are combined. Occasionally such a church also opens and operates a kind of outpost program, often in a store-front setting, in which it may seek to offer both religious and social work services.

One of the most unique adaptive efforts has been the East Harlem Protestant Parish initiated by Union Theological Seminary students in one of the most congested areas of New York City. In this parish a group of ministers work as a team. They use several old church buildings and store-front centers. By concentrating on a sidewalk ministry they take the church out onto the streets and into the community where the people and problems are. Financial subsidy is provided by several denominations and through private contributions. Without making a distinction between them, as is done in the "institutional" church, social work objectives and traditional religious objectives are so intermeshed in the program as to be almost indistinguishable.

Illustrating a slightly different approach is Trinity Parish of the Protestant Episcopal Church which operates the Lower East Side Mission in New York City primarily as a vast experiment in religiously oriented social group work with the youth of the street gangs in an area of high delinquency and conflict.[22]

Many other types of missions are also being operated in numerous places. While some still lean heavily toward traditional evangelizing patterns, the major tendency increasingly seems to be toward ministering to need in a spirit of humanitarian concern without immediate reference to evangelistic objectives. Included in a vast assortment of other programs are settlement houses, recreation centers, camping programs, services to migrants and transients, Goodwill Industries and other aids to the physically handicapped, the YMCA and the YWCA, The Salvation Army, and the like.

One of the most interesting present trends is toward the provision of chaplaincy services in a variety of settings where such services have not previously been available to any considerable extent. Included among these settings are prisons, juvenile reform and treatment centers, mental institutions, hospitals, children's homes, homes for the aged, industrial plants, and similar places. Though there is great variety in what the chaplains do, and though they serve officially as representatives of religion, their actual duties

---

[22] C. Kilmer Myers, *Light the Dark Streets* (Greenwich, Conn.: Seabury Press, 1957).

are often related as much to social work as to specifically religious objectives.

At the local church level nurseries, clinics, recreation programs, youth centers, golden age clubs, and the like, are being organized. In many instances, local church committees exist to sponsor a variety of services to community institutions and agencies.

Another significant evidence of the impact of welfare needs and social work practices on the churches is the great amount of attention which is currently given in the theological seminaries to the training of ministers for counseling responsibilities. Most reputable seminaries now make this an important aspect of ministerial preparation. The counseling for which this emphasis is designed is not, moreover, the traditional type, that has to do primarily with matters pertaining directly to religious faith and belief. Instead, the emphasis is on preparation for counseling that deals primarily with a variety of psychological and social adjustment problems similar to or identical with those which command the attention of social workers in regular social agency settings. Furthermore, the theories and techniques which are taught ministers with respect to counseling are essentially identical with those incorporated in the training of social workers. It is necessary to add, however, that the theories and techniques are usually not taught so thoroughly in the seminary as in the school of social work and that they are sometimes not too well integrated with other emphases in the minister's total training experience.

Some theologians looked askance at this development. They feared that it would tend to weaken the minister's theological undergirding. Recently, however, there is considerable feeling that ministers need much more training in the skills of social work than they are receiving, since an increasing proportion of pastoral responsibilities have to do with the types of welfare needs (family counseling, personal counseling, group work, community organization, etc.) for which the skills of social work were specifically developed. Several major denominations have made provisions to insure that at least a few of their ministers regularly obtain training in a school of social work after graduation from the theological seminary. There seems to be a growing trend in this direction.

The dynamic nature of the struggle for effective adaptation to welfare needs is indicated at the denominational level by the number of major agencies of social welfare which the denominations have set up. The following brief summary of arrangements in a few of the major denominations is indicative:

The American Baptist Convention maintains a Council on Social Progress, and has within its Home Mission Society a department of "Christian Centers," a Division of Institutional Ministries, and a Juvenile Protection Service. The American Lutheran Church has a Board of Charities, and a Commission on Research and Social Action. The Church of the Brethren has a Brethren Service Commission, including a Department of Social Welfare. The Congregational Christian Churches have a director of health and welfare in their Board of Home Missions and a Council for Social Action with specialized leadership in such fields as Christian citizenship, international relations, and industrial, agricultural, racial, and cultural problems. The Disciples of Christ, International Convention, has a Department of Social Welfare with Divisions of Social Education and Community Service, and a Benevolent Association to administer homes for children and the aged. The Evangelical and Reformed Church has a Commission on Health and Welfare Services and a Commission on Christian Social Action. The agency of the Evangelical United Brethren is called the Commission on Christian Social Action. The Lutheran Church, Missouri Synod, has a Board of Social Welfare. The Mennonite Church maintains a Board of Missions and Charities. The Methodist Church has a Board of Christian Social Concerns, a Board of Hospitals and Homes, a Woman's Division of Christian Service, and a Division of National Missions which carries on many services through departments of City Work, Town and Country Work, and Goodwill Industries. The United Presbyterian Church in the U.S.A. maintains a Division of Social Education and Action in its Board of Christian Education; an Office of Health and Welfare for neighborhood houses, chaplaincy, and institutions; and a Department of Education and Medical Work in its Board of National Missions. The Presbyterian Church in the U.S. has a Division of Christian Action in its Board of Education and a Division of Homes and

Christian Welfare in its Board of Church Extension for the over-sight of homes for children and the aging. An extensive program is carried on by the Protestant Episcopal Church through its De-partment of Christian Social Relations, which is organized in the three divisions of (1) Health and Welfare Services, (2) Christian Citizenship, and (3) Urban-Industrial. The Southern Baptist Con-vention has a Christian Life Commission. The United Lutheran Church has a Board of Social Missions. The National Lutheran Council maintains a Division of Welfare, which co-ordinates the welfare work for two-thirds of the Lutherans.

The quest for adaptive techniques is also reflected in the various co-operative arrangements which are being worked out at the inter-denominational level. The National Council of Churches maintains a Department of Social Welfare in its Division of Christian Life and Work, and similar departments are sponsored in state and local councils of churches.

The Department of Social Welfare at the national level sponsors annually the Church Conference of Social Work, which is an open forum held in conjunction with the National Conference on Social Welfare. At intervals of about three years, also, the Department brings together the health and welfare associations of its constituent bodies to consider new developments of common interest at a National Conference on Churches and Social Welfare.

Much growth and experimentation are occurring, too, in the state and local councils, where attention is being given to such diversified and specialized activities as court work, the operation of centralized "intake" and referral services, casework with children, training in group work, camping programs, and the maintenance of institutional chaplaincies.

At least twenty-five cities already have councils of churches with departments of social welfare in which professional staffs are employed to co-ordinate and direct welfare activities. These de-partments are frequently supported by Community Chest funds, and serve as representatives of the churches in local councils of community agencies.[23]

---

[23] Johnson and Villaume, *op. cit.*, p. 446.

Another form of co-operative arrangement, often sponsored by the council of churches, is the federation of Protestant social agencies, which takes place most often at the local level in order to further mutual concerns and to strengthen the agencies in their struggles for recognition and support.

These, then, let it be said in summary of this section of our discussion, are a few of the general evidences that the church is aware of the changing definitions of social welfare, is still keenly interested in ministering to welfare needs, is consciously attempting to embrace the new skills and insights of modern social science and social work, and is struggling to discover and maintain its proper role and function in the changing welfare scene. Indications are that some useful adaptive techniques are being acquired, but the quest continues at a rapidly mounting pace.

In Terms of New Bases of Support

A major source of the churches' distress with respect to direct participation in social welfare work is in the fact that their economic resources show a progressive decline in relative adequacy. This is not to say that they are receiving fewer contributions for the support of their welfare programs, but it is to point out that what they receive represents a rapidly shrinking proportion of the total amount being spent in society for social welfare.

While government expenditures are astronomical by comparison, a 1940 report of the United Stewardship Council's study of church income compared with the income of private philanthropy showed that the churches cannot even begin to compete with the economic strength which private philanthropy commands. The average annual expendable funds of private philanthropy in America over a seventeen-year period, it was shown, were more than three times as much as the twenty-two leading denominations had received as total denominational income in their best year on record.[24]

---

[24] John Price Jones, *Yearbook of Philanthropy, 1940* (New York: The Inter-River Press, 1940), pp. 13, 16 (as reported in Buell G. Gallagher, "Welfare Work: Ally or Alternative?" in Randolph Crump Miller [ed.], *The Church and Organized Movements,* Vol. II [New York: Harper & Brothers, 1946], p. 117).

This, of course, poses grave problems for the churches as they seek to maintain even a semblance of relevance to welfare needs through social services.

So far, efforts to reduce the severity of this great economic handicap have not been strikingly successful, though some minor gains have been achieved. It would be unrealistic to expect that, with all the other responsibilities they have to carry, the churches could, under existing circumstances, increase their benevolent giving sufficiently to put their welfare programs on anything resembling financial parity with public and private non-sectarian philanthropies.

Under the pressure of need for additional financial support, church-related social agencies have turned, in many instances, to the Community Chest in quest of funds. Chest regulations, however, usually impose strictures on "religious" or sectarian emphases in agencies receiving such funds. Consequently, churches tend to feel frustrated in and somewhat alienated from their objectives in many of the situations where such funds are accepted. Inter-denominational work through local councils of churches seems to fit into the Chest subsidy arrangement better, however, than do the denominational agencies.

With an eagerness almost suggesting desperation churches have been turning, also, to the acceptance of tempting opportunities for government subsidies in connection with many of their welfare programs. Such subsidies appear to be increasingly available in connection with schools, hospitals, and other institutions, as well as a variety of other agencies and services. It may be, too, that the fact of the government's making them available to the churches reflects a sense of need for the churches to keep a hand in the welfare field. Indeed, the subsidies may indicate a hopeful direction for future developments. Many church leaders are beginning to have serious misgivings, however, and are wondering if the churches, in their eagerness to secure financial assurance for their continued welfare activity, are not carelessly surrendering the values represented in the traditional Protestant principle of separation of church and state. A question exists, also, as to whether government subsidies may not eventually prove unduly restrictive of the freedom of church agencies in the pursuit of welfare objectives which seem important to them.

While church agencies are not the only ones that are perplexed over the question of the appropriateness of accepting government funds for the operation of voluntary agencies, they must be no less alert than the most responsible of other agencies to the seriousness of the implications in such acceptance. Family Service Agencies, for example, have been weighing carefully, in a manner which church agencies may well emulate, the advantages and disadvantages of accepting unrestricted grants from government funds. In a recent statement proposed for consideration in the Family Service Association of America, the following points were outlined:

POSSIBLE DISADVANTAGES OF ACCEPTING UNRESTRICTED GRANTS:

1. Danger of upsetting balance of program.

2. Public funds, in any case, will not meet existing financial deficits or justify the effort and time involved in seeking them.

3. Such funds may prove temporary.

4. Chests and United Funds may be encouraged to default on their primary obligation for financing voluntary agencies.

5. Such trends may impede development of public services.

6. It is inappropriate to use unrestricted public funds until public-private agency responsibilities are redefined.

7. Acceptance of unrestricted funds implies responsibility for full-coverage service.

8. Do services limited to sectarian groups, or organized so that lay boards may not have complete freedom to set policies or who may not be fully responsible to the whole community, have a right to accept general tax funds?

POSSIBLE ADVANTAGES OF ACCEPTING UNRESTRICTED GRANTS:

1. Provide opportunity to interpret to and secure understanding of program from a broader group in the community.

2. Permit official recognition of and support for the unique community value of family casework.

3. Strengthen family agencies and make it possible for them to

participate in the handling of special problems requiring intensified family casework, when these problems are of special concern to the community and require attention on behalf of the taxpayers.

4. Extend specialized services of the voluntary agency which are sometimes needed by public agencies.

5. Finance experimentation.

6. Demonstrate services which might later be incorporated into public agencies.

7. Demonstrate service which might later be incorporated into voluntary agencies and supported by Chests or United Funds.

8. Augment staff to utilize particular family agency skills and' provide experience in reference to services for specific groups, such as to persons released from mental institutions or to their families.

9. Permit additional staffing and preferential services to particular governmental units or other institutions.

10. Reimburse (foster homes, etc.) for particular services traditionally centered in the family agency in certain communities.[25]

Equally significant, perhaps, and surely as far out of line with tradition as the accepting of funds from government, is the fact that church-related agencies have turned to the expedient of financing themselves in large measure through fees and other charges for their services. Data supplied by 1,011 agencies in a 1954 study conducted by the National Council of Churches indicated that approximately four-fifths of the total operating income of these agencies was so-called "earned income." Service fees from individuals amounted to more than three-fourths of total operating income, and those from public funds and other sources considerably overshadowed income from investments in accounting for the remainder of the four-fifths "earned" total. At the same time, contributions of religious organizations to these agencies amounted to only 5.4 per cent of their total operating budgets. Even when hospitals, which received 89 per cent of their total income from service fees, were excluded, the figure for the contributions of religious organizations to the support of the remaining agencies

---

[25] From "Considerations Involved in the Use of Public Funds by Family Agencies" (A proposed statement; mimeographed) (New York: Family Service Association of America, January 21, 1960).

amounted to only 15 per cent of the operating budgets of those agencies.[26]

It is not to be wondered at, therefore, that the report made note of the bitterness of agency executives over the fact that the church seemed especially ready to claim credit for sponsoring and initiating welfare programs, but very reluctant to give them adequate financial support, "or even to solicit such support energetically from lay church people." This tendency toward bitterness, it added, is made especially acute by the feeling that church-relatedness often prevents the agencies from obtaining support from public funds which might otherwise be available to them.

A question may well be raised, however, concerning the extent to which agencies relying heavily on government grants, on Community Chest funds, or on fees charged for services, actually represent genuine expressions of Christian compassion and charity.

In Terms of Church and State Relations

What has been said in the preceding section about the churches' acceptance of government subsidies is related to one of the most profound dilemmas with which Protestant churches are currently confronted in their welfare programs and philosophy. It is the dilemma of how to define the respective roles and spheres of responsibility of the church and the state. Great confusion exists in the minds of churchmen on this point, and an impressive amount of inconsistency in practice is evident.

One of the major reasons for this confusion is that there is not, and apparently never has been, a consistent Protestant understanding of the doctrine of separation of church and state. Neither Luther nor Calvin seemed to feel that such separation was necessary. John Wesley remained until his death a priest in a state tax-supported church. Protestantism in England and some of the Scandinavian countries still functions through state tax-supported churches.

Since, however, many of the Protestant groups that constituted the early settlements in North America were motivated to come

[26] Bachmann (ed.), *op. cit.*, Vol. II, pp. 127, 143.

here by persecution at the hands of state churches, they held, in connection with their religion, an understandably strong bias against any official ties between the state and the church, as well as against any interference by the state in the exercise of religion. This bias, undergirded by a mixture of emotion and logic, assumed decisive significance as the influence of these early groups permeated and achieved dominance on the American scene in the formative years of the nation's history.

Concurrently, there was a strong anti-established-church sentiment among the agnostic rationalists and humanists who figured conspicuously in the intellectual life of the young nation.

Consequently, the doctrine of the separation of church and state, as the editor of a prominent Presbyterian journal comments, "may well be more indigenous to the United States as a civil polity than to Protestantism as a religious community." Certainly it is true, as this commentator adds, that "in this country Protestants tend to be divided in their convictions, depending upon what the issue is that is at stake." For example, he continues, "they tend to be *for* Bible-reading in the public schools, so long as it is a Protestant Bible that is read, and definitely *against* what is to them 'sectarian,' but to the Roman Catholic is 'Christian' teaching about the Virgin Mary."[27]

So acute has become the awareness of the general confusion and inconsistency in thinking on church and state relations that the subject is currently receiving prominent attention in major discussions under the auspices of interdenominational groups, such as the National Council of Churches, and in the governing bodies of many individual Protestant denominations. The 172nd General Assembly of the United Presbyterian Church in the U.S.A., meeting in 1960, even went so far as to appoint a special committee to conduct consultations and work out a statement designed "to interpret the meaning of the doctrine of separation of church and state in the light of the Reformed tradition, so as to clarify the rights and responsibilities of religious groups in our pluralistic society."[28]

---

[27] *Social Progress,* July, 1960, p. 28.
[28] *Ibid.*

Pressure toward clarification of the Protestant position on church and state relations is being stimulated by a combination of several circumstances in connection with social welfare. For one thing, the phenomenal growth of government welfare programs has resulted in such an overshadowing and appropriation of services rendered by the church in many of the areas of the church's traditional concern that churchmen are provoked to ask whether or not the government may be going beyond its proper functions and invading areas of church responsibility. At the same time, the Roman Catholic Church, having become thoroughly assimilated and indigenous to the American scene, is with increasing aggressiveness articulating and seeking implementation of its far more coherent and strongly contradictory point of view. A further and still more perplexing consideration is the fact that the pressure of needs and demands seems to be moving the society inexorably toward such continued expansion of public welfare services as could pose a threat to many democratic values for which the church feels a concern that goes far beyond anxiety over its institutional status and prerogatives. Finally, out of all these conditions arises a poorly defined fence-straddling relationship of "co-operation" between government and voluntary welfare services under church and other auspices that becomes ever more complicated and adds greatly to the confusion.

A brief look into some of the facts that lie back of these four "pressure points" seems in order.

The growth of government welfare services is fairly easily traced. Prior to the Great Depression of the 1930's, public social welfare was relatively small in scope and almost wholly on the local, county, and state levels. The depression, however, forced the federal government to step into the picture to help meet financial needs of the unemployed. Now almost all financial assistance is given to needy people by government, much of it with Federal funds. Social security is the "nest egg" upon which nearly all the population rely for physical comfort in old age. Public welfare has become a major aspect of government at all levels and is training and using a large proportion of all social workers. Public agencies are providing for the majority of children who must receive care outside their own homes. Most mental hospitals, and an increasingly large proportion of all other hospitals, are government owned. Most of the research in health and welfare is being undertaken by government agencies or with government funds.

While there are 4,000 agencies and institutions owned by or clearly related to Protestant churches, spending over $1 billion annually and having capital assets of about $3.5 billion, they are dwarfed by comparison with government agencies, institutions, and financial outlays. For example, government expenditures for health and welfare, including social security benefits, currently considerably exceed $20 billion annually, while in 1955 churches contributed only $380 million to church-supported health and welfare activities, and the total amount raised in 1956 through all the efforts of the United Community Funds and Councils of America was only $322 million. A recent report points out that voluntary philanthropic contributions to health, welfare, education and religion, rose from $4 billion in 1950 to $7.8 billion in 1959, but that, by way of comparison, health and welfare voluntary expenditures in 1958 totaled only $2 billion as over against government expenditures of $24 billion in the same field.[29]

Protestant church leaders, viewing this rapid growth of government welfare services, and knowing that voluntary contributions could be sharply reduced by another depression or by a shift in the policy of taxation, are understandably anxious as to what may be the future of church-related services. They sense that if the church has prerogatives which the state should respect in the welfare field, those prerogatives must be quickly and clearly specified and vigorously defended. At the same time, these churchmen are anxious to maintain a constructive rather than an obstructionist relationship to all welfare services that fall properly within the province of government responsibility.

In the midst of this concern is the provocative fact that the Roman Catholic Church and its leaders have a clear, well-

---

[29] Thomas Karter, "Voluntary Agency Expenditures for Health and Welfare from Philanthropic Contributions, 1930–1955," *Social Security Bulletin,* February 1958; also, statement of Robert E. Bondy to a conference of executives, National Social Welfare Assembly, Inc., June 15, 1960.

organized, and carefully thought out position with respect to church and state relations in social welfare. This position is subsumed under the broad general principle of "subsidiarity."

Subsidiarity, according to the Catholic view, is a principle derived from the theological doctrine of the freedom of man. Man's freedom is necessary in order for him to fulfill his responsibility to God for his moral life and thus secure eternal salvation. God is the source of man's freedom, not the state; but the state should be the guarantor of freedom. Government programs should, then, be limited to accomplishing only those purposes for the common welfare which the people cannot accomplish for themselves either personally or through their family units or larger natural associations. Voluntary agencies, including church-related voluntary agencies, are such natural associations, and must therefore be regarded as living expressions of the people's desire, as well as of their right, to help themselves through mutual effort. In welfare, as in education, it logically follows that voluntary agencies have the prior right to existence and activity, as compared with government agencies. Government, Catholics hold, is an artificial instrument created by the people to do what natural associations cannot accomplish.

Elaborating upon this line of logic, the Roman Catholic Church holds that the two important roles of government in respect to social welfare are (1) the promotive and (2) the protective. The promotive function of the government, which is its primary function, is to encourage and make the fullest possible use of voluntary associations. This should be done in connection with voluntary educational and welfare agencies, for example, before any government-operated direct service structures are created. Government should always express its educational and welfare concern, whenever possible, through the voluntary agencies. Practical means to this end, in the American situation, are purchase of service arrangements, subsidies for building construction, and the like. The government's protective function, which permits it to render direct services to people, should be exercised only as a last resort. It is legitimate only after all efforts to serve the people through strengthening voluntary agencies have failed. When it is employed there should be recognition that an extremely regrettable step, which threatens the God-given freedom of men, has been taken. In any case, even when direct governmental services are required, responsibility for them should be kept at as local a level of government as possible.

This makes it eminently clear that the Catholic Church, while it accepts the possibility that certain assumptions of responsibility for the people's welfare by the national government may be necessary, assigns basic importance to voluntary agencies as the principal repository of democratic welfare philosophy.

Many Protestants who arrive somewhat haphazardly at a point of view similar to that of the Catholic Church on matters pertaining to social welfare are surprised to learn that it is a Catholic position. Moreover, they are shocked to discover its implications for education and church-state relations in many other facets of national life. Usually such persons are quick to realize, when they consider the matter carefully, that there is too much ambivalence in their theology, philosophy, and value concerns for them to be able to maintain the position all the way through to its dogmatically logical conclusions.

In general, Protestant emphases have differed considerably from those of the Roman Catholic Church. For example, Protestants have not looked upon welfare work as a legalistic religious obligation. Good works are not to them a means of their salvation, but a grateful and joyous response to God's love. Their salvation, they believe, is assured by their faith in God's love as revealed in Christ, and a good and purposeful life on earth, as well as eternal life in the hereafter, flows from their personal relationship with God through Christ. Protestant church-related social agencies or schools are therefore only natural expressions, or extensions, of the spontaneous impulses to Christian charity which arise in the hearts of individual Christians and in the fellowship of the church. Furthermore, use of these agencies or schools by church members is entirely optional. Humanitarian concern for the general welfare of the whole person, rather than a limited focus on the salvation of the soul or a special theological responsibility for the administration of saving grace, is the controlling objective.

Other factors of significance that must be taken into consideration in appraising Protestant policy are (1) the Protestant doctrine of vocation and (2) the views regarding government which are held by most Protestant churches.

The doctrine of vocation has had great influence in shaping Protestant attitudes toward non-sectarian public and voluntary agencies. According to this doctrine, God calls all Christians to serve Him. Since this is so, a man who is called by God to serve Him in government, in a non-sectarian agency, or even in a grocery store, can render Christian service that is just as acceptable to God as is the service of a man called to work professionally in the church.

Linked significantly with this conviction concerning the sacredness of vocation is a generally held view that government, far from being an artificial instrument of the people, is one of the orders of creation ordained by God. In this view the church is seen as having both eternal and temporal responsibilities, but the government is seen as being also charged with temporal responsibilities. These government responsibilities are primarily those of maintaining justice and order, and of promoting the common welfare. Recognizing that government has such responsibilities in God's order of creation, and that they may overlap the church's concerns for men's welfare, Protestants are not so consistent as Catholics in stating their views of what government should or should not do. As a matter of fact, they seldom judge the situation from a doctrinal viewpoint unless matters of conscience, as they see them, are involved. Consequently, Protestants tend to accept a broad interpretation of government's responsibility for the social welfare.

Some of the contrast in Protestant and Catholic views on these matters is apparently due to differences in the manner of interpreting what Richard Niebuhr designates as the relationship of Christ to culture. Catholics tend to see Christ as being "above" culture, while Protestants incline more toward the views that Christ and culture are in a paradoxical relationship to one another, or that Christ is the transformer of culture.[30]

---

[30] H. Richard Niebuhr, *Christ and Culture* (New York: Harper & Brothers, 1951).

As indicated at the outset of this discussion of church-state relations, another of the pressures of concern which Protestants feel for clarification of their position arises from their sense of uneasiness over the possible threat to democratic and spiritual values implied in the continued expansion of public welfare services. Protestants fear the loss of individual freedom that may accompany centralization of responsibility in government. They know that a "welfare state" can become paternalistic, authoritarian, and oppressive. They believe that the individual should always carry a maximum amount of responsibility for his own welfare. Furthermore, it is difficult for them to see how voluntary responses to God's love can be adequately expressed through charity arrangements authoritatively provided by government on the basis of its powers of taxation.

"The gravitation of welfare to the state," says the editor of *Christianity Today,* in the January 18, 1960, issue, "may leave the churches some token of voluntary participation. The state's substantial control of human welfare means that in time government action will progressively narrow the role of the churches in *diakonia,* and the churches will have to console themselves mainly as centers of private devotion. . . . The socialist state . . . subtly transforms human 'wants' into human 'rights.' . . . Instead of hailing state welfare programs as an extension of Christian social ethics, it is high time Christian clergy and laymen consider the premise that state welfare programs are inherently anti-Christian."

Many other Protestants, however, are not so sure about these matters. Some are inclined to feel that it would be un-Christian for a vast, complexly interdependent, affluent society such as ours to insist on leaving provisions for the common welfare to laissez faire processes in the haphazard expression of voluntary impulses on the part of individuals, local congregations, local communities, special interest organizations, or other relatively atomistic groups. They do not consider that corporate effort through government channels in a democratic society necessarily negates either democracy or individual freedom. To them there appears to be nothing worse in what people do together through their government than in what they do separately as individuals or as local groups.

While these Protestants want to maintain democratic safeguards as a check on government, they accept the necessity of broad planning and co-ordination of welfare services through the central agencies of government. They consider that Protestantism has too long emphasized a narrow, individualistic orientation, to the neglect of the corporate emphases and social imperatives of the Christian gospel. Government in this democracy, they believe, could be greatly improved and more fully trusted with responsibilities for social welfare if Christians committed themselves fully to the performance of their duties as citizens and if the church functioned responsibly in a positive relationship to the institutions of government. Out of negativism and failure to be good citizens at the corporate level of government they do not see success coming in provisions for the total social welfare at the local or personal level.

Limitations of space preclude an adequate discussion of the final "pressure point" cited at the beginning of this analysis of the church's quest for new role definitions in church-state relations. The pressure referred to is that resulting from the increasing confusion and uneasiness of conscience arising out of expediency arrangements of "co-operation" between the church and the state. The problem relates particularly to the offer and acceptance of government funds for the support of church-related educational and welfare agencies and services. It is becoming troublesomely acute because such arrangements are rapidly multiplying, and because numerous hazards are increasingly evident in connection with them. Above all, it is an embarrassing and annoying problem because these arrangements expose the fact that the Protestant denominations do not have a fully articulate philosophy with which to justify them.

The extent of government financial subsidization of church-related agencies, within present patterns of loosely defined "co-operation," is extremely difficult to determine. All evidence indicates that it is of great magnitude. Beginning with the traditional subsidy of tax exemption, it has expanded in an almost phenomenal number of directions.

128 COMPASSION AND COMMUNITY

One of the most common types of subsidy is that known as "purchase of service." Rather than expand public welfare services, government authorizes public agencies to purchase specialized services from voluntary agencies, such as hospitals, old people's homes, children's agencies, and even missions for transient men. In consequence, voluntary agencies often are largely financed in this way. For example, many Protestant children's agencies receive from 30 per cent to 100 per cent of their operating budgets in this fashion.

Such purchase of services is made by many branches of government at national, state, and local levels. The total amount thus contributed to sectarian welfare agencies runs into hundreds of millions of dollars annually. Notation should be made, however, that it is not all a pure subsidy, that works only in favor of the agencies. Many agencies complain that they are having to sell their services to the government at less than cost. Still, they do it because in many instances this is the only way they can continue operating.

Among the best-known federal subsidies are those provided by the Hill-Burton Hospital Survey and Construction Act. Of the more than $1 billion allocated thus far under this act, about 20 per cent has gone to church-related agencies. Roman Catholic agencies have received 80 per cent of this portion, Protestant agencies 15 per cent, and Jewish agencies 5 per cent. Because the bill was recently amended to permit subsidies for construction of nursing homes and of infirmaries for homes for the aged, further extensive allocations may be expected.

The federal Grant-in-Aid Program, which exceeds $5 billion a year, is being widely used by church-related agencies for new programs and new construction in institutions of higher learning, for health and welfare services, and for vocational rehabilitation. Goodwill Industries, for example, a Protestant church-related organization, received $1 million in a period of three years.

Liberal government loans constitute another type of subsidy. FHA-insured forty-year mortgages, for example, are available to cover 90 per cent of the cost of erecting housing for old people.

Most loans under this arrangement to date have been obtained by religious organizations, among which Protestant organizations are especially prominent.

State and local funds are often given as lump sum subsidies of old people's homes, children's homes, hospitals, and other church-related agencies. That annual operating budgets also benefit considerably from these sources was revealed by a survey made by the National Council of Churches in 1955. At that time, sixty-nine agencies were receiving $1,250,000 in such annual contributions.

Beyond the national scene, sectarian overseas agencies also are sustained in large measure by the government. The International Cooperation Administration contracts with sectarian agencies to carry forward programs of community development, health, education, and agriculture in other nations. In addition, hundreds of millions of dollars' worth of surplus food, contributed by the government, is distributed by the National Catholic Welfare Conference, Church World Service, and other sectarian (as well as some non-sectarian) relief agencies.

Though government subsidies help harassed Protestant agency executives meet their budgets, many churchmen are seriously pondering the long-range implications. Will subsidies lead to loss of the agencies' freedom? Is it ethical to use public funds for sectarian religious emphases? If religious teachings are not incorporated in services rendered, what justification is there for the agencies' existence? Where is the Christian charity in programs paid for by government? Is it ethical for the church to pretend that it is offering services when government is paying the bill? What would become of the church agencies if government services should be withdrawn? Are Protestants "just grabbing money because money is available?" Does approval of such arrangements as "purchase of service" lead logically to approval of state support for parochial schools? Are Protestants ready to join with Catholics in support of the principle of subsidiarity, or should they clearly establish and support some other position? In any case, how can Protestants make what they do make more sense in terms of their religious and political ideals, as well as in the arena of elementary logic?

In Terms of a Proper Emphasis

Finally, it seems fitting to conclude these observations concerning the church's quest for new role definitions in social welfare by adding that it is engaged in a serious quest for a definition of what constitutes a proper emphasis in its welfare activities. This phase of the quest was quite evident in the discussions which took place in both of the great conferences sponsored by the National Council of Churches.

Much of the difficulty in this quest for a proper emphasis revolves around the reconciliation of the church's long-standing traditional emphases on almsgiving and charity with the new scientific and humanistic emphases on therapy, rehabilitation, protection of individual integrity, social justice, and the general welfare. It would be an understatement to say that churchmen often appear to be suffering from conflicting emotions concerning what expression to give to the impulses of Christian charity. Direct personal almsgiving is still preached and practiced in many quarters, as is manifest when baskets are being distributed to the needy at Christmas and Thanksgiving. At the same time, there are serious misgivings in the churches concerning such practices. Many efforts are being made to shift church emphasis increasingly toward therapy, rehabilitation, and social action, designed to give needy persons maximum assistance in achieving the ability to help themselves.

As has already been intimated in comments previously made in this chapter, one of the great issues in the mind of the church seems to be whether its welfare activities should be conducted on a basis of purely humanitarian motives or whether they should be under the discipline of carefully defined sectarian (denominational or "religious") objectives and interests. To the thoughtful churchmen who find neither of these alternatives acceptable, the broader issue is how to keep welfare activities wholesomely religious without permitting them to become narrowly sectarian.

The Findings Committee at the 1957 Atlantic City Conference on Policy and Strategy declared that churches and Christians should engage in social welfare "out of gratitude in response to

God's act in Jesus Christ as an expression of faith" and "as an essential part of our Christian witness," and that "the social welfare mission of the church cannot be evaluated in terms of its success in making Christians out of those whose need is served."[31] However, this did not exactly settle the issue. Social work continues to be used in some church quarters for evangelizing purposes. There are also many indications of great concern over protecting the status of Protestant interests and emphases in the welfare field. Though this is understandable in view of the mounting strength of Catholic and Jewish charities, and in the light of the marked secularism of public welfare, it serves rather to underscore the church's difficulty at this point than to release it from the dilemma.

Many are the indications, too, that the church is seeking to determine where to place the emphasis in the programming of its welfare activities in relation to what is being done by other agencies. Since there have been no significant comity arrangements or clearcut divisions of labor, giving the church a mandate for specific welfare responsibilities, confusion in this regard is both understandable and inevitable. Discussions which reflect this confusion usually revolve around whether the church should duplicate, and possibly compete with, other agencies in an effort to add a "plus" which the other agencies are not providing in their services; whether the church should restrict itself to filling in the gaps of unmet need not cared for by other services; whether the church should carry on experimental work and conduct demonstration projects designed to aid in pioneering toward the improvement of all welfare services so that they will minister adequately to "the whole man"; or whether the church's responsibility lies in some other direction.

One of the greatest issues in the church's struggle for a proper emphasis, however, has to do with whether welfare work should be done within a theological framework, relying heavily on biblical authoritarianism as the guide to individual therapy, or within a scientific and humanistic framework which aims at helping individuals to help themselves. It must be added, of course, that

---

[31] *Policy and Strategy* (*op. cit.*), p. 9.

many churchmen are refusing to see this as an either-or proposition and are earnestly seeking a logical and meaningful blending or harmonizing of the theological, scientific, and humanistic emphases in a single frame of reference which will give added dimension to all three.

The Church in the Administration
of Social Welfare

What is happening in church-administered welfare services? Are churches relaxing or increasing their welfare efforts? Are they accepting or rejecting modern social work methods? To what extent are they using professional social workers trained in modern techniques?

Before attempting to answer these questions, it should be noted that much Protestant social work is not done under the direct sponsorship of the churches. Many agencies and institutions which were originally begun by the churches have, in keeping with the Protestant conviction that social welfare is a community responsibility, been released to public or independent auspices. Many other agencies, the YMCA and the Salvation Army being good examples, sprang up independently but are so obviously related to Protestant traditions and emphases that they merit classification alongside church-related services.

While it would be desirable to give consideration to those agencies only that are under direct church control, it is not always possible to single them out in the factual summaries which are available. In any case, it appears that developments in the agencies affiliated with Protestant traditions but independent of church control have been similar to those occurring in agencies under church administration.

If churches are relaxing in their welfare efforts, the statistics certainly do not indicate the fact. On the contrary, much evidence is available to support the conclusion that most Protestant denominations are now giving increased attention to the establishment of health and welfare agencies under their own auspices. Best current estimates are based on projections of figures obtained from a National Council of Churches survey in 1954 covering denominations representing 70 per cent of the nation's Protestant membership. According to these estimates, about 4,000 Protestant agencies and institutions throughout the nation serve about 17,000,000 people annually. A majority of these services have been established in the last thirty-five years. Their capital assets amount to about $3.3 billion, and their annual current expenditures run to more than $1 billion. They employ about 200,000 persons full time and another 45,000 part time, and are estimated to use as many as 100,000 volunteer workers.[32]

It is also estimated that a breakdown of the statistics on the number of Protestant agencies would show about 800 services for children, 700 homes for the aged, about 600 hospitals, and 120 family welfare agencies. The more than 1,700 other agencies are distributed among a variety of categories representing settlement houses, residence halls for young women, neighborhood houses, group work services, chaplaincy services, services to the handicapped, and the like.[33]

Though there is no way of knowing exactly how extensive has been the adoption of modern social work philosophy and techniques by the church-related agencies, all indications are that there is a widespread inclination toward such adoption. Practices out of line with the prevailing standards in secular social work are definitely on the defensive, and most of the stronger agencies have long since determined to abandon them as rapidly as possible in an all-out effort to achieve excellence according to the secular standards. This is not to say that no criticism of secular social work exists, but that such criticism as occurs takes place within a general framework of acceptance. Meanwhile, church-related agencies are rapidly adopting the latest casework, group work, and administrative practices, and are seeking to add as many trained social workers to their staffs as they can obtain.

That there are certain handicaps in achieving such objectives, however, is undeniable. For one thing, the limited finances of many agencies make it almost impossible for them to do standard work.

---

[32] Johnson and Villaume, *op. cit.,* p. 444; also, Bachmann (ed.), *op. cit.,* Vol. II, pp. 123–126.
[33] *Ibid.*

In many instances agency control is so intertwined with church politics that it is difficult to prevent administrative offices from being usurped by untrained people who are not fully sympathetic with the maintenance of the highest standards. Furthermore, the church's long and honorable tradition of using voluntary, untrained workers for many types of work for which modern standards prescribe trained personnel is not easily changed and still represents values which the church is understandably reluctant to discard. On the fringe, too, there are, of course, some agencies that are still so oriented to the early church emphases on direct almsgiving and the use of welfare programs for the purpose of evangelism that they resent and resist the encroachment of standards not congenial to these objectives.

The handicaps are gradually being overcome, however, and many church-related agencies are outstanding in their pioneering work to raise social work standards even higher than they tend to be in the general profession.

The fact must be admitted, nevertheless, that, in general, the social work of the churches still has a long way to go before it can be said to have arrived at the minimum levels of competence which social work standards prescribe. For instance, research done under the auspices of the National Council of Churches in preparation for the 1955 Conference on the Churches and Social Welfare showed that in a sampling of 1,117 agencies only 451 were employing professionally trained social workers, and that of the 1,641 social workers employed by these 451 agencies, only 675 (41 per cent) were holders of accredited professional degrees.[34] It also found a decrease in the proportion of social workers with accredited degrees highly correlated with measurable increases in the amount of religious control over the agencies. In addition, the report pointed out that church-related agencies have gloried in the "dedicated" worker, placing almost no limits on the hours and types of service which might be demanded of him, while professional social work has labored to establish standards which protect

---

[34] That this is not, however, a condition unique to church agencies is reflected in the fact that only about 4 per cent of the workers in the vast program of public welfare are said to be fully trained.

the social worker from exploitation and demoralization. The report comments, too, on the fact that church-related agencies have a widespread reputation for having low professional standards and that it is hard to believe that this reputation is "without some confirmation in fact."[35]

Trends and Problems

In the efforts which the churches have made and are making to retain effectiveness in the welfare field a number of significant trends and serious problems are in evidence.

Among the trends, the following deserve special mention:

1. A trend toward increasing concern with the theological bases of social work and with the more effective integration of social welfare into the primary objectives and emphases of the churches.

2. A trend toward deep concern to bridge the gaps of separation between the church and secular social work.

3. A trend toward expansion of church-related welfare activities—a trend which may eventually be defined as irresponsibility on the church's part in the face of increasingly competitive welfare coverage by public and other non-sectarian services and in view of reduction in its relative strength and resources for such expansion.

4. A trend toward anxiety with reference to maintaining the integrity of and a place for Protestant social agencies—a trend which seems to be causing considerable wavering from the traditional Protestant conception of social welfare as essentially a community responsibility, and a leaning toward status-protecting efforts to give distinctive definition to Protestant social services and to direct these services toward specifically Protestant objectives.

5. A trend toward increasing acceptance by the churches, both in theory and in the operation of their welfare programs, of the criteria and standards prevailing in the secular discipline of social work.

6. A trend toward willingness on the part of the churches to compromise many of their traditional values and convictions (such

---

[35] Bachmann (ed.), *op. cit.,* Vol. II, pp. 148–150.

as those pertaining to separation of church and state, and the freedom to use welfare services as a part of evangelism) in order to maintain a not-very-well-defined position in the welfare field.

Some of the more serious problems are suggested by such questions as:

1. Should the church willingly yield its welfare responsibilities to the growing strength of secular agencies, committing itself to a program of gradual withdrawal from direct participation in welfare activity, or should it resist encroachments and seek to retain a place for itself in welfare administration?

2. If the church is to stay in welfare work, should it use the same social work criteria and skills as other agencies, or should it develop its own patterns and objectives and attempt to do a distinctively different job?

3. Should the church engage in activity duplicating and competing with the welfare work done by other agencies, or should it adjust its services to the objective of filling gaps uncared for by other community services?

4. Should the church design its welfare services to minister primarily to the needs of its own members and constituency, or to be equally available to all persons in the whole society?

5. Should the church in its welfare efforts place principal emphasis on conducting pioneering experimental or demonstration programs which might lift the level of social work generally, but which public agencies are not so free to undertake?

6. In view of its relatively limited economic resources, should the church undertake only those social service responsibilities which it can reasonably expect to discharge in a clearly superior manner?

7. Does the church actually have a unique responsibility and a distinctive contribution to make in the welfare field, or is it merely struggling to retain vestiges of its traditional prestige in the insistence on continuing its own separately administered programs?

Though these questions are obviously difficult enough to answer, further dimensions of the church's problems are suggested by at least two other, even more provocative questions which are currently being raised in the discussions of these matters.

The first question is: Is welfare work an ally or an enemy of the church? The reasoning back of the question considers the claim that philanthropy is often a substitute for justice, a pittance gift tendered in lieu of more equitable provisions in wages, pensions, employment, non-discriminatory social arrangements, and the like. Involved in the consideration, also, is the charge that the church, in promoting emphases on benevolence, may be blunting its ethical sensitivity through making paternalism a "moral equivalent of brotherhood."[36] The implication is that the prophetic ministry of the church as an influence for needed social change may be hindered rather than helped through the church's extensive identification with social work.

The second question is even more shocking and extreme in that it asks: Is the church itself, however unwittingly, actually standing in the way of human welfare?[37] That such a question is being asked is probably of more significance than any exposure of fact to which it leads. Nevertheless, its seeming absurdity is considerably modified by data resulting from studies which have attempted to measure the amounts of religious activity in communities as compared with objective evidence of community welfare. The most striking example of such study is that of E. L. Thorndike, who, during the 1930's (and it must be remembered, of course, that conditions may have been considerably altered since that time), gathered data on a sampling of cities and came up with the conclusion that the more religious activity there is in a community the less adequate are the community's provisions for social welfare. Where church membership was high, for example, he found more slums, lower wages, more health problems, less adequate public services, and the like; whereas, in situations where church membership was lower and less attention was apparently paid religion, the indices of community welfare were higher.[38] Another study made a

---

[36] Gallagher, *op. cit.*, pp. 102–103.

[37] *Ibid.*, p. 103.

[38] E. L. Thorndike, *Your City* (New York: Harcourt, Brace & Co., Inc., 1939).

similar comparison of the states and arrived at the same conclusion.[39]

Summary and Conclusions

Because charity has always been so important a part of its emphasis, it was inevitable that the church would become deeply involved in the patterns of change which are developing in modern social welfare. That the involvement is real and extremely perplexing is very evident.

For one thing, the necessity of adapting almsgiving to the requirements of a vast, highly organized corporate process in which Christian ideals of humanitarianism have been generally accepted has not been easy. Almsgiving through the impersonal channels of corporate processes may provide the individual with an escape from the genuine personal involvement which Christian commitment should require. On the other hand, insistence on more direct forms of giving to the unfortunate may reflect unworthy motives of merit-seeking satisfaction on the part of the giver and an effort to escape from broader social responsibilities suggested by the unfortunate gift-recipient's plight.

The church is faced with the problem of keeping individual consciences sensitive to the requirements of charity, and individual lives committed to the expression of charity in genuine personal involvement. It is also under the necessity of guiding men into an understanding of how it may take more of God's grace to support with taxes, benevolences, and continuously concerned good will, corporate programs aimed at an organized ministry of mercy and justice than it does to give alms directly to the unfortunate persons who happen to come within the individuals' immediate purview.

Moreover, the church has sensed the trends toward sensatism,[40] materialism, and secularism in the society as a whole. In view of

---

[39] A. L. Porterfield, "The Church and Social Well-Being," *Sociology and Social Research*, January-February, 1947. Both studies are interestingly summarized in Harvey Seifert, *The Church in Community Action* (New York: Abingdon-Cokesbury Press, 1952), p. 11.

[40] *Sensatism* is a term being used to describe the tendency toward placing an exaggerated emphasis on the values of sensory experience.

these trends, it is understandably anxious that the expanding corporate programs of welfare services give the fullest possible consideration to all the needs of "the whole man," including the requirements of the spiritual side of his nature as well as those involved in his physical and social well-being.

Another aspect of the involvement has been related to the question of the continuing place for the church's own separately administered welfare services. These services represent a long tradition of response to need when other services were not available. They have long been an integral part of the church's functioning. They represent a great investment in money, sacrifice, and personal heroism. What will become of them?

It has been the main burden of this chapter to show that the church, as represented in the Protestant denominations, has, on the whole, reacted positively to the situation in modern social welfare through expanding its efforts, through modifying its objectives, and through attempting to adjust its practices to the new professional social work standards. At the same time it has been necessary to make note of the fact that the church appears to be suffering from a feeling of the threat of displacement in the welfare field, and that it is extensively involved in a serious search for new role definitions for itself as its programs are overshadowed and many of its traditional functions are usurped by greatly expanded secular services. To say that it has been something of a traumatic experience for the church to discover that it has lost centrality, not only in the administrative practice of social welfare but also in the dominance of social work philosophy, and that it has sometimes been chagrined and confused at finding itself criticized for seeming to lag behind and to cling to outmoded methods and objectives, is to put the matter altogether too mildly.

Nevertheless, despite embarrassment and occasional flashes of resentment, Protestant churches are steadfastly continuing to demonstrate a sense of mission in connection with social welfare and are sticking with their purpose to maintain, despite all odds, a dynamic relevance to the welfare field. By and large, the churches are pleased that society has taken to heart so seriously the concerns for human welfare which they have always championed. At the same time they are anxious to retain a place for themselves in the practice of social welfare. Furthermore, the churches are anxious to keep all welfare efforts sufficiently oriented to spiritual objectives to assure an adequate ministry to the needs of "the whole man."

It will be noted that this chapter has not dealt with the church's participation in action programs designed to bring about needed social changes as a part of the expression of its interest in social welfare. The omission is not due to oversight, but to the intentional reservation of this topic for discussion in another connection. Let it suffice here to say that while the church has maintained an interest in social action for social change, it is being bypassed at this point, also, on the welfare scene as social action and social planning are increasingly made an institutionalized part of the professional discipline of social work. Whether the church is dragging its feet at this point or merely being outdistanced by superficial exuberance in secular developments of the moment is a matter meriting serious consideration. At least one church spokesman has been led to deplore the fact that the church seems to be cursed by "social ineffectuality," which often allows it to operate in communities without changing those communities in ways that they should be changed.[41]

Comfort may be taken in the fact, however, that many thoughtful observers are in agreement with the leading social scientist who recently said that though it is less actively involved as welfare functions have become more specialized, the church continues, through its constituent groups and individual members, to provide "the emotional dynamic that keeps many helpful programs going from year to year." Moreover, he added, religious groups "continue to be the inspiration behind much of the idealism" which permeates the humanitarian appeals on which all our welfare services are based.[42]

---

[41] Seifert, *op. cit.*, p. 15.

[42] Irwin T. Sanders, *The Community: An Introduction to a Social System* (New York: The Ronald Press Company, 1958), p. 320.

There can be no doubt that the churches are still needed and wanted in welfare work. It would be a calamity if they were suddenly to withdraw from what they are now doing. Though it has been necessary for the welfare field to expand beyond their resources in directions of independence and specialization, the churches need not feel resentful or lose their sense of relevance. There is still much for them to do that need not be either duplication of the work of other agencies or competitive with them.

Finally, churches should rejoice that at last they are being freed to concentrate their ministry to people where Jesus so obviously wanted to focus His efforts. As the general public assumes increasing responsibility for material assistance, the churches are released to give fuller attention to people's non-material or spiritual needs. To the more difficult tasks of helping to bring understanding, encouragement, purpose, self-respect, comfort, and confidence to the masses of individuals caught up in the stresses and strains of today's changing world, the churches are increasingly being challenged. To the rough frontiers of modern man's desperate need in the realms of personality, social adjustment, values, and faith, they are being more insistently called.

QUESTIONS FOR DISCUSSION

1. In the light of the churches' increased benevolence giving and expanding welfare services, what logic is there in the suggestion that the church's influence in the welfare field may be declining?

2. What part do you believe the church should continue to have in the social welfare of the future?

3. Should the church insist that more of its ministers receive social work training?

4. Under what circumstances should a local church include social work in its program? In what types of social work should a local church engage?

5. What should be the purpose of the church's welfare activities?

6. How can the church overcome some of the mistakes it has been making in its welfare efforts?

Follow-up Suggestions

Individual

Find out what welfare services your local church sponsors. Is it doing more or less now than in the past? What standards are maintained in the work being done? Compare your church with other local churches. What reasons do church leaders give for the welfare work they are doing?

Group

Arrange a tour of church-sponsored social agencies within reasonable travel distance. Study facilities and program. Inquire as to staff, standards, objectives, bases of support, problems, needs, and the like.

Contact national headquarters for information on all aspects of welfare services under your denomination's auspices. Request literature, pictures, charts, posters, data on trends and the like. Arrange an attractive and informative display of these materials in a conspicuous place at your church.

IV: The Church's Relationship to Social Work and the Social Worker

Though the church has lost the position of dominance in the administrative practice of social welfare and in the articulation of the philosophy of social work, it can take justifiable pride in the fact that it had much to do with the origin and development of both. It should not permit itself to become easily or unnecessarily alienated from either. That a certain amount of alienation has already taken place is undoubtedly true, but there is no reason to assume that it is of insurmountable proportions.

It is not surprising that changes and adjustments in attitudes and practices have sometimes seemed to come easier in the new, experimental social work settings outside the church than in the older, more traditional institutional processes which have sustained the church's continuing interest in welfare programs through the years. Should it be surprising, then, that it is possible to detect that a certain amount of estrangement has arisen between the church and the newly independent discipline of social work, as well as between ministers and professional social workers?

In any case, the important consideration is that the administration of social welfare is an indispensable profession in this complex age, and that there is urgent need for the church and the members of this profession to work together in the closest harmony. It is encouraging to see that leaders in both the church and the welfare field are beginning to recognize this, and that efforts are being made to work through the estrangements to a better basis of mutual understanding, appreciation, and practical co-operation. Beyond the somewhat hesitant moves so far made in this direction, however, great need exists for a fuller and franker confrontation of differences and misunderstandings The need, too, is for more of the spirit of genuine humility which it takes to confess faults, recognize limitations, and maintain the attitude of learners.

The church certainly needs more of the vitalizing strength which could flow into it through a fuller opportunity to appropriate the exceptionally high level of motivation and commitment in the lives of the thousands of dedicated people who form the ranks of social workers. Also needed by the church is the broader relevance which an embracing identification with the great and growing programs of humanitarianism in social work would give it.

Social work, on the other hand, could undoubtedly benefit from a consciously closer and more harmonious identification with religious values and frames of reference, and from a practical working relationship with the church which would foster a more efficient use of these values and frames of reference in ministering to the needs of people.

Most important of all, distressed persons in this complicated world have complex needs that relate to every area of their lives. Because these needs are not neatly compartmentalized in their experience as physical, social, psychological, or religious, neither the church nor social work can expect to minister to them adequately without ministering to them in the unity of purpose and effort that is only possible in the sincerest and fullest co-operation.

A brief summary of some of the patterns of relationships, areas of estrangement, points of conflict, and possibilities for improved co-operation, will constitute the remainder of this chapter.

The Church and the Discipline of Social Work

To the church, despite its faults and failures, is due much of the credit for inspiring and nurturing the impulses which gave birth to modern social welfare and to the discipline of social work. More than this, as has already been documented in previous chapters of this book, these developments emerged largely out of programs the church had long operated, and probably would not have occurred without the groundwork which these church programs had laid for them.

It is significant to note what a prominent role ministers of the church played in the earliest developments of the modern social work discipline. For instance, it is to the Rev. Thomas Chalmers (1780–1847), a minister of Glasgow, Scotland, that credit is usually given for having developed the individualized approaches and person-centered philosophy which undergird the present concepts of "case work." He evolved and called attention to these through the actual organization and operation of his large parish in a poor section of Glasgow. In doing so he pioneered in one of the first major breaks away from the wasteful, demoralizing, categorical, inhumane, poor law practices. Approximately fifty years later, another minister, the Rev. Henry Solly, inspired by Chalmers' theories, made a recommendation concerning the co-ordinating of the activities of the many private and public charities. As a result, the first Charity Organization Society was formed in London in 1869. This society devoted itself not only to co-ordinating charity activities but also to implementing Chalmers' principles in the effort to reduce pauperism among persons in need of relief. The Rev. Richard Green and The Rev. Samuel Barnett were prominent among the members of this society who came to be well known as the Charity Organization Movement rapidly spread to many other cities throughout Europe and America.[1]

The Rev. Joseph Tuckerman was launched in Boston in 1826, with the backing and support of Unitarianism, on a pioneering "ministry at large" to the underprivileged and unchurched masses. This has been called the first example of religious social service in America on a scale of significance, and is sometimes credited with having been the beginning of the development of most of the principles of scientific charity.[2]

---

[1] Friedlander, op. cit., pp. 25, 41.
[2] Charles H. Hopkins, op. cit., p. 4.

Many other such examples could be cited to illustrate the fact that the church was directly related to some of the most significant beginnings and subsequent developments of social work. Altogether they underscore the logic in the observation that the church is "the mother of social work in the western world,"[3] and that most welfare activity in the United States is undergirded by religious philosophy and fundamentally represents an expression of religious heritage.[4]

Social welfare may, indeed, be interpreted as "the active outreach of love in society,"[5] regardless of whether it is administered under church auspices. Many churchmen are viewing it as such. Social work in the context of this definition is, then, a dedicated, disciplined, skillful application and communication of love through the welfare programs and agencies. It may be added, however, that while neither the church nor social workers are likely to be inclined to quibble with such a statement, both are embarrassed by the fact that much of the good being done in our society seems to be getting done without much love. Superficial charity often makes giving a condescending and heartless matter of trying to get rid of the sight of misery, and professionalization inclines toward the production of charity-machines that grind out impersonal alms and assistance in cold, machine-like fashion.[6]

Recognition of the value of love properly communicated may be considered one of the important areas of agreement and overlapping concern between the church and the profession of social work. The obvious difficulty which each encounters in trying to achieve and maintain a proper communication of love leaves room for the criticisms of each other which occasionally arise in both. One of the great needs is for increased appreciation of the fact, both in the church and in the profession of social work, that love-based concern constitutes the foundation of both and that both remain under a

3 Johnson and Villaume, *op. cit.,* p. 441.

4 Victor Obenhaus, *The Responsible Christian* (Chicago: University of Chicago Press, 1957), pp. 121, 124.

5 *Ibid.,* p. 136.

6 Gustave Weigel, "The Present Embarrassment of the Church" in *Religion in America,* by John Cogley (ed.) (New York: Meridian Books, Inc., 1958), p. 241.

requirement of much further creative endeavor in order to learn the better techniques needed for the more effective implementation of this concern.

Mutual acknowledgment of the validity of love as a healing and redemptive force, however, is only one of the points at which understanding can be improved through recognition of the common ground which the church and the social work profession occupy.

A recently published text outlining the concepts and methods of social work lists the following values as those subscribed to by social workers in American culture:

1. A conviction of the individual's dignity, integrity, and inherent worth.

2. A conviction concerning the individual's right to self-determination, even to the extent of determining what his needs are and making his own choices as to how they shall be met.

3. A conviction concerning the importance of providing equal services and equal opportunities for all persons, on the basis of individual need and capacity, regardless of race, religion, social status, or party affiliation.

4. A conviction that all help rendered the individual must be pointed toward encouraging him to assume his full share of social responsibilities.[7]

The same text goes on to say that within this framework of basic values social work labors to help individuals, groups, and communities toward achievement of the highest possible degree of physical, mental, and social well-being, and that it differs from the other helping professions in that it operates in consideration of *all* factors influencing the life of the individual, the group, or the community.[8]

The most remarkable thing about these statements is that they might very well have been made by a spokesman of religion concerning values and objectives of the church as most of the churches conceive of their purposes in relation to much of what they are trying to do in behalf of individuals, groups, and the social welfare. In fact, the statements serve to confirm the observation made by a

---

[7] Walter A. Friedlander (ed.), *Concepts and Methods of Social Work* (Englewood Cliffs, N.J.: Prentice-Hall, Inc., 1958), pp. 2–6.

[8] *Ibid.*, p. 7.

spokesman of religion in an almost equally recent book to the effect that there is universal agreement, in both the church and public welfare, that need must be met, hunger assuaged, humanly caused insecurity eliminated, family disintegration halted, and the injured of body and mind healed.[9] It is therefore important, continues this spokesman, that there be recognition, both in the church and in secular welfare work, that the ultimate ends pursued in social work and social welfare "are fundamentally religious in nature."[10]

A statement adopted by the First Conference on the Churches and Social Welfare, held at Cleveland in 1955 and referred to in the preceding chapter, pointed out that both the churches and social welfare are in agreement that their over-all objective is the same, namely that of helping man achieve his greatest potential. Subsidiary to this objective, it affirmed, both are involved in concern for the identification and realization of the highest possible personal and social values; both believe in man's dignity, intrinsic worth, freedom within the law, and right to the opportunity to achieve the abundant life; both seek to enable him to enjoy the maximum happiness possible in this imperfect world.[11]

While all this is true, even more true than parochially-minded churches and secularly-oriented social workers have sometimes been willing to admit, it would be misleading to leave the subject at this level of consideration. For the larger truth is that, despite these broad areas of overlapping agreement, a number of significant areas of disagreement and misunderstanding between the church and professional social work are apparent.

One of the main sources of difficulty is in the realm of philosophy and theology. At the very time when social work was receiving its biggest boost with the expansion of welfare programs in the 1930's, the American churches were beginning to experience the full impact of disillusionment and pessimism which had been building up in the theological circles of both Europe and America through the debacles of World War I, the Great Depression, and the terrible aftermaths of these. A radical shift was taking place in the minds of

9 Obenhaus, *op. cit.*, p. 133.

10 *Ibid.*, p. 134.

11 Bachmann (ed.), *op. cit.*, Vol. III, p. 191.

churchmen away from the buoyant optimism which had characterized the earlier social gospel movement, with its tendency to place
so much easy faith in man and in the inevitability of social
progress. A new Bible-centered "realism" was replacing the earlier
leanings toward humanistic optimism. The churches were becoming
less confident of man's capacities and potentialities, and were beginning a vigorous insistence that his autonomy is limited, that he
is dependent on God's mercy and grace, and that only God can
restore his lost dignity to him. Social work, on the other hand, was
moving into vastly enlarged opportunities for control over material
and environmental factors affecting distressed people's lives. It was
enthusiastically embracing the discoveries in psychology and psycho-
analysis which made it possible to help individuals strengthen their
egos and improve their command over their own destinies. Where
the church was moving away from faith in man, social work was
building up an enthusiastic and relatively unqualified faith in him.
The rifts in understanding which resulted have sometimes produced
the impression in social work that the church is too judgmental and
authoritarian to be able to help disorganized people. Similarly the
church has been given the impression that social work is a form of
idealistic social humanism which does not take sin and man's sinful
nature sufficiently into account.[12]

Another, closely related area of difficulty has to do with the
church's feeling that most social work is too secularly oriented to be
conscious of or able to help with the individual's basic spiritual
problems, while social work, viewing the matter in a psychological
rather than a theological context, holds a remarkably similar attitude
toward the church. Is not the church for many people a kind of institutionalized conscience or superego, ask some social workers, and
therefore almost disqualified for helping people with some of their
deepest problems? How can they tell their problems to representatives of the church and feel that there is an "accepting attitude?"
Can the church really communicate acceptance of the person while
not accepting his behavior? What chance has the church to help the
individual whose main problem is that he is already too sick and

---

[12] See Johnson and Villaume, *Social Work Year Book, 1957,* p. 423,
from which most of this is adapted.

disorganized from the over-burden of his feelings of guilt to be able to help himself, or even to accept help without skilled assistance?

Considerable estrangement is reflected also in evidences of an attitude in the church which, as intimated in comments earlier in this chapter, reacts negatively to what is considered to be the coldness, aloofness, impersonalism, and professionalism of social work; whereas social work sometimes seems to feel that the church is too superficially sentimental in its dealings with people in need, too carelessly authoritarian to respect their dignity and integrity properly, and too frequently inclined to use its charity as a means of acquiring use of people for institutionally defined and narrowly conceived "religious" ends.

Further dimensions of the areas of disagreement were succinctly spelled out in the following summary of differences identified by the 1955 Cleveland Conference on the Churches and Social Welfare:

A. The difference in importance placed by social welfare on the physical requirements of people as contrasted to the greater emphasis which the church places upon the spiritual.

B. The freedom which is accorded social workers (depending in part upon their denomination) as to the importance they place upon the religious and other cultural factors in any given situation and how they deal with them. This is in contrast, perhaps, to religion which accepts the obligation to improve the person helped and to persuade him to accept the Christian way of life.

C. The difference which sometimes exists between the church and social welfare in the priority of qualifications required for any welfare position. Welfare places competence and skill as the first priority in all such employment, whereas the church often places "a Christian love for humanity" as the first requirement.

D. Social work extends help to whoever needs and can accept it. It imposes no test of worthiness, repentance, or declaration of faith. This attitude is sometimes questioned by the church as though sin were condoned and invited.

E. In its pronouncements on Christian obligations, the church sometimes appears to exploit those in need by the appeal for help which it makes to its members and sometimes by the form in which this help is extended. Social welfare is not so much concerned with the motivations which induce people to help (these may come from other sources than Christian) but only that they have this motivation and that the help extended will not do damage to those to whom it is extended.

F. The inadequacy of religion in the personal lives of many social workers causes the church to question whether they can deal with the "whole" human personality. Question is also raised as to whether this "religious illiteracy" is the result of inadequacies in their professional education.[13]

Nevertheless, despite the reality of these differences and misunderstandings, and despite considerable validity in the criticisms each offers of the other, there are encouraging evidences that the church and the profession of social work have never been so far apart as an enumeration of the differences seems to indicate, and that a better relationship of appreciation and understanding is developing between them. It appears that the matters eliciting most criticism are increasingly being recognized on both sides as evidences of unnecessary narrowness. In nearly every case they reflect perspectives distorted by misinformation, misinterpretation, oversimplification, and the like. The more mature and better-informed persons in both the church and social work are identifying them as distortions and are growing more concerned to keep them interpreted as such.

As was pointed out in one of the early social welfare textbooks, it is possible for religion and social work to realize a "splendid fusion," where religion is interpreted broadly enough to embrace the individual's physical, psychological, and social rehabilitation, along with his spiritual regeneration, and where social work is conceived of as something more than a narrow technical specialty.[14] The quest for this "splendid fusion" seems to be gaining in tempo with such current trends as the following, which have been evoking comment recently: a tendency of the church to pioneer in social work that other agencies are not in position to do for the improvement of the

---

[13] Bachmann (ed.), *op. cit.,* Vol. III, p. 192. Used by permission of the National Council of Churches.

[14] C. C. North, *The Community and Social Welfare* (New York: McGraw-Hill Book Co., Inc., 1931), p. 14.

profession; a trend in the church toward demanding that those who
work in church-related agencies have social work training equally
as good as, or even better than, that prevailing in the best professional social work circles; a small but fairly steady movement of
social work students into theological seminaries and of theological
students into schools of social work; and a growing interest of
social workers in assessing the religious foundations of the tasks in
which they are engaged.[15]

In a very significant article recently published in the journal,
Social Casework, the administrative head of the University of Tennessee School of Social Work discusses "Religious and Spiritual
Values in Social Casework Practice" with admirable insight and
sincerity of concern. The author's comments revolve around the
human needs that find expression in religion, the contribution which
religion makes to the inner life of the social worker, the historical
interrelatedness of religion and social work practice, and the importance of the social worker's being able to help the client make
affirmative use of his (the client's own) religion. She affirms the
value of a faith "that God in his mercy and knowledge is working
through life"; points out how the social worker's own values play a
part in his professional practice; reports that the social work profession is increasingly recognizing its inability to solve the world's
problems alone and is seeking ways of sharing responsibilities with
other groups; reviews the necessity of the social worker's having a
mature understanding of religion so he can be aware of how he uses
his own religious faith and capable of understanding when a client
needs the help of a skilled spiritual adviser; and challenges social
workers to dedicate themselves more earnestly to the task of acquiring the skills necessary to help their clients appropriate the values
available to them in religious faith and a proper use of the resources
of religion.[16]

Thus, it is to be hoped, the breaches are slowly being closed between these two important representatives of resources vital to the
fulfillment of human need in this increasingly complex age. It is

---

[15] Obenhaus, *op. cit.,* p. 129.

[16] Sue W. Spencer, "Religious and Spiritual Values in Social Casework
Practice," *Social Casework,* December, 1957. Reprinted in *The Journal of
Pastoral Care,* Vol. XIII, No. 1, Spring, 1959, pp. 13–23.

imperative that these positive trends toward rapprochement and understanding be further accelerated with all possible effort.

Certainly there need not be a conflict between the church and the profession of social work over which can help people best, when all that both can do is so obviously needed, and when the skills and emphases in both are so obviously complementary. Social work can help the church communicate the acceptance, understanding, and forgiveness which the church believes to be in God's grace for every individual; and the church can help social work maintain and communicate a framework of values, faith, and purpose without which there can be no successful structuring of man's ego within the area of his autonomy, and no ultimate stabilization of the changing and demoralizing social order. Social work can and must recognize that man is a spiritual being with value needs, and it must strive to give a broader and more mature consideration to these aspects of his nature. At the same time, the church, which stresses concern for the spiritual welfare of the individual, must recognize that spiritual development cannot occur in a vacuum but must be solidly based on the availability of the physical, social, and psychological necessities of life. It must see the careful, skillful meeting of these needs as essential to the development of spiritual maturity in the individual, including his ability to accept God's grace, to see meaning and purpose in his life, and to achieve a responsible level of concern for other people.

Even the problem of sin and guilt need not impose impossible barriers to mutuality of understanding and approach. For better or worse, man has conscience and it would be calamitous if his conscience should be negated or silenced. Where there has been some oversimplification and unrealism in religion's easy assumption that guilt of conscience is readily curable by repentance and forgiveness, can it be denied that there is equally unrealistic oversimplification in treating such guilt as if it were only a medical or social adjustment problem? The problem in the traditional approach of religion has not been in its recognizing guilt, but in its restricted understanding of causation and responsibility, and in its sometimes harsh judgmentalism toward them. Moreover, this ignorance and judgmentalism have often been linked in religious men with pious hypocrisy, stemming from failure to understand their own guilt, especially that of their involvement in the guilt of others. Social work and the related scientific disciplines have been entirely justified in condemning this, but they must stay on guard against their own equally superficial tendency to ignore the possibilities of causative aspects of guilt-producing behavior that are not simply physical, environmental, or socially-interactional. Especially must they stay on guard against their apparent inclination to oversimplify the requirements of conscience in terms of value-relatedness and consistency.

At points like this, religion, science, and social work must grow in willingness to admit their shortcomings, must try to learn from each other, and must co-operate in seeking more effective ways of working together.

Promising progress along these lines has been made in some of the steps which the church has already taken—for example, in: (1) the formation and support of the Department of Social Welfare in the National Council of Churches; (2) the organization, in 1930, of the Church Conference of Social Work; (3) the organization, in 1934, of the Association of Church Social Workers; and (4) the combination of these interests in 1953 in an organization known as Christian Social Welfare Associates.

To the extent that they represent inclusive, integrative emphases these arrangements can make a valuable contribution to overcoming the barriers between the church and the non-church-related segments of social work; to the extent, however, that they represent a spirit of separatism and divisiveness they may be expected to contribute to further alienation and conflict. It is to be hoped that they will devote themselves unceasingly to bridging such gulfs as still remain between the church and every responsible element of so-called secular social work. When it comes to meeting human need out of concern for the worth of persons, there should be no room for distinction between sacred and secular effort.

The Church and the Social Worker

The church has a unique opportunity and responsibility in its relationship with social workers. In few, if any, professions other than that of social work are so large a proportion of the personnel to be found with motivations and commitments so fully in harmony with the vocational ideals which the church has long proclaimed. Indeed, there is more than coincidence implied in the observation that a disproportionate number of social workers are the children of ministers.

The social worker needs the church's sympathetic understanding, support, and encouragement. He is often underpaid, overloaded with work, relatively low in social status, and baffled by the complexity of the problems with which he daily struggles. At the same time he usually has a high sense of mission, is conscientiously trying to do a good job, and feels that he is involved in a program that is just as concerned for the welfare of people as is the church. When he is a member of the church, as he usually is, he is inclined to feel that he is engaged in work that is fundamentally religious even though it may be in a secular setting; and where he is aloof from or has broken with the institutional church he often feels, possibly with some justification, that the work he is doing is truer to the real spirit of religion than is the church.

In any case, he needs to know that the church understands him, that it is fully aware of the importance of the work which he is doing, and that it appreciates the sacrifices, skill, and devotion which he is giving to his tasks. If concern for what is ultimate in the realm of values is an element of faith, as theologian Paul Tillich considers it to be, then the church can recognize the social worker as a religiously motivated man of faith, regardless of his formal religious affiliations. Though it may sometimes be felt that he is not religiously all that he might be, he should, in complete fairness, be given the full credit which is due him, so that he may be strengthened for and encouraged to all the spiritual growth of which he is capable.

The church is, of course, increasingly recognizing and paying tribute to the professional social worker through using him in preference to untrained volunteers from among its members for the staffing of its own social services. In this trend, his skill and integrity matter more than his religious affiliation, and it is not uncommon for a Catholic or Jewish social worker, or one with no religious connection, to be employed by a Protestant agency. The day when the church could be happy with the use of "dedicated ignorance" in its welfare programs is rapidly drawing to a close, and this in itself indicates that the trained social worker is becoming firmly established in the church's esteem.

A footnote should probably be added, however, to the effect that there are still points at which the relationship can be improved. For instance, where social workers have struggled long and hard to achieve professional standards that would assure them against exploitation in terms of hours and workloads and permit them to do the highest possible caliber of work, the church has been accustomed to stress complete personal dedication, unselfishly sacrificial service, and "going the second mile" to render at least a modicum of service to all the need in sight. As might be expected, these emphases occasionally come into conflict. While some cross-fertilization may be helpful to both, the church will do well to concede that the maintenance of high professional standards in social work is of greater importance, in the long run, than whatever temporary gains can be achieved through encouraging social workers to assume larger responsibilities than they can discharge without sacrificing quality and experiencing personal and professional demoralization.

The Church and the Lay Christian in Social Work

Since most social workers are members of some church, and since social work has been so much a part of the core of church teaching and tradition from the beginning, the church is under heavy obligation to give special attention to its lay members who are engaged in social work. The fact that a measure of secularization has taken place in social welfare since it outgrew church auspices, must not be permitted to obscure this responsibility, or to deter the church from the discharge of this manifest duty.

It may even be remarked that there is something odd about the fact that the church has not maintained a more consistent definition of the social worker's vocation as an especially sacred "calling," to be ranked alongside that of the minister, the missionary, and the director of religious education. There was surely early and sufficient precedent in the office of deacon, as established in the church of the first century, for so ranking the profession.

At any rate, the church cannot afford to become aloof from or indifferent to social welfare. Moreover its greatest opportunity for maintaining a dynamic welfare relatedness is through its members who are in the profession of social work. It is obvious that public and non-sectarian private agencies must increasingly be depended upon to meet the growing welfare needs of complex society. Equally obvious is the fact that if the church is to have a witness in the welfare field it will have to provide this witness in ever increasing measure through its lay members who carry responsibility in these agencies.

The important question for the church is how it can identify these social worker members and single them out for the special help and encouragement which they need. At the same time there is the question of how the church can make a larger place in its own program of voluntary activities and services for the special talents and skills which these members possess.

Great need exists for the church at the local, denominational, and interdenominational levels to find out who the social workers are in the ranks of its membership. Having identified them, the church should take the steps necessary to begin disciplined conversations with them on what their needs are, what kinds of help they most desire, and what services they are best prepared to render the church. It should also seek to discover how the church's responsibilities toward these workers and the whole field of social welfare should be defined. The more local, continuous, and comprehensive such conversations can be, the better.

Without narrowness of intent or any attempt to exploit the welfare field outside its own bounds for sectarian purposes, the church should attempt to communicate to its laymen in all phases of social work that it considers them a very special branch of its ministering concern for people in need. It should help them to feel that wherever they go in response to need they are the church, and that beyond all tangible forms of assistance they may be able to give they are privileged most of all to help mediate the grace of God to persons who are of such infinite worth that God claims them for

His own children. The church should make special effort to aid
these laymen in every possible way to acquire the religious knowledge, spiritual maturity, inner confidence, and insightful skills which
will enable them to be the church in this highest sense and to do its
redemptive work in an efficient and adequate manner.

The church should take joy in seeking out occasions for giving
special public recognition to the social workers both of its fellowship and of the entire community. They deserve honor as the "gate-
keepers" of the community's welfare, as guardians and protectors
of the weak, and as obedient servants both of human need and of
society's charitable will. The church will bring credit upon itself in
according them the honor they are due.

It should not be difficult to find ways of honoring social workers
in the ordinary process of church functioning. Many of the special
events in the regular church calendar provide admirable opportunity for paying public tribute to various categories of these public
servants who labor devotedly to provide for the community's welfare. Church group programs and educational activities can be
greatly enriched through carefully planned use of social workers
who have ability to communicate their insights and to share something of the challenges they are experiencing in their work.

Social workers could make especially valuable contributions on
many important church boards and committees. As trained specialists, they should be as carefully and deliberately selected for these
assignments as is the banker, for instance, for a place on the finance committee. In many instances it would be appropriate to
include among the various fellowship and service organizations of
the local church or district group of churches an organization of
social workers, and to provide for regular conversations between
them and the church leadership. Commissioning and consecration
services such as those for persons going into missionary work, the
chaplaincy, religious education, the armed services, and the like,
would be highly appropriate for individuals entering social work as
a vocation; and an occasional day of recognition and dedication
such as that annually accorded teachers in the church school would
certainly not be out of place.

There should be real possibilities, too, in church-sponsored retreats or lay institutes designed especially for social workers after the pattern the church has used so successfully in other connections. Such retreats or institutes could contribute particularly to helping raise the level of communication and understanding between church leaders and members of the social work profession. They might also be a means of helping social workers develop an adequate perspective on how to bring the resources of Christian faith more effectively to bear upon the moral and ethical dilemmas which they are confronting in social welfare practice.

In its planning for emphases in this direction, however, the church should be careful to include all social workers who are a part of its constituency, and not merely, or even primarily, those who are serving in church-related agencies. In so far as possible, it should also seek to include all social workers in the community without respect to agency sponsorship or religious affiliation and without proselytizing designs upon them. The purpose should be to lower to an absolute minimum all barriers of division that separate the church from any part of this great ministering profession or the programs of welfare for which it is responsible.[17]

The church has some important messages to convey to social workers. It also has some important lessons to learn from them. Let there be mutual overtures toward that relevance to truth and human need that is compatible with the hopes and purposes of the Kingdom of God. Let there, especially, be a mutual renewal of the important quest for that dynamic quality of unselfish, deeply personal involvement in meeting the whole needs of individual human beings, as well as of society collectively, that was so magnificently demonstrated in Jesus of Nazareth.

---

[17] Good precedents are being set for the local church at this point in the fact that many local councils of churches, through their Department of Social Welfare, are sponsoring groups that bring together social workers and religious leaders of the community for discussion of topics of mutual interest. The National Council of Churches also sponsors many groups and conferences that bring together social workers regardless of whether they are affiliated with church-related agencies. The Second National Conference on the Churches and Social Welfare, to be held in 1961, is an "open," or non-delegated, conference to which all interested social workers are invited.

The Church and the Recruitment
and Training of Social Workers

One of the most important responsibilities which the church has for social welfare is in the recruitment and training of properly motivated people for the social work profession. This is a role for which the church is uniquely equipped, and the need for its services along this line is increasingly great.

It is estimated that more than half of the social work positions in the United States are being filled by persons without professional social work training, and that there are probably as many as 10,000 unfilled vacancies. Every indication is that the demand will continue to outstrip the supply of trained workers for a long while to come, in view of the rapidly growing acceptance of social work's value. A serious crisis impends in the welfare field unless a more adequate program of recruitment is developed.

Since the profession of social work, in the modern sense, is relatively new, and the job requirements and opportunities are not well known to the general public, many young people are making their vocational commitments to far less meaningful activities without having been challenged to give this profession the serious consideration which they should. The church should intensify its efforts through every available channel to see that all young people are informed of the opportunities and needs, and that they are given utmost encouragement to consider the social work profession as a place of service worthy of their highest Christian commitment. Moreover, while the need for trained workers in church-related social agencies is especially acute, the church's vocational challenge to youth with respect to social work must carefully be kept on a broader base than merely that of recruiting personnel for the church's own agency services.

Beyond recruitment itself is the very great need to help those persons recruited to obtain the training they need. At least two years of expensive graduate study are involved; and beginning salary expectations are usually not much higher than for many better-known types of work not requiring graduate school preparation. More generous provisions for scholarships and fellowships are greatly needed. The church will indicate how important it considers skilled competence in the profession by the attention it gives this need in the disposition of its funds.

If the religious foundation of social workers' training is important, the church must also find better ways than those it has been using to make provision for this phase of social work training. Except for those under Catholic auspices, very few of the fifty-nine accredited schools of social work in the United States and Canada are affiliated with universities that are even nominally under church sponsorship. In fact, those at the University of Denver and Boston University, both Methodist related, were the only ones specifically identified as currently functioning under such sponsorship in the report prepared for the 1955 National Conference on the Churches and Social Welfare.[18]

Though schools of social work are very expensive to operate, it may be that more of them should be established in connection with church-supported universities. Whether or not this is done, however, more attention must be given to the religious needs of students enrolled in schools of social work having no direct relationship to the church. This may be accomplished, in part, by (1) carefully planned extracurricular religious activities provided on or near the campuses for these students; (2) internships in church-related agencies; (3) conversations between church leaders and schools of social work faculties on how religion may be fitted properly into the curricular structure; (4) promotion of exchanges of students between seminaries and schools of social work; (5) contributions of good literature to the libraries of these schools, interpreting the place of religion in social work; and (6) such other means as the church, out of deep concern, may be able to devise.

The Minister and the Social Worker

An element of estrangement between ministers and social workers seems to have existed from the beginning of social work's becoming established as a profession independent of church control. Ministers were, of course, the professional guardians of the church's prerogatives in the welfare field, and were inclined to be especially sensitive to the displacement trend as welfare expanded beyond the adminis-

---

[18] Bachmann (ed.), *op. cit.,* Vol. II, p. 41.

trative oversight of the church and became more and more secular-
ized. To them fell the responsibility of defending many of the sacred
traditional emphases, as well as the time-worn practices against
which reaction was taking place as social work became more scientifically and secularly oriented.

Ministers were disturbed by what they considered, often with
much justification, to be superficiality and error in the experimental
efforts of those who practiced the new profession. They resented the
disdain and irreverence with which some social workers seemed to
treat religion and the church, as well as the tendency on the part of
the fledgling profession to arrogate unto itself a monopoly of authority and wisdom in matters pertaining to welfare practice. They were
nonplussed by cutting criticisms of their own profession's long-
established methods and practices.

Social workers, on the other hand, were struggling for recognition as a profession capable of skilled, responsible, scientific study
and treatment of persons and problems involved in the social welfare. They were under the burden of proving that they were able
to make effective, disciplined use of the best available scientific
knowledge concerning social processes and human behavior. To
them most ministers appeared to be neither very cognizant nor very
appreciative of the scientific principles which the profession of social
work was seeking to apply to the treatment of personal and social
ills. Because of the minister's position as professional leader of the
church, in which old-line charity practices had been developed and
maintained, social workers saw him as a jealous guardian of most
of the outmoded, unscientific methods and philosophies from which
they were seeking emancipation. Social workers resented the clergy-
man's persistence in unscientific definitions and practices, his seeming indifference to many values which were assuming increasing
significance to them, and his often ill-concealed hostility toward
what they were doing.

It must be remembered, of course, that these developments were
occurring, for the most part, in the first three or four decades of the
twentieth century, when the long-smouldering conflicts between
science and traditional religion were coming to a head. Social work
began achieving the stature of an independent profession following

World War I; the Scopes "monkey trial," that pitted the old tenets of religious fundamentalism against the new, scientific theories of evolution, took place at Dayton, Tennessee, in 1925; and Reinhold Niebuhr began making religious thought intellectually respectable to modern, scientifically-minded man in the 1930's.

In the intervening years many adjustments in religious thought and perspective have occurred. Ministers of today are by no means so unacquainted with nor so unsympathetic toward science and its principles and procedures as they were when social work began to seek identity as a profession. Communication between religion and the scientific disciplines involved in social work has improved remarkably. At the same time, social workers appear to have begun to move beyond the first flushes of excitement in their new-found independence. In doing so, they are achieving a maturity which enables them to ask the kinds of insightful questions concerning their discipline which lead them back toward a more meaningful relationship with religion. The time is rapidly coming, if it is not already here, when the minister and the social worker can and must join hands in a co-operative fellowship of mutual understanding and appreciation.

It would be incorrect, however, to imply that there no longer exist any elements of tension between ministers and social workers. Both professions continue to be plagued and handicapped by a considerable amount of hostility toward each other. Both must accept responsibility for helping to eliminate the causes of the hostility if the needed improvement in relations is to take place.

While generalizations are always dangerous, and untrue in part, it appears that many social workers are still seeing ministers as:

1. Having uncertain educational backgrounds.

2. Being inclined to be carelessly sentimental in dealing with needs.

3. Relying too much on spiritual exhortation rather than on scientific skills and insights.

4. Making legalistic, judgmental, authoritarian approaches to people in ways that are dangerous and often damaging.

5. Disagreeing radically among themselves as to what are the basic criteria and essential emphases of religion.

6. Failing both in the matter of making adequate diagnostic distinctions between the types of persons and problems coming to them and in maintaining a disciplined recognition of the limitations in their individual skills and abilities to help people.

On the other hand, many ministers, it appears, are still seeing social workers as:

1. Being too strictly humanistic in their point of view.

2. Having an overly simplified and overly optimistic view of human nature.

3. Failing to take God, sin, salvation, and the spiritual side of reality sufficiently into account.

4. Seeking to substitute social adjustment for the more profound re-orientations of life which people need.

5. Trying to eliminate the symptoms of guilt in persons without getting at the guilt itself and the reasons for it.

6. Ignoring the fact that people have religious needs and that many of their problems stem from deprivation in the area of these needs.

Ministers will do well to understand that most social workers are not antagonistic to religion. Some social workers are inclined, however, to feel uncertain as to what can be expected of the average minister in the way of standardized procedure in dealing with persons and their problems. Their impression is that the minister's tendency most often is to be moralistic and authoritarian in his approaches to people with problems, and that he relies too much on verbal admonitions rather than on skills and insights. All the training of social workers, on the other hand, has conditioned them against these approaches and techniques. In particular, social workers have been taught not to be judgmental in dealing with people, but to be accepting and as objectively helpful as possible. Their conviction is that, out of respect for the integrity of the individual with whom they are working, they should never seek to impose their will upon him, and that they should, therefore, carefully refrain from using any kind of manipulative or authoritarian techniques. Because so much of what the average minister does suggests that he does not operate consistently within this framework of concern, social workers find it difficult to relate to him sympathetically.

When ministers seriously seek to understand why social workers seem hesitant or hostile in their relations with them, they will discover that the roots of the difficulty tend to run in the following general directions:

1. A feeling of difference as to interpretation and methods.

While it is recognized that the goal of both professions is that of helping persons to greater adequacy and fullness of living, social workers often feel that the minister is trying to get the individual to rely on supernatural forces outside himself, whereas they are trying to get him to understand and accept himself and to build on the foundation of his own (God-given?) strength and resources. In other words, social workers expect the miracle of regeneration to arise from within the individual as he learns to make better—that is, more insightful and creative—responses to himself and to the total revelations of reality outside himself. As social workers frequently see it, the minister seems to be working toward a more supernatural regeneration, which does not always occur as desired, and when it does not, may leave the individual in a worse plight rather than a better one.

2. A feeling of difference concerning the approach to guilt.

Social workers are keenly aware of the fact that many persons, some of them overly conscientious religious adherents, become disorganized because of extreme guilt feelings. Recognizing that these persons come for help because they are already overburdened with guilt, social workers try to stay professionally on guard against doing anything to add to their guilt load. Their responsibility as social workers, it is felt, is neither to condone nor to judge, but to help the guilt-laden person to see and understand all that is involved in his guilt and to learn how to handle it in the most positive and constructive fashion possible. Helping him to find the strength to handle his problem is the objective, rather than leading him toward a specific resolution which the worker prescribes. The minister, as social workers tend to see him, does not appear to understand the mechanism of guilt in human personality, often oversimplifies it, and frequently treats it in ways that merely add to the individual's already dangerously great burden of it.

3. A feeling of difference with respect to recognition of the necessity of maintaining safeguards and precautions for the protection of the client's integrity and worth.

Social workers conscientiously strive to restrict themselves to the problems the client brings to them and cautiously seek to refrain from intrusion into other areas of his experience unless invited to do so. In other words, they are as hesitant to go probing as they are to offer their own solutions to his problems. Because they do not wish to encourage dependency, their purpose is to come to his aid only when he invites their assistance, and to help him gain the strength to work through his difficulties to his own resolutions of them. Furthermore, they are especially fearful of the hasty application of limited psychological insights by persons inadequately trained in their use, and for this reason, insist on making referrals wherever possible to specialists with the competencies required for the treatment of each particular problem or disorder. Though they recognize that the minister means well, many social workers suspect that he is not usually so careful in these respects as they insist that members of their own profession must be.

4. A feeling of difference with regard to the degree of certainty concerning the criteria of religious judgment.

To many social workers these criteria seem very vague, variable, and sectarian. Since their professional responsibility is to minister to all persons on the basis of need, regardless of religious backgrounds, they tend to disqualify themselves for dealing with problems specifically in the area of religion. Though some of this disqualification may stem from their own confusion and uncertainty concerning religious values, a major part of it derives from a disciplined respect for the client's right to self-determination in matters of religious belief and affiliation. In their view the minister appears much more rigid and restricted in his religious attitudes, and much more impelled to seek to impose his particular religious perspective and value judgments upon the client.

It is a mistake, of course, to assume that all social workers hold such attitudes as those enumerated above, or that these are the only directions in which estrangement difficulties can develop. Moreover, upon encountering the attitudes, many ministers will probably feel justified in disagreeing with them or in denying that they have any foundation in fact. The more important matter is, however, that ministers be able to recognize the validity of the value concerns to which the social workers' criticisms pay homage, even though those criticisms are undeserved on the ministers' part. It is on the validity of these value concerns that increasingly better inter-professional relations can be structured.

Meanwhile, ministers must bring themselves to admit that some of the criticisms are merited. They can undoubtedly improve in their usefulness to God and humanity through giving serious consideration to correcting the faults which their colleagues in social work are helping them to identify.

A minister should realize, too, that he does not have to break the pastoral relationship with an individual when he refers him to a therapist or social worker for specialized help. In fact, if he has established good relations with the specialist to whom he makes referral he will usually find his pastoral relation enhanced rather than hindered through the referral. A far surer way of bankrupting his pastoral relationship with the individual is to neglect proper referral and do a sloppy job trying to meet the person's needs within the restrictions of the average pastor's inadequate time and training.

In a recent lecture to ministerial students, Mr. Isadore Seamans, Executive of the Health and Welfare Council of the National Capitol Area, Washington, D.C., made the following practical suggestions which all ministers would do well to act upon:

1. Pay a call on the Welfare Council where you live.
2. Ask the Council for an enumeration of local problems.
3. Volunteer for membership on one of the Council's committees.
4. Visit some of the key agencies in the community; identify with them; get on the board of one of them, if possible.
5. Know your church-related welfare agencies, and get them to take a look at themselves to see if they are providing the services needed, in the best possible ways.

He might have added that the minister should know the social workers in his congregation, visit them where they work, and confer with them on matters relating to their special skills and interests.

Summary and Conclusion

The purpose of this chapter has been to review the current status of the relationship of the church to social work and the social worker. The focus has been on exploring the common grounds of agreement, assessing the extent of breaches in understanding, and suggesting ways of repairing the breaches. Special attention has been given to the responsibilities of the church and of its ministers with respect to improving the relationships which exist.

The burden of the chapter has been to express the conviction that the church and social work, as well as the minister and the social worker, have too much in common, and are too greatly needed in co-operative approaches to the vital tasks of helping people in this complex and turbulent age, to let anything come between them, or to permit themselves to harbor any estrangements which prevent them from functioning in the closest possible team-work relationships.

It is evident that both the church and professional social work are having difficulty in keeping their values "on straight" in the fostering of charitable impulses and the administration of social welfare in the vast impersonalism of modern, highly organized, mass society. They can both continue to learn from each other, if they will, and they must realize that they are mutually involved in a task of such gigantic proportions as to demand more of them than their current deficiencies would allow them to produce even if they were functioning in the most ideal patterns of co-operation, to say nothing of how far short they will continue to fall to whatever degree they indulge in separatism.

Obviously, in terms of modern insights and value convictions, highly specialized skills are more needed today than ever to meet the complex needs of persons in this increasingly complex society. At the same time, it is equally evident that a dynamic expression of love in terms of deep personal involvement in the meeting of needs of distressed persons becomes ever more difficult to maintain. Both the church and social work must stay alert to these conditions, and must strive to meet the challenge of them in every way possible. Both must labor to meet the whole needs of man in as skillful and adequate a manner as possible.

While supporting the high standards sought in professional social work, and trying to help social workers maintain a religious quality of personal interest in their clients, the church must seek fresh, new ways of encouraging untrained individuals to become personally involved in doing the kinds of things which they are qualified to do as Christians concerned for persons in distress. The purpose should be to supplement, not to interfere with or substitute for, the labors of the social worker. Social work will do well to assist the church in such effort.

QUESTIONS FOR DISCUSSION

1. Should the church claim credit for the development of the modern professional discipline of social work, or did the discipline develop as a reaction against the church's carelessness and mistakes in the practice of social work?

2. When does social work qualify as a Christian profession?

3. What common ground, if any, is occupied by Christian theology and the philosophy of modern professional social work?

4. How could the minister and the social worker co-operate to help a person suffering from emotional illness, or from difficulties in social adjustment?

5. What have been the church's greatest shortcomings in its relationship to the practice of social work?

6. What steps should the church take to improve its relationship with professional social work—especially with that part of the profession which is not embraced in church-sponsored agencies?

FOLLOW-UP SUGGESTIONS

Individual

Interview two or three pastors on the subject of what their experiences have been in making referrals of parishioners to social agencies. Have the pastors been pleased or displeased with the results? What attitudes are expressed toward the agencies and the social workers who function in them?

Following these interviews, talk to a comparable number of social workers about their experiences in trying to work with ministers and churches in efforts to meet the needs of clients. Have the results been gratifying or unpleasant? What attitudes are expressed toward ministers, churches, or religion?

Group

Sponsor a luncheon for local ministers and social workers. Involve leaders of both groups in the planning of the program. Make the objective one of helping members of the professions get better acquainted with each other in order that they may better communicate with each other across professional lines about mutual problems and concerns.

Make a survey of the community to (1) find out how many local pastors are serving on boards or committees of important social agencies and community welfare programs; (2) ascertain how many local churches have effective social service or Christian social relations committees; and (3) discover what use local churches are making of the social workers who belong to their congregations.

V: The Local Church and Social Agencies in the Community

A certain professor is said to have made a habit of declaring, "If it isn't local, it isn't real."[1] Such a statement is particularly appropriate in discussions of the church, for it is at the level of the local church that all the meaning of the church universal comes into concrete expression.

Special responsibility rests upon the local church, therefore, to give expression to social welfare concern in a careful and consistently Christian way. Under the peculiar conditions of modern community life this responsibility entails special obligations with respect to the manner in which the church relates itself to the social agencies which carry the major administrative burden for community welfare. In the quality of the relationships which its interaction with these agencies helps to build in community life is one of the local church's most forceful prophetic articulations of hope for the coming of the kingdom of God.

Dangerously misleading implications are embraced in the statement often made to the effect that "The church is in the community, yet not of it." Though the intention in this statement is to suggest that the church must maintain a tension with the community which leads toward ever more ideal conditions in community life, it often results in detachment and social irresponsibility. A dynamic

---

[1] Albert T. Rasmussen, *Christian Social Ethics* (Englewood Cliffs, N.J.: Prentice-Hall, Inc., 1956), p. 202.

interrelatedness exists always between the local church and its community—an interrelatedness which no amount of disclaiming can negate. The church is both in the community and a part of the community. Not only is it the community's conscience, as it is often declared to be; it is also one of the community's working organizations. What it is and how it behaves as a working organization affects every other agency in its social environment and makes a serious impact on the functional structure of all community relationships. What it fails to say or do may often be more influential than what it actually says or does.

Though the church must not have a narrow conception of community which shuts out the broader reaches of the world or a comprehensive awareness of needs in the whole family of humanity, it must not fail to recognize that all community service begins in the local setting. What it hopes to do for the world at large it must carefully devote itself to accomplishing at home. In the manner in which it gives itself to the needs close at hand, it expresses its truest sentiments concerning need anywhere.

Moreover, the mere preaching of ideals or the offering of conscience-pricking criticisms will never be enough. The church that serves effectively in its community must join the team of groups, agencies, and individuals who strive for improvement in the community's welfare. Such a church must commit itself to the kind of practical and co-operative "blood, sweat, and tears" working involvement through which alone social redemption can be expected to occur in community life.

A minister who is especially sensitive to these imperatives for the local church, because he comes out of a background in social work education, in community organization, and in the office of president of a council of social agencies, comments that his experience has given him the following very vivid impressions:

1. That it is remarkable how many agencies in every community are concerned for so many of the values which figure in the church's concern.

2. That the needs in every community are so great that all the agencies struggling with them are up against almost overwhelming odds.

3. That it is nothing short of marvelous what a dynamically concerned and co-operative pastor and congregation can mean to the organization and functioning of the community agencies striving for the common welfare.

4. That there is too often a tragic lack of adequate communication and understanding between the church and community social agencies.

Because the church is interested in the whole man, it must work constructively with all the agencies and institutions which affect his welfare. Especially must it recognize, appreciate, and develop good communication and working relationships with those agencies which share any measure of its concern for the worth and welfare of persons. As the National Conference on Policy and Strategy in Social Welfare pointed out, the church can carry out its relationships to the community's institutions and agencies through: (1) coordination of its services with their services; (2) mutual sharing in the use of personnel, skills, and facilities; (3) joining with them in planning, research, and fund raising; and (4) co-operating with them in striving for good interpretation and communication.[2]

To do less than this would hardly be worthy of the church. Behavior short of such an ideal would not seem to be in keeping with the mind and spirit of Christ, whose living body the church seeks to be in the community. How the church can equip itself for the task and best proceed in discharging its responsibilities in the matter will be the focus of attention for the remainder of this chapter.

Understanding Itself and Its Opportunities

Involved in its spiritual preparation for its tasks is the church's obligation to seek an understanding of itself as an organization functioning in the structure of community life. Each local church should evaluate the role it is playing, and try to ascertain whether this is the role that it really wants to take or that it should be taking. The ancient admonition to "know thyself" is probably as appropriate for a church as it is for a person.

Self-understanding may be promoted through conscientious ef-

---

[2] *Policy and Strategy* (*op. cit.*), p. 14.

forts to be objective in self-evaluation with respect to the common tendencies and temptations to which churches are sometimes prone to yield. Some of the more obvious and serious of these tendencies and temptations which have special relevance to the present discussion may be described as follows:

1. The tendency of the church to identify not with the community as a whole but only with selective elements in it.

Where this occurs, of course, the church, however unwittingly, helps to deepen the cleavages and sharpen the conflicts that prevent community integration. The church that seeks the wholeness of the community must identify itself in every way possible with the whole community. To include only certain social classes, certain occupational groups, certain neighborhoods, or certain races in the center of its concern is to be less than the church needs to be if it is to have a truly healing ministry amidst the conflicts and injustices engendered in community life. It is, furthermore, to invite justified criticism from those agencies which labor for the unity and welfare of the whole community and of all the persons in it.

2. The tendency toward "self-centered parochialism."

The church that fails to see and serve needs beyond the narrow confines of its own restricted neighborhood or select constituency is both dangerously myopic and tragically callous and egocentric. Yet there is a constant temptation to the church to become so engrossed in its own self-generated, self-centered, and self-enhancing activities within a radically circumscribed context that it loses the sense of challenge to be self-emptying in its consecration to the tasks of carrying the gospel to "all the world." The parochially self-centered church represents, then, a community blind spot, an island of isolation, a vote for anarchy and weakness. It reveals a thick-skinned insensitivity to the broader aspects of welfare needs on the level of the total community, and implies a basic attitude bordering on social irresponsibility.

3. The temptation of the church, on the other hand, to focus its social concerns as far away from its local setting as possible.

It is easy for the church to become so involved in the local status quo, and to develop so many vested interests to protect there, that it feels it cannot afford to take an aggressive part in local struggles for justice or for more equitable welfare provisions. Direct involvement would be too troublesome and too costly. As a substitute, and sometimes to divert attention from its own home-base shortcomings, it may yield to the twin temptations to fight social injustice that is vague and generalized, or that is located in some remote place where other people will have to carry the burden of direct involvement.

4. The tendency of the church to gravitate toward middle-class smugness.

Because America is dominated by a middle-class psychology, the church tends to yield unconsciously to pressures toward middle-class norms. In consequence, it is always in danger of drifting so far away from the less privileged status groups that it experiences difficulty in understanding their predicament. Almost a third of the nation's people are said to be in substandard income brackets that hardly qualify them for middle-class identification; and working-class people, as represented by their relative proportions in church membership, appear to be losing interest in the churches. Furthermore, studies have shown that church positions of leadership and authority are almost invariably dominated by middle-class and upper-class persons—all of which strongly suggests that unless the church stays on guard against the tendency, it may find itself smugly voicing middle-class sentiments and unable to sympathize with needed welfare programs designed for persons who fall into less privileged categories.

5. The temptation of the church to insist on playing a "prima donna" role.

Like many other agencies in society, the church is sometimes tempted to insist, after the fashion of a spoiled "prima donna," on playing the spotlight role that receives most of the credit for cooperative community efforts in which it participates. If it cannot dictate the pattern of activity or be in the primary leadership role, it may be inclined to sulk, criticize, or withdraw its support. In order to enjoy a sense of unchallenged stardom it may attempt to operate its own independent welfare programs quite apart from serious consideration of what the total community needs are, or of what are the purposes, programs, and policies of other agencies.

In so doing it may easily enter into ill-advised efforts that are superficial, inadequately planned, beyond its limited resources, or even damaging. When these fail, instead of acknowledging its shortcomings with respect to co-operation and careful planning, the church may console itself by nurturing a martyr complex, which assumes that its efforts were noble ones that would not have failed except for the lack of understanding and support from an indifferent laity or from other persons and agencies in the community.

6. The tendency of the church to neglect defining itself and its work very carefully.

Because Protestant churches emphasize voluntarism as the basis of membership, they tend to think of themselves as collections of people assembled through mutual interests and preferences, rather than as agencies of strength charged with social and divine responsibilities for a specific ministry within a specific area. Consequently, the local church seldom has very well-defined parish boundary lines or a very clear conception of what its total responsibilities are to all the people in its neighborhood. Its ministry becomes selective, beamed to the insiders who have been attracted into the fold, and fails to take the community as a whole into serious consideration. It is a ministry considered to embrace objectives relating to the spiritual, physical, and social welfare of persons; but these objectives may only be hinted at in the vaguest possible ways, and never spelled out concretely, in the routine operation of a traditional church program. With vague definitions of its parish, a vague focus on its community, and a vaguely structured program the local church is inviting ineptitude and irrelevance.

Though many other tendencies and temptations to which the church is subject could be identified, these will suffice for purposes of illustration. The church that is faithful in its stewardship will carefully seek an understanding of itself in such matters, and will sincerely strive to correct whatever faults it may detect in its behavior. Moreover, it will be constantly laboring for a clearer conception of its total opportunities and obligations in community life.

Accepting Its Responsibilities

It is not enough, however, for the church to know itself and its opportunities; it must be wholeheartedly willing to accept its responsibilities. While these responsibilities are numerous, extensive, and pointed in many directions, several important ones have a special bearing on the church's relationship to welfare conditions and social agencies in the community. To some of these attention will now be briefly given.

The Responsibility to Be Concerned

The whole gospel for whole persons embraces the whole of community life. In its concern for the whole man the church finds it imperative to be concerned for all those agencies and influences that contribute to his wholeness.

Because the church's concern for persons leads it into concern for their physical, psychological, and social, as well as their spiritual, welfare, it must lead it, too, to a sensitive appreciation of the importance of all the social agencies which exercise a stewardship of skills and resources for ministering to any of the facets of human need. The church cannot be true to itself and be indifferent to any agency that appreciates the worth of persons and ministers to their needs; neither can it be indifferent when needs are going unmet because of conditions that prevent the appropriate agencies from making adequate provision for them.

The Responsibility to Be Informed

Every local church has a responsibility to keep itself informed not only about welfare needs in the community but also about the agencies and services available for meeting these needs. Information on such matters should be carefully, systematically, objectively, and continuously gathered. Without it the church cannot intelligently plan its program or carry out its ministry.

Because there are unique conditions, of which the church should be aware in every community, and because the problems and needs of any community are constantly changing, no church can ever be free of the imperative to be a community-focused, fact-finding, and fact-using church. Tragedy befalls both church and community where sentimentality, hunches, and guesswork are substituted for reliable knowledge.

In seeking information the church should, of course, look carefully at its immediate neighborhood, but it should not stop with neighborhood or parish boundaries.

State-wide problems, needs, and services are also essential considerations, regardless of the church's size or location; and beyond the state, in turn, are the region, the nation, and the world. The church with a truly Christian compassion for humanity in its heart will not set narrow limits on its quest for knowledge of need wherever need exists; nor will it be content to be ignorant of or unidentified with the organized forces of humanitarianism which struggle anywhere to meet need.

It is with the church's relationship to needs and agencies in the local community, however, that the present discussion is principally concerned. The church must begin where it is, and is not likely to be more enduringly effective anywhere than it is at home.

A careful survey of the needs of all the people in the community is essential. It is seldom necessary, however, for the individual church to undertake to gather all the needed data firsthand. Many important items have already been covered by studies conducted under auspices of various branches of government, chambers of commerce, business corporations, public utilities, the public schools, councils of churches, councils of social agencies, and the like. Information on these items is usually available for the asking. Even when a firsthand study seems necessary it is better, wherever possible, to do it in co-operation with other churches.

In any case, the church needs to know how the various segments of the community's population compare with one another, and how the community as a whole compares with other communities, the state, and the nation with respect to such important matters as: (1) employment opportunities, income, and working conditions; (2) housing, sanitation, and general living conditions; (3) family life, marriage, divorce, juvenile delinquency, and child welfare; (4) health and medical care; (5) educational opportunities and achievement; (6) recreational advantages; (7) age, sex, racial, and ethnic composition; (8) segregation, discrimination, and other evidences of injustice; (9) vice, crime, and law enforcement; (10) accessibility to all needed private and public facilities; (11) adequacy of welfare provisions; and (12) availability of adequately staffed and supported social agencies.

In addition to such a general knowledge of community conditions, it is especially important that the church know the programs, policies, and key personnel of the major social agencies serving in the community.

Most important of all, perhaps, the church should be acquainted with the local council of social agencies, and should learn much through it concerning the network of available services and the extent of unmet need for which provisions are still to be made. Where the council operates one, the church should be familiar with and make full use of the social service exchange.

Back of most of the private agencies in the community will usually be found the Community Chest or United Givers' Fund, which raises a major portion of the money to support them. The church should know the Chest or Fund—how it is organized, how it is administered, what its policies are, why it includes support of some agencies and not of others, how it decides which agencies receive what proportions of the funds raised, how well it is succeeding in its fund-raising goals, and the like.

In nearly every community, too, there will be found sectarian services supported by local churches or by denominations. The church should be thoroughly conversant with these, especially with those to which it gives any measure of its own support.

In addition to contacts made regularly by the pastor and key church leaders, visits and study tours to the important institutions and agencies should be a consistently maintained part of the program of activities for the entire church constituency. Furthermore, staff members of the important agencies should be included in the programs of all church groups as frequently as possible, and church volunteers should be encouraged to help the agencies in whatever ways their services may be needed.

An up-to-date list should be on file in every church office of all important local social agencies, together with addresses, telephone numbers, and names of key personnel. Supplementing this should be a file of current materials being regularly received from the agencies. The church should, of course, request to be put on agency mailing lists.

In every way possible, the church should seek representation on councils, commissions, boards, study groups, and in organized movements aimed at assessing community needs and developing more adequate services.

It is inexcusable for a church to be functioning in a community and not be able to speak with maximum assurance and accuracy on conditions pertaining to the community's welfare. Surely no other organization in community life has a greater responsibility to know and be concerned about such vital facts. It should be in the church that people are stimulated to ask the most serious questions, encouraged to co-operate in seeking the most adequate perspectives, and strengthened in the possession of the most reliable data concerning community needs and services. To know what is happening to families, children, youth, the sick, the crippled, the homeless, the hungry, the imprisoned, the ignorant, the oppressed, and the poverty stricken should be placed on a parity with study of the Bible. To know the agency personnel and community leaders who carry the burden of local social work should be made to seem of no less importance than knowing about the ancient prophets and kings. To know the adequacy of public welfare grants, community chest subscriptions, and social agency resources should be underscored with emphasis equally as great as that placed on understanding the church budget.

The Responsibility to Be Properly Organized and Oriented

Obviously the church cannot maintain the continuous fact-gathering process suggested in the preceding paragraphs without making specific organizational arrangements to assure that it will be done. Beyond the mere gathering of facts, too, is the larger task of helping the congregation make the fullest and best use of accumulated data in redemptive community action. In this broad area of responsibility lie requirements not only for the most careful organization but also for the greatest skill and dedication of which the church leadership is capable.

The minister has definite obligations to know key social workers and agencies, to participate in community organizational efforts, and to keep himself reasonably well informed concerning community needs and problems. Still, the minister should never be expected to substitute for the congregation's need to have an organized unit of its own lay members charged with responsibility to go into these matters in depth and detail, and to follow them through with consistency and persistence. Much more should be done than the minister's crowded schedule and necessarily divided interests can ever permit.

In every congregation there should be some type of committee or commission[3] established for the specific purpose of keeping the congregation informed concerning community needs and problems, and of giving careful leadership in expressing Christian ethical concern through constructive action. Such an organizational unit should work in the closest possible relationship with every other unit in the total organizational structure of the church. It should be the pastor's "right hand," in a sense, and the official board's chief counsel. At the same time, it may serve as a major source of assistance and guidance in the programs of missions, evangelism, Christian education, and social service.

Though such a committee or commission may well give attention to needs that stretch far beyond the confines of the local community, it should always maintain a major and dynamic community focus.

In large churches situated in complex communities the committee or commission should have several subcommittees[4] to help

---

[3] It may have any one of many titles; the name is of little consequence as long as the function is clear. In some churches it is called the "Christian Citizenship Committee," in others, the "Social Action Committee," or "The Commission on Christian Social Concerns."

[4] Significant possibilities: (1) Committee on Ministry to Courts and Institutions, (2) Social Work Committee, (3) Research and Survey Committee, (4) Family Life Committee, (5) Committee on Juvenile Delinquency and the Welfare of Children and Youth, (6) Committee on Crime and Law Enforcement, (7) Committee on Housing and Urban Renewal, (8) Committee on Problems of the Aged, (9) Committee on Legislation, (10) Committee on Alcohol Problems, (11) Committee on Employment and Economic Life, (12) Community Organization Committee.

it keep in close contact with developments in specialized areas of need, and maintain the proper educational and actional emphases with reference to each. In the church of average size a single unit may suffice. Even the smallest rural church, however, should have at least one lay person especially designated for this type of responsibility.

Effective organization along these lines, and the development of leadership for the exercising of such practical Christian influence has been labeled "a matter of spiritual life or death for a church."[5]

In the final analysis, however, it is the general attitude of the church upon which the success of all organizational arrangements rests.

The pattern and effectiveness of the organization for community relevance, for example, will always depend upon the manner in which the minister and congregation interpret the social imperatives of the Christian Gospel. If these imperatives are understood to be an integral part of the total Gospel, and if the church maintains enough alertness to its responsibilities to justify its identification as a church, interest in the social agencies and welfare conditions will be easily sustained.

The church must see itself not as set over against society and the ways of life in culture but as a working unit in society and culture, striving for the transformation of social relationships in terms of the highest revelations which have been delivered through every channel of God's grace. As it does so, the church will find its way beyond the negativism that condemns everything secular. It will develop a positive appreciation of the fact that social work, whether or not under church auspices, is an important ally in the struggle to conserve and enhance values of paramount significance.

The Responsibility to Plan Its Welfare Activities Carefully and to Do a Good Job of Them

The church still has many welfare responsibilities and is usually involved in welfare activities of some kind. It must manifest the greatest care, however, in the manner in which it conducts itself with reference to them. In no other way can it earn the respect of

---

[5] Rasmussen, *op. cit.*, p. 180.

professional social workers or be influential in relationships with the community's social agencies.

Only in demonstrating that it is as sensitive to values and as perceptively anxious as the best of social agencies to protect values can the church bring credit upon itself and validate its claims to speak with authority. Exploitation of the needs and sufferings of the unfortunate to promote institutional objectives, to enable the smugly privileged to indulge in subtle self-congratulation, or to purchase sporadic relief from the guilt feelings born of persistent neglect, is as unbecoming as it is unethical and un-Christian. To distribute charity so carelessly as not to distinguish between genuine and pretended need, between symptoms of merely physical deprivation and those that speak of problems that lie deeper in the mind and spirit, or between the methods that enhance and those that destroy the personal integrity of the recipient, is to raise justified doubts as to maturity and responsibility. To classify all non-material problems in a generalized "religious" category and apply a standardized "religious" therapy to them all alike is to suggest, not great religious faith but something quite the opposite—naivete, perhaps, or laziness, or stubborn indifference to the helpfully differentiating truths and skills revealed in science.

The church with a reputation for rummage sales, soft-touch handouts, morbidly sentimental holiday distribution of food baskets, and charity as bait on sectarian hooks, will be able to command no more respect in social work circles than it deserves.

The church's help in welfare work is greatly needed and will always be appreciated when it is rendered in a superior manner. Where the church is not prepared to conduct formal welfare activities on the highest level of meaning and value, however, it will usually be better for it to place such responsibilities in the hands of persons and agencies more adequately equipped. Even where such persons and agencies are not already present, it may be better for the church to invest its energies in helping the community to secure them than for it to thrust itself hastily into the gaps of unmet need in an ill-prepared manner which may handicap the community in making the more adequate provisions that the conditions will ultimately demand.

Meanwhile, where a sense of higher obligation imposes acceptance of such wise precautions the church will discover that its spiritual imperatives remain unimpaired. It will continue to find endless opportunities for the informal activities of inspiration, helpfulness, encouragement, motivation, and love, which are the heart of welfare concern and without which there would be no adequate foundation for any welfare program.[6] The maintenance of good relationships with the community agencies carrying the main burden of social work—relationships that foster free communication, mutual understanding and respect, and full co-operation—the spiritually sensitive church will recognize to be of far greater consequence to the community's ultimate welfare than anything to be hoped for from independent or competitive activities sloppily conducted under its own limited auspices.

The Responsibility to Co-operate

Since the church cannot stand alone and care for all the community's needs, it should praise God for the resources and strength possible through unity even in the midst of division and diversity. Furthermore, the church should accept with enthusiasm its opportunity and responsibility to help lead the community in a co-operative quest for the good life which is increasingly possible under the providence of God. At this point, possibly more than any other, the church is uniquely equipped to provide community leadership. It is commissioned to maintain an open fellowship, to be concerned in love for the welfare of all, and to function in a responsible relationship both to God and man. In addition, the church

---

[6] One large urban church has been exploring the frontiers of these less formal service opportunities with a plan which seeks to assign a church member who has been through a trying experience, such as a bout with cancer or business failure or bereavement, to function as "buddy" to another person who is involved in a similar experience. Other churches are experimenting with a variety of schemes, such as the Big Brother plan, for using volunteer workers under skilled supervision in providing friendly assistance to boys exposed to high delinquency risk. While these are far from utopian, they suggest that the church will always be able, without bringing itself into disrepute, to find valuable ways of continuing direct expression of its welfare concerns, even where it may not be in a position to offer formal welfare services in keeping with the highest professional standards.

clearly symbolizes the noblest impulses and highest aspirations of all persons in the community, and is blessed with a rich historical endowment of general respect and affection. In it, as nowhere else in society beyond the family, is co-operation based on love and mutual regard specifically identified as a primary bond of institutional life.

The church can, if it will, therefore, be a powerful catalytic agent that helps the diverse community elements to combine in patterns of mutuality that increasingly open doors for the inflowing of redemptive grace. Where it fails to be such an agent, it automatically becomes, at least in one important respect, a part of the community's problem rather than a part of God's answer to the community's need.

If the church is to serve as the community's conscience, which it is often said to be, it must recognize that it is dynamically involved in the processes through which are produced the community's psychic attributes. A community is essentially a psychic or spiritual phenomenon, almost comparable to the personality of an individual, and when there is an absence of the co-ordination which makes effective teamwork possible it may be said to be suffering from a schizoid affliction. If its conscience is to contribute more to it than debilitating conflict, incoherence, or paralysis, it must be a conscience carefully welded to integrative behavior.

It is of the utmost importance, then, that the local church devote itself to fostering the fullest possible measure of co-operation between itself and the social agencies in its community. Church and social agency co-operation is called for by the logic of obviously complementary mutual concerns. It is full of promise for the improvement of the general welfare. It is also the main line of hope for a balanced program of concrete therapy that can bring healing and wholeness to the lives of the individuals of whom the community is composed. That there is great "need for building rapport between the church and other community organizations and agencies"[7] has been dramatically demonstrated in far too many tragic instances.

---

[7] Samuel W. Blizzard, Jr., "Let the Church Serve Its Community," *Social Progress*, March, 1950, p. 2.

The church must remember, however, that rapport is not built on a definition of co-operation that insists on "getting others to do it my way," or that says "let's all get together and help me get what I want." Real co-operation is a matter of giving as well as receiving. The church must hold itself convincingly ready to go more than halfway in encouraging the relationship. It must be prepared, too, to be patient and persistent in the practices through which co-operation is nurtured. The understanding and trust on which alone genuine co-operation can be based cannot be created by fiat, by the formation of committees, or by setting up elaborate organizational machinery. Time is required for growth in such matters, and much strenuous effort must be invested in creating the essential supporting conditions. Only the church that is more interested in accomplishment than in receiving credit, and more concerned for the community's good than for success in exercising dominance, will be prepared to make the necessary sacrifices.

There is, it may be added, a special obligation on the church to assume the initiative in fostering community co-operation. Religion has frequently demonstrated a penchant for being one of the most divisive influences in community life. Few, indeed, are the communities that cannot recite a history of conflict related to denominational competition and to argument over doctrine, to say nothing of battles between conservative religious traditionalism and the forces of science, rationalism, secularism, and "worldliness." It would be no more than proper, therefore, for the church to undertake to make amends by proving that it is capable of a maturity that transcends petty rivalries and negative judgmentalisms in a sincere concern for the higher values to be realized in what is unifying and positive. In such maturity, expressed through appreciative co-operation with all helping agencies in the community, the church will be able to earn the right to make constructive criticisms with reasonable expectation that they will be given a serious hearing.

The place for co-operation to begin, of course, is between the local congregation and other churches. To replace rivalry and open conflict with passive tolerance is not enough; even a pattern of mutual support for unilateral action is inadequate. The well-integrated community must have churches that have the will and the working patterns for unity of action. Where the will exists, the resultant working pattern is usually in the form of an interchurch committee of ministers and laymen representing the various congregations, or of a local council of churches.

The council of churches is an especially valuable means of extending the co-operative outreach of individual congregations in large communities. Where it would be impossible for each church to have direct contact with all the social agencies, for instance, and to have representation in the council of social agencies, so. as to know about and assist in programs designed for the community as a whole, the council of churches can have such contact and representation and can keep all the churches informed concerning significant developments. Moreover, the council of churches, or even an interchurch committee where no council exists, provides the advantage of a single, conveniently accessible, at least semi-authoritative body, prepared to serve as spokesman and delegate for the churches in community affairs.

The 1955 Cleveland Conference on the Churches and Social Welfare raised the question of how the local church, serving as initiator, participant, co-ordinator, and facilitator, can help create a constructive teamwork relationship between itself and other churches and community organizations. In answer, the following suggestions were proposed:

1. That social work should be looked upon not as a competitor of the church, but as one of the important means through which the church can do its work.

2. That social workers be looked upon not as persons trying to interfere with the pastoral responsibilities of the church, but as dedicated people, many of whom are members of the church implementing their Christian vocation in the welfare field, and as such, meriting recognition as persons doing church work.

3. That when unmet need is found, instead of rushing in to provide its own service, the church first draw together social agency personnel, and representatives of government, other churches, and community planning bodies for consultation on how the needs can best be met.

4. That the church seek the establishment of effective teamwork relationships with the social agencies through the pastor and key laymen assuming responsibilities in community agencies and in social planning, through having social workers appear before church groups to interpret their methods and responsibilities, and through co-operating with (and helping to create where none exists) the community welfare council.

5. That the church be on the lookout for specific projects on which it can co-operate with social agencies in expressing concern and taking concrete action.

6. That all such local groups as the council of churches, the council of churchwomen, and the community social planning council, be stimulated to provide leadership to churches in social welfare activities and to foster co-operation between churches and social agencies in meeting community needs.

7. That the church express its community welfare concerns in ways that contribute to the unity of the community, especially by recognizing that institutions and agencies do not have to be under church control in order to meet welfare needs in a Christian fashion.

8. That the church, in instances where they are needed, undertake experimental or pilot projects, after proper consultation with community agencies, but be willing to maintain high standards in them and to keep them open to community evaluation in regard to their continuing need and relevance.

9. That even in rural areas where social workers are few or non-existent, the church make use of resource persons and guiding materials from colleges and universities, statewide government agencies such as the departments of health, education, and welfare, and county and statewide private organizations such as the Crippled Children's Society and the Mental Health Association.[8]

The 1957 Atlantic City Conference on Policy and Strategy in Social Welfare reiterated most of these points and added others, some of the more important of which may be summarized as follows:

1. That the church must accompany the preaching of the Word and the life and worship of the congregation with practical pro-

---

[8] Bachmann (ed.), op. cit., Vol. III, pp. 166–167.

grams of Christian service in such areas as health, social work, recreation, youth services, and social education and action.

2. That the church recognize that most social work must be done by non-church agencies, and that it urge its members to support these agencies in every way possible, especially by serving as volunteer workers, as board members, and in other policy-forming capacities.

3. That whenever possible and appropriate the church, either alone or in co-operation with other churches, should supply skilled pastoral care and chaplaincy services both for the staff and the clients of non-church agencies.

4. That the church should initiate and encourage continuing conversations between its representatives and social workers.

5. That the church, in faithfulness to the doctrine of the priesthood of all believers, should openly recognize that the Christian motive for social welfare may find expression in services, both professional and voluntary, rendered by church members in any agency, whether church or non-church.

6. That the church should make maximum use of existing social and health services in the community, developing good referral habits and serving as a major referral source.

7. That the church should specialize in enlisting, training, and using volunteers for assignment in social agencies and for work in its own program.

8. That the church should seek to recruit persons from among its members for the social work profession, and should encourage them with spiritual and financial support while they are in process of securing the necessary training.

9. That the church should concentrate on motivating and educating its entire membership through study and discussion groups, field trips, study tours, workshops, institutes, work camps, service projects, and the like, as well as through prophetic preaching and discerning pastoral leadership, on matters pertaining to welfare needs and the work being done by social agencies.

10. That the church should interpret charity and all welfare activities carefully as expressions of faith "done out of gratitude in response to God's act in Jesus Christ."

11. That the church should be alert and courageous to support persons and groups in the community who fight for just causes, however unpopular.

12. That the church should especially help its members to understand the work of public health and welfare agencies so they will be able to function intelligently as citizens with respect to them.

13. That it be recognized as vital that the church concentrate on developing lay leadership and action within itself and in the community.[9]

While these summarize most of the more important aspects of the church's co-operative responsibility, the possibilities for additional suggestions are almost limitless. The church could, for instance, keep a large group of well-trained solicitors or house-to-house canvassers standing in readiness at all times to assist in important community campaigns for funds, surveys of need, education for action, and the like. It could sponsor annual receptions or dinners for social workers in general or for the staffs of particular agencies in order to foster good will and better understanding through personal acquaintance. It could secure copies of the local social service directory from the council of social agencies and place them in the church office and library, and in the hands of all responsible church officers. It could regularly feature exhibits in the church foyer or library interpreting the work of particular local agencies.

If the goal toward which co-operation is pointed is the production of a good community program of social work, it may be that a word should be added as to what would be the characteristics of such a program. Paraphrasing and amending the words of an early text on the community and social welfare so as to include consideration of the church's role, we can say that the following would be the important characteristics. The support and control of the agencies (and of the churches?) is representative of the interest and thought of the community. The attitude of the agencies and of the churches toward one another is one of mutual assistance rather than of competition. The services of the agencies and of the churches are closely co-ordinated with one another. Any particular type of service rendered by the agencies or the churches is available for all the members of the community who need it. All addi-

---

[9] *Policy and Strategy* (*op. cit.*), pp. 9, 12, 13, 14, 15, 16, 19, 21–23, 33, 39, 45.

tions to the social work of the community, whether by the church
or by some other agency, are made in the light of a full knowledge
of all the needs of the whole community and with the approval of
at least a majority of the social-work interests of the community.[10]

In view of all this, there is biting poignancy in the comments recently made by a Methodist layman who is the executive director
of the United Givers' Fund for one of the nation's largest metropolitan areas. Said he, in words to this effect: "The American way
is the way of free enterprise, but it is also the way of a voluntary
spirit of co-operation. The Protestant tradition has been to see to
it that the community has the necessary social services to care for
all the people's needs; yet the Protestant churches do not always
support the United Givers' Fund vigorously. Is this lack of enthusiasm due to the fact that the UGF does not stress Protestant
charities as such? Should we have 'Protestant charities,' or should
we look upon all community agencies as the arm of the church?
Is it possible to support both adequately?"

The Responsibility to Nurture the
Wholeness of the Community

Implied in all the preceding statements is the general responsibility of the church to devote itself unceasingly to the task of nurturing the wholeness of the community. When the community is adequate, integrated, and approximating what it ought to be, it is
easier for individuals in it to be adequate, integrated, and approximating what God wants them to be.

Social work is increasingly moving toward the concept of the
"therapeutic community"—the type of community that possesses
and is so organized as to contribute to all its members the spiritual
and physical health and wholeness which save persons from demoralization. It is at this point that the church can and must relate
itself most meaningfully to all that the social agencies represent,
recognizing that the "therapeutic community" is what the church
at its best has stood for through the centuries.

A good community has balance, co-ordination, and what has
been called "a continuing soul." Chiefly it is built out of the spirit

---

[10] C. C. North, *op. cit.*, p. 24.

of the people as that spirit expresses itself through all their shared relationships. Such a community is a manifestation of how the grace of God flows through the intermeshed relationships of our "unescapable mutuality." It follows, too, that the social work of any community is, as has often been said, merely an expression of the organized good will of the community.

Understanding, good will, brotherhood—the qualities of life that characterize a good community and that the church has long stressed as central emphases of the Christian gospel—are the indispensable requirements of an adequate welfare program. Individuals experience few needs of a social welfare nature that are not cared for where these qualities prevail in community life. The church, therefore, as it fulfills its mission to help create a spirit of love and brotherhood, as it inspires and nurtures the will to work together toward the highest goals, and as it demonstrates the reality of truly Christian fellowship, makes a contribution of incalculable worth to the welfare of all persons and the success of all social agencies composing the community's corporate structure.

Giving Itself Away in Redemptive Service

Perhaps the best way of all for the church to relate itself to the social agencies of its community is through completely and unselfishly giving itself, with all the intelligence, skill, and material resources of which it is possessed, to the meeting of the human needs which called the social agencies into being. The fact that social complexity has made the agencies necessary does not excuse the church from any measure of the utmost involvement. Detachment, irrelevance, and engrossment in selfish institutional concerns that do not come to grips with human need in a realistic manner can be the greatest of barriers between the church and all the forces that wrestle daily against overwhelming odds in the community arena of need.

The church must realize that concentration on finding and preserving its institutional life can mean losing that life, and that losing its life in Christ-like service can result in finding all the meaning that makes its institutional existence worthwhile. The church must recognize that it cannot effectively preach the Good Samaritan

Gospel without heeding the injunction to "go thou and do like-wise."

This inevitably means that it must be a functional rather than an institutional church. The functional church, it has been re-marked, spends just as little time as possible on institutional machinery and details of routine, and concentrates on projects which contribute directly to the purpose of transforming men and communities. Far from being program-centered and denomination-minded, it is person-centered and community-conscious. Its pri-mary focus is not on doctrinal and historical background, but upon the application of the gospel's dynamics in the contemporary scene. Consequently, it is not so rooted in tradition that it cannot experi-ment with new procedures designed to achieve a greater relevance. It does not restrict religion to certain pious personal practices, but sees it as embracing every area of life. Finally, the functional church moves beyond verbalisms to supplement careful discussion with practical action.[11]

Because the church is an influential organizational unit in com-munity life, it cannot shift its responsibilities to its individual lay and clerical members. The church, as a corporate body, builds buildings, employs staffs, adopts policies, and does many other things. It must, as a corporate body, address itself unselfishly to community needs.

Summary and Conclusion

Consideration has been given in this chapter to the subject of how the local church should relate itself to the social agencies in its community. Since the purpose has been to discuss only the church's side of responsibility in this interactional relationship, the equivalent obligations which the social agencies should feel have not been treated, though they may be equally important.

The discussion has been organized around three major headings. The first had to do with the church's obligation to understand it-self and its opportunities, particularly in the matter of staying on guard against its weaknesses and temptations, knowing its com-

---

[11] Seifert, *op. cit.,* pp. 19–25.

munity's needs, and becoming thoroughly acquainted with the local social agencies. The second stressed the importance of the church's accepting its full measure of responsibilities with respect to welfare needs and the social agencies, in terms of being concerned, being informed, being helpfully organized and oriented, being careful and thorough in its own welfare undertakings, being fully co-operative and supportive, and being unequivocally devoted to nurturing the wholeness of the community. The third considered the value of the church's being functional rather than institutional, and as such, giving its life away for Christ's sake and the gospel's in the redemptive tasks of meeting the human needs which are a major part of the church's concern as well as the reason for the existence of the social agencies.

That there is great need for better relationships between churches and social agencies at the local level can be little doubted, and it has been treated here as a self-evident assumption.

From the discussion it should be clear: that there is much the local church can and should do to relate itself more helpfully and meaningfully to the social agencies in its community; that the church should look upon these agencies as major allies in the tasks of redemptive service; and that the welfare of the community as a whole is significantly dependent upon the quality of understanding and co-operation that exist between the agencies and the church.

While the local church has religious concerns that may stretch beyond the bounds of social welfare they do not function apart from welfare considerations and should not be used as excuses for escaping involvement in the practical aspects of the local welfare struggle. Moreover, while it is always the business of the church to provide inspired prophetic leadership, recognition must be given to the fact that leadership in the life of complex modern communities involves the special skills and obligations of dynamic co-operation through which alone effective leadership is evolved.

QUESTIONS FOR DISCUSSION

1. Should the church actively support public and private non-religious social agencies in its community? Why? If it should, in what ways?

2. What should the church do about a local social agency that is reported to use methods or engage in practices of which the church does not approve?

3. Should the church take an active part in local struggles to provide better incomes, better housing, better working conditions, better schools, better health and medical care, better family services, elimination of discrimination, and the like? Why, or why not? If it should, how should it proceed?

4. Is your church more interested in the problems and points of view of middle- and upper-class people of the community than it is in the problems and points of view of the people of the working class and lower income groups?

5. Do churches, in terms of their over-all influence, tend to divide or to integrate communities?

6. Are the churches and the social agencies working together effectively in your community? What common objectives do they appear to be consciously sharing?

FOLLOW-UP SUGGESTIONS

Individual

Inquire of your pastor as to what opportunities for social service are provided in your local church. Volunteer your support if there is a place where you can be helpful. Make constructive suggestions if the church's current arrangements seem inadequate.

Call the council of social agencies in your community and inquire about opportunities for voluntary workers. If there is no nearby council office, visit a local hospital, social agency, or welfare institution. Ask what the needs are and what you can do to be helpful.

Group

Confer with local social workers in order to identify the most acute welfare needs in the community. Consider the feasibility of forming a congregational or interchurch service organization to help the agencies and welfare forces meet the needs. Plan ways of calling the needs to the attention of all official bodies of local churches.

Appoint a committee to study and report on the effects of state and national legislation on local welfare services. Instruct the committee to give particular attention to the most recent pertinent bills that have been introduced in Congress or in the state legislature.

VI: Needs and Services in Special Areas of the Church's Concern

This chapter is devoted to a brief survey of the status of social welfare needs and services in a few of the more important areas with which the church should be especially concerned. While no exhaustive treatment is possible, it is hoped that these sketches of the dimensions of needs, problems, and services will stimulate serious-minded churchmen to further study of each item, in much greater depth and detail.

Though there has been no particular effort to establish a definitive list of the areas of social need which should command primary attention of the churches, the areas considered here may be compared with the seven identified by the National Council of Churches' 1957 Atlantic City Conference on Policy and Strategy in Social Welfare as those which should "have priority . . . on the heart of the churches today." Briefly summarized, these seven were: (1) housing, (2) racial and intergroup relations, (3) family life, (4) world order, (5) services for the aging, (6) educational opportunities, and (7) mental health.[1]

Family and Child Welfare

One of the broadest and most important areas of needs and services with which the church should be concerned is that having to do

---

[1] *Policy and Strategy* (*op. cit.*), pp. 32–33.

with the welfare of families and children. While only brief attention can be given here to a few of the major aspects of this complex area, it is obviously a topic that should be high on any priority list of the church's concerns.

Marriage Stability

A total of 610,000 divorces were granted in the United States in 1946. This all-time high amounted to almost one divorce for each three new marriages that year—one of the highest rates for any nation in history. By 1959 the number had been reduced to 393,000, which amounted to a rate of one divorce for approximately each four new marriages. Temporarily, at least, the situation seems to be fairly well stabilized at about this 1959 level, although the long-range trend since the Civil War has been one of an almost steady increase at an average rate of approximately 3 per cent a year.

An untold number of other marriages are marked by great tension and conflict.

Much of the difficulty seems to stem from: (1) the rapidly changing roles of both men and women in society as a whole; (2) the fact that the psychological-emotional factors involved in affectional response have become the almost exclusive basis for marriage; and (3) the carelessness and difficulty associated with mate selection in the stresses and strains of a highly mobile mass society.

An obvious need is for better educational guidance and preparation for marriage.

Adequate services of counseling and assistance for persons preparing for marriage, and for those whose marriages are in difficulty, are also greatly needed.

The legal grounds for divorce are quite varied and unrealistic, seldom recognizing the reasons for marriage failure that the behavioral sciences would identify as most important.

Child Welfare and Child Care

Children, the nation's most valuable resource, are still being left largely to the fate which their families are able or willing to provide for them. This despite the fact that many parents have had no training for their parental responsibilities, are unable to earn enough to meet the economic needs of their children adequately, or are too demoralized to care sufficiently about their children's welfare. Consequently, we have: (1) a rapidly increasing juvenile delinquency rate that brings about 2,000,000 juveniles to the attention of the police each year; (2) reports that one-half of the nation's children are being reared in one-sixth of the nation's families which receive only one-tenth of the nation's income,[2] and that 9,000,000 children live in families with annual incomes of $2,000 or less;[3] (3) great numbers of children ill-fed, ill-housed, ill-clothed, and with medical and dental needs inadequately provided for, to say nothing of their emotional distress because of neglect and improper treatment; (4) a very great proportion, sometimes estimated as high as 50 per cent, of the most intelligent youth never receiving a college education; and many other tragic reflections of family inadequacy and community neglect.

Public welfare grants, helpful as they are, in the program for Aid to Dependent Children are not really adequate, even when maintained at the maximum level for which federal funds are available to the states on a matching basis. The average per family in January, 1959, was $106.92. Yet many of the states fall far below the federal maximum. Alabama, for example, paid only $27.97 in a recent month, while Wisconsin paid $164.27. Since the grants are not available in cases where the mother works or where a father who is capable of working is in the home, serious problems are inevitably created by them. Children suffer deprivation in a marginal existence, mothers are tempted to turn to prostitution or other unwholesome practices to earn hidden income supplements, and fathers without work often are motivated to desert their families in order to make them eligible for relief grants.

Children whose families fail them so completely that they become public charges are in serious jeopardy. It is generally agreed that adoption or foster home placement is ordinarily best for them.

---

[2] From a leaflet issued by the Planned Parenthood Federation in 1954.
[3] Research Division, National Education Association, *Estimates of School Statistics, 1958–59* (Washington, D.C.: National Education Association, 1958), p. 27.

Legal technicalities, however, make many ineligible for adoptive placement, and those that are eligible are subject to many forms of exploitation due to very loose regulations covering adoption procedure. Many private arrangements are still possible, and both private and public agencies are involved in formal casework placements. Many times, too, the child falls victim to the strong competition between sectarian religious groups. While adoptive placement of very young children of the white race is usually relatively easy, placement of non-white children and of all older children is nearly always more difficult.

Foster home care for dependent children not eligible for adoption is usually hampered, also, by a number of factors. For one thing, the money for foster home support has to be provided locally and is seldom available in more than token amounts. On the other hand, even where money is available it is extremely difficult to get good homes to accept children for foster care.

The result is that great numbers of children are still being herded into an amazing variety of institutions operated under both private and public auspices. City, county, and state children's "homes," "shelters," and "schools" are operated with public funds. Almost every religious body has its quota of similar arrangements, as do many lodges, fraternities, and other non-sectarian private organizations. The institutional structures are often quite impressive and the titles attractively euphonious. The tragic fact is, however, that many of the children incarcerated in them ought not to be there, and that there is little effective standardization or control over the programs and services which the institutions offer.

Economic Security for the Family

In view of the fact that child-rearing is of such great importance to society as a whole and imposes such large burdens on the families that undertake it, and in consideration of the fact that families are the basic social units, upon the stability of which all social welfare depends, there have been a growing number of proposals to put better economic supports under the family. Some of these have suggested a system of family allowances from public funds, such as Canada has, based on the number of children in the family.

Others have favored differential pay for workers who are family heads, as is practiced in certain European countries. Some look to more liberal public welfare grants and social security benefits, or to higher minimum wage levels.

A guaranteed annual wage has been advocated by several segments of organized labor.

Increases in unemployment insurance compensation and extension of payments beyond the present twenty-six weeks limit have also been proposed.

Despite high national averages, it is disturbing that almost a third of the nation's families are living on submarginal incomes, and that a very high proportion of the nation's children are in these families.

Controversies and Criticisms

Many controversies and criticisms are associated with current provisions for family and child welfare. Only a few examples can be cited here, as follows:

It is argued by some persons that the Aid to Dependent Children grants of public welfare encourage illegitimacy by making it possible for a woman to obtain an economic reward for bearing a child out of wedlock. This, of course, seems an extremely dubious contention in view of the inadequacy of such welfare grants, and may be only a disguised way of expressing opposition to the principle of public welfare. In any case, it is doubtful that healthy moral values can be bought so cheaply, or that mothers and children should be permitted to starve simply because they are illegitimate.

It is also argued that residence requirements for public welfare eligibility impose undue hardship on highly mobile families, and that ineligibility of families where a potential wage-earner is present causes desertion and family break-up. Counter arguments cite the necessity of protecting public funds and guarding against undue dependency and demoralization.

Much controversy exists over whether or not planned parenthood should be encouraged and birth control information and materials should be made more generally available. In some quarters it is felt that public clinics should provide such services to help relieve parents of excessive burdens of childbearing and child-rearing. By and large, middle- and upper-class groups already have access to such materials and knowledge, but the poorer classes do not.

Controversy and criticism also focus on the fact that many institutions for children seem to have vested interest reasons for staying in operation and trying to hold on to their quota of children, thereby possibly preventing other, better arrangements from being worked out.

A final example is the contention that most of our public welfare arrangements for family and child welfare still stigmatize and demoralize the recipients, and should be replaced with a more comprehensively positive program designed to increase rights and security without imposing stigmas, discrimination, or demoralizing definitions.

Agencies and Services

Among the agencies which may be involved in family and child services in the local community, the following especially should be looked for: the public health service, the public welfare service, the family service agency, guidance clinics, marriage counseling services, social work services in the public schools, housing agencies, planning and renewal agencies, nurseries and day care centers for children, homes and institutions for children, organizations involved in group work with children and youth, and organizations promoting family life education or research. Courts and detention centers for children and youth, as well as lawyers and courts handling divorce and domestic relations problems, should also be considered.

The following are a few of the more important national agencies representing interest in family and child welfare as indicated:[4]

Giving the churches relevant guidance:

National Council of the Churches of Christ in the U.S.A.
Division of Christian Life and Work

---

[4] For the addresses of most of the agencies included in this chapter indebtedness is expressed to the excellent listing in Charles F. Kemp, *The Pastor and Community Resources,* published for the National Council of Churches by The Bethany Press, St. Louis, 1960.

Department of Social Welfare
475 Riverside Drive
New York 27, N.Y.
   (Also the Division of Christian Education, Department of
   Family Life)

Agencies of the federal government:

Children's Bureau
   (Also the Bureau of Public Assistance)
Social Security Administration
Department of Health, Education, and Welfare
Washington 25, D.C.

Federal Housing Administration
Housing and Home Finance Agency
811 Vermont Avenue, N.W.
Washington, D.C.

Voluntary organizations concerned with marriage and family counseling:

American Association of Marriage Counselors, Inc.
150 East 35th Street
New York 16, N.Y.

American Institute of Family Relations
5287 Sunset Blvd.
Los Angeles 27, Calif.

Planned Parenthood Federation of America, Inc.
501 Madison Avenue
New York 22, N.Y.

Voluntary organizations with a general interest in family services:

AFL-CIO Community Services Committee
9 East 40th Street
New York 15, N.Y.

American Public Welfare Association, Inc.
1313 East 60th Street
Chicago 37, Ill.

Family Service Association of America, Inc.
215 Fourth Avenue
New York 3, N.Y.

National Council on Family Relations, Inc.
1219 University Avenue, S.E.
Minneapolis 14, Minn.

Voluntary organizations with special interest in child care and services to children:

American Association of Psychiatric Clinics for Children
1790 Broadway
New York 19, N.Y.

American Humane Association, Inc.
Children's Division
896 Pennsylvania
Denver, Colo.

Big Brothers of America, Inc.
Suburban Station Building
Philadelphia 3, Pa.

Child Study Association of America, Inc.
132 East 74th Street
New York 21, N.Y.

Child Welfare League of America, Inc.
345 East 46th Street
New York 17, N.Y.

National Child Labor Committee, Inc.
419 Fourth Avenue
New York 16, N.Y.

National Congress of Parents and Teachers
700 North Rush Street
Chicago 11, Ill.

National Education Association of the U.S.A.
1201 16th Street, N.W.
Washington 6, D.C.

Unwed Mothers and Their Children

An estimated 201,700 children were born out of wedlock in the United States in 1957. This amounted to 47.4 per 1,000 of all live births, as compared with a ratio of 37.9 per 1,000 of all live births in 1940.

Many problems are represented in this fact—for the mothers, the children, and society.

The mothers, their parental families, their children, and the many families that are anxious to adopt their babies, need special attention.

From very harsh and judgmental treatment of both mother and child, society has been moving toward a much more tolerant and protective attitude of humaneness and compassion. Legislation is increasingly giving both mother and child improved legal status, requiring support from the father where he can be identified, seeking carefully to regulate adoption and legitimatization procedures, and making state agencies responsible for protecting welfare interests.

Conditions, however, are still far from ideal. Male parents still manage to escape assuming most of their legal responsibilities. Forced marriages that usually only complicate difficulties still occur. Shelter care and medical services for mothers and babies are still far from adequate. Casework services are insufficient to give the mother and her parents the guidance and counsel needed to enable them to make wise decisions with reference to the situation, especially as to what shall be done with the baby. The excessive demand on the part of prospective adoptive parents keeps a powerful black market in babies operating to force the mother into a hasty decision to release her baby for unsupervised adoption that may be very unwise both for her and the child.

Wise control of adoptive placement of the child is a particularly difficult matter. Though limited casework services and financial assistance are provided through the department of public welfare, and supervision of adoption is usually made its responsibility, the department is nearly always seriously restricted in making arrangements that remotely approach the ideal. Consequently, private agencies assist in important ways with shelter and medical care during and immediately following confinement and delivery, with more intensive casework, and with adoptions. Many communities, however, do not have the private services needed. Especially great deficiencies often exist in services to non-white mothers and children.

Private services are being provided by many local groups, and many sectarian religious organizations. The Florence Crittenton Homes, operated in most of the larger cities with Community Chest and other private support, are especially well known. Voluntary agencies interested on the national level are:

The Salvation Army
120–130 West 14th Street
New York 11, N.Y.

Florence Crittenton Home Association
608 South Dearborn Street
Chicago 5, Ill.

Maternity Center Association, Inc.
48 East 92nd Street
New York 28, N.Y.

Health and Medical Care

American society is experiencing a mounting crisis with respect to health and medical care. The crisis has to do not so much with inadequacy in the quality of our medical technology as with variations and inadequacies in the distribution of medical services. Physicians and hospitals are so unevenly distributed that many sections of the country, particularly the rural areas, are greatly disadvantaged in getting elementary needs met, while in some of the larger urban areas there is a relative abundance of these resources. Medical costs, too, have risen very rapidly and impose an extremely heavy burden upon those families and individuals whose incomes are limited. How to improve the distribution of services in keeping with the nation's resources and democratic ideals is a major question.

Of the approximately 15,500,000 men given physical examinations in connection with the selective service program during the era of World War II, more than 40 per cent were rejected as unfit for military service. [5]

---

[5] C. H. Greve, *Physical Examinations of Selective Service Registrants During Wartime*, Medical Statistics Bulletin No. 3 (Washington, D.C.: National Headquarters Selective Service System, 1944), p. 45; also Bulletin No. 4 (1946), p. 4.

As late as 1956 the United States still ranked eighth from the top among the major nations leading the world in terms of the lowest infant mortality rates. At the same time it was sixth from the top in terms of lowest maternal mortality rates, and eighth in terms of the longest life expectancy.[6]

A survey made in 1952–1953 indicated that approximately one out of every hundred American families each year spends 100 per cent or more of its total income on personal health services. This amounts to about 500,000 families. Almost the same number spend between 50 per cent and 100 per cent of their total incomes for such services. Contrasting with these 2 per cent of families so heavily burdened, were 5 per cent which had no expense outlay for health, and a total of 53 per cent of all the nation's families which spent under 5 per cent of the family income on health.[7]

Another study showed that while 58 per cent of the families paid only 18 per cent of the total cost of medical care for all families in a year, an unlucky 10 per cent of families struck hardest by illness paid almost 41 per cent of the total cost for all families.[8]

Though there were 1,428,943 hospital beds available to the nation in 1958, some states had more than twice as many per 1,000 population as did others. Moreover, 174,663 of the beds were classified by state planning agencies as "not acceptable" because of fire, health, and other hazards. Of 221,435 beds available in "Skilled Nursing Homes," 108,416 were "not acceptable" on the basis of similar hazards.[9]

Whereas in some states, until very recently at least, as high as 95 per cent of all births were occurring in hospitals, and virtually all others were being attended by a physician outside the hospital, in other states less than half were occurring in a hospital and almost

---

[6] Statistical Office of the United Nations, *Demographic Yearbook, 1957* (New York: United Nations, 1957), pp. 200–209, 362–433, 558–572.

[7] Odin W. Anderson, *National Family Survey of Medical Costs and Voluntary Health Insurance* (New York: Health Information Foundation, 1954), pp. 25, 46.

[8] Committee on the Costs of Medical Care, as reported in the *Social Work Year Book, 1949*, p. 303.

[9] U.S. Department of Health, Education and Welfare, *Summary of Health and Vital Statistics*, Public Health Publication No. 600.

a fourth were being attended by a midwife or by no trained person at all.[10]

About 17,000,000 Americans are suffering from mental or emotional disorders, and 300,000 are currently entering mental hospitals for the first time each year. At the present rate, one out of every ten of today's children will spend part of his life in a mental hospital. The approximately 750,000 patients now in mental hospitals constitute a total greater than all patients in all other hospitals combined at any given time. Nearly all mental hospitals are seriously overcrowded, however, have long waiting lists, and are terribly understaffed. At least 350,000 more beds are needed.

Such data are only samples of the many which can be found to attest to the fact that much needs to be done to protect the American people's health and to improve the quality of the medical care which they are receiving. Only the highest income groups, it appears, are presently able to benefit fully from our marvelous medical science. Low income groups suffer the most days of sickness and disability per capita but receive the least medical care.[11]

Bills providing for compulsory national health insurance, paid for through contributions assessed on earnings, have been introduced regularly in Congress since 1939. They have always been strongly and successfully opposed by the American Medical Association, commercial insurance companies, drug houses, and a few other groups. Arguments against the plan have been based on opposition to "socialized medicine."

Government, however, is already heavily involved in medical and health services that might well be labeled "socialized medicine" even though they are not so comprehensive as national health insurance would be. About 70 per cent of all hospital beds, for example, are situated in government hospitals.[12]

The inadequacy of government programs for health services and research, however, has given rise to a great many private founda-

---

[10] *Social Work Year Book, 1949,* p. 303.

[11] *Ibid.*

[12] Franz Goldmann, "Medical Care," *Social Work Year Book, 1951,* p. 303.

tions and organizations supported by voluntary contributions. The great plethora of such organizations, despite their individual value, has become something of a perplexing fund-raising problem for communities throughout the land.

Voluntary insurance plans, represented chiefly by Blue Cross and Blue Shield, have attempted to substitute for compulsory national health insurance, but offer only a very limited coverage for a limited portion of the total population at rates that have steadily climbed to discouragingly high levels. The plans are local, and reciprocity arrangements are not always satisfactory. Administrative efficiency in the operation of the plans varies widely. Rural areas are not covered so well as urban. Unemployed, retired, and indigent persons are usually not covered. Extended chronic illnesses are not provided for; neither are illnesses not requiring hospitalization. Numerous restrictions are placed on drugs, X-rays, and laboratory and other hospital services, and benefits are given on a cash indemnity rather than a guarantee-of-services basis. All in all, voluntary insurance plans still make it practically impossible for the individual citizen to purchase more than a shock-absorbing modicum of protection against bankruptcy in the risks of relatively short-term illnesses.

Among the many emphases to which the church may well direct its energies in the health and medical care field are the following: (1) The importance of the individual's recognizing that his body is the temple of his soul, and caring for it accordingly; (2) the importance of society's making maximum provisions to assure that every person who needs it will receive the best of medical care; (3) the necessity of planning and programming at the national level in order to obtain the equitable distribution of medical care that is needed; (4) the imperative that a balance be maintained between the democratic values of freedom, equality, justice, and responsibility, in connection with the provision of medical care, in view of the fact that "life, liberty, and the pursuit of happiness" are "unalienable rights"; (5) the responsibility of society to seek the elimination of all socially imposed health hazards; (6) the continuing need for relentless experimental efforts to discover better medical techniques and better agencies and services for distributing medical care.

At the local level the church should be in touch with and understand the policies of (1) the Medical Society, (2) the Mental Health Society, (3) the Dental Society, (4) the Public Health Service, (5) the Department of Public Welfare, (6) the Hospital Association, (7) the health insurance agencies, such as Blue Cross and Blue Shield, (8) the public school health programs, and (9) such voluntary health agencies as the Cancer Society, the Tuberculosis Association, the Heart Association, the National Foundation (formerly for Infantile Paralysis), and the like.

The Department of Health, Education and Welfare, Washington 25, D.C., is the main source for information concerning programs of the federal government. The Public Health Service, and the Social Security Administration's Bureau of Public Assistance carry most of the Department's responsibility for health and medical services.

The National Health Council, Inc., 1790 Broadway, New York 19, N.Y., serves as a co-ordinating body for the numerous voluntary health organizations.

The United Nations World Health Organization is the directing and co-ordinating authority on international health work. Its regional office for the Americas is Pan American Health Organization, 1501 New Hampshire Avenue, N.W., Washington 6, D.C. Its National Citizens Committee is located at 1790 Broadway, New York, N.Y.

A few other important addresses are:

American Medical Association
535 North Dearborn Street
Chicago 10, Ill.

American Public Health Association, Inc.
1790 Broadway
New York 19, N.Y.

National Association for Mental Health, Inc.
10 Columbus Circle
New York 19, N.Y.

National Council of Churches
Department of Social Welfare
475 Riverside Drive
New York 27, N.Y.

The Handicapped

Handicapped persons[13] between fourteen and sixty-five years of age in the United States number about 6,000,000, to say nothing of the many children under fourteen. Disease, accidents, and congenital conditions add an annual increment of between 250,000 and 500,000.

About half of these handicapped are in need of and could use services to enable them to work and become self-supporting. Only about 80,000 per year are actually receiving such services, however, despite a greatly expanded state-federal vocational rehabilitation program.

The other half, though they could not be fitted for productive labor, are in need of various kinds of care in their homes which they are unable to provide for themselves.

Most of the disabilities are caused by disease or accident. In fact, only about 5 per cent are considered to be the result of congenital defects. Moreover, because of heart trouble and other conditions associated with aging, the greatest amount of difficulty occurs at about the age of fifty years.

State agencies supported by both federal and state funds carry on a variety of vocational rehabilitation services without limitation as to the type of handicap. Cases are analyzed, medical services are provided where the individual cannot afford them, special education or training is given, tools are furnished, and jobs are found or the individual is set up in a business of his own.

This program of vocational rehabilitation is spelling the difference between demoralizing dependence and self-respecting independence for thousands of individuals. The program is still seri-

---

[13] Most of the information in this section was obtained through interviews with Mr. Joseph La Rocca and Mr. Robert Van Hyning of the Office of Vocational Rehabilitation, U.S. Dept. of Health, Education, and Welfare.

ously handicapped, however, by lack of sufficient funds, a great shortage of trained personnel, inadequate research in the development of new techniques and devices for overcoming handicaps, the reluctance of employers to provide jobs for handicapped persons, and a paucity of sheltered workshops where special work arrangements can be made for the more severely afflicted.

Numerous voluntary agencies have also arisen to help meet the needs of the handicapped. These agencies are training a large portion of the specialized personnel required, are carrying on most of the pioneering experimental work, and are providing for many extreme cases needing more personalized services than public agencies can ordinarily give.

One of the most meaningful recent developments has been the expansion of the disability benefits of the Social Security Act. Provision is now made for "freezing" or insuring the disabled person's retirement benefits, for beginning payment of his cash benefits as soon as he becomes fifty years of age, and for paying cash benefits to his dependent disabled child. These benefits are distinguished by the fact that they are "earned" rather than provided as a form of charity.

While many communities are providing special schools, classes, and other facilities for the mentally retarded, the blind, and those afflicted with cerebral palsy and other crippling conditions, in vast areas of the nation such provisions are very scant or entirely lacking.

The church should be carefully organized to identify and provide a continuous ministry to handicapped individuals and their families. Either the pastor, some other individual, or a committee, should maintain a file of information on organizations, agencies, and institutions which provide services for various kinds of disability problems. To be able to make a proper referral promptly is often a service of the greatest importance.

It is especially important for the church to be thoroughly familiar with the basic service resources which are available when disastrous disability strikes an individual or a family. Among these are the local Department of Public Welfare, the local Public Health

Service, the local Social Security office, the nearest Vocational Rehabilitation Agency office, and the local voluntary agencies that are relevant.

The church can encourage employment of the handicapped; it can assist in the establishment of rehabilitation workshops for the training of the handicapped; it can educate its constituency concerning the needs of the handicapped and the inadequacy of resources for meeting these needs; and it can help in providing needed resources. Most of all, however, the church can specialize in providing the spiritual intangibles which may sometimes be more important than material assistance. It can help the individual and his family to maintain courage, faith, and hope, and to keep up community contacts. Often it will have to help interpret the handicap as not being a punitive act of God. Always it will need to be standing by in a spirit of loving concern as helper, counselor, and friend.

The following are among the more important sources of information and assistance:

Department of Health, Education, and Welfare
Office of Vocational Rehabilitation
Washington 25, D.C.

American Association on Mental Deficiency, Inc.
Mansfield Depot, Conn.

American Foundation for the Blind, Inc.
15 West 16th Street
New York 11, N.Y.

American Rehabilitation Committee, Inc.
28 East 21st Street
New York 10, N.Y.

American Speech and Hearing Association, Inc.
1001 Connecticut Avenue
Washington, D.C.

Goodwill Industries of America, Inc.
1229 20th Street, N.W.
Washington, D.C.

National Association for Retarded Children, Inc.
99 University Place
New York 3, N.Y.

National Association of the Deaf, Inc.
2495 Shattuck Avenue
Berkeley 4, Calif.

National Society for Crippled Children and Adults, Inc.
2023 West Ogden Ave.
Chicago 12, Ill.

The Aged

Until very recently the population of the United States has been characterized by exceptional youthfulness.

The picture is now rapidly changing, however, toward a great weighting of the population in the older age brackets.[14] Whereas there were fewer than three million persons 65 years of age or older in the nation in 1900, there are now more than fifteen million, and by 1975 there will be about twenty million. Percentage-wise, these figures represent 4.1 per cent of the total population in 1900, 8.1 per cent in 1950, and 11 per cent of the estimated population for 1975. Every day produces a net gain of about 1,000.

Problems have greatly multiplied with the increase of the aged in the population. Some of the problems are due to old age itself, but many of them result from changing social conditions which impose handicapping definitions on old age.

Increasingly the nation's major health problems are those associated with the degenerative diseases characteristic of old age—cancer, heart trouble, and the like. Yet over half of the persons 65 years of age or over currently have no health insurance protection.

---

[14] Indebtedness is acknowledged to the following sources for information in this unit: Federal Council on Aging, *Aiding Older People,* May, 1958; Federal Council on Aging, *Federal Publications on Aging* (1958); *Aging,* No. 57, July, 1959, U.S. Dept. of Health, Education, and Welfare; Welfare Council of Metropolitan Chicago, *Community Services for Older People* (Chicago: Wilcox and Follett Co., 1952); Robert J. Havighurst and Ruth Albright, *Older People* (New York: Longmans, Green, and Co., 1953); and Fink, Wilson, and Conover, *op. cit.,* Ch. 13.

Providing economic security for the long years of unemployment following retirement—years of increasing ill-health and helplessness—becomes an ever more paramount concern. Pressures are rapidly building up, also, for more special provisions for housing, nursing care, and public and private casework and group work services specifically designed for the aged.

To the usual problems of older people, American society adds a number of extra burdens. American social attitudes put a premium on youth and interpret growing old as a tragedy. Toleration and pity, rather than respect and prestige, tend, therefore, to be the lot of the aged. Consequently, persons growing old usually experience loss of work, loss of status, feelings of rejection, and a general sense of uselessness or worthlessness. Many go to great and ridiculous extremes to try to preserve the appearance of youth, and many become psychologically disorganized as age forces itself upon them despite their resistance.

Organized interest in the problems of aging has been developing rapidly in recent years. The American Geriatric Society was formed in 1942 to study the diseases of old age. The Gerontological Society was organized in 1944, on a broader base of concern for all aspects of aging—biological, economic, psychological, and sociological. The First National Conference on Aging was held in 1950. The first White House Conference on Aging was held January 9–12, 1961, under the theme: "Aging with a Future—Every Citizen's Concern."

Among the important welfare considerations to be kept in view in connection with the problems of aging are the following:

1. Helping the older individual maintain a zestful, creative interest in life.

2. Providing maximum opportunity for continued usefulness.

3. Protecting integrity, independence, personal sovereignty, and self-respect.

4. Maintaining normal social contacts and experiences.

5. Supplying love, appreciation, and a sense of worth.

6. Making adequate provision for economic needs, physical care, and medical services.

Though many things are being done for the aged, provisions are as yet by no means adequate. Retirement is being arbitrarily forced upon people who are still vigorous and healthy. Many of the aged are bankrupt and humiliated by economic dependency which they were helpless to prevent and can do nothing to remedy. Many are clinging to shreds of pride in a marginal existence of bare subsistence. Many are lonely, conscious of being an unwanted burden on their families, and bored with lives of idleness and emptiness. Many are deposited helplessly in shabby, sub-standard nursing homes to wait for death. Many are being enticed or forced by circumstances into institutional depositories which encourage their return to infantilism and deprive them of the continued sovereignty and creative responsibility which could keep their lives meaningful. Many, seeking to maintain themselves in independence and self-respect, are paying a terrible price for their determination—a price reflected in physical discomforts, unmet medical needs, and psychic disturbance.

The church must help society make responsible provision for the needs of the aged. To do so it must maintain an experimental, creative attitude, for the situation is extremely dynamic, and ideal answers to many of the problems are by no means apparent.

All community agencies should be encouraged to expand their services for the aged, and should co-operate in community action aimed at providing a sufficiently broad range of services to meet the varied and special needs of older persons. The aim should be to help the aged individual get his needs met in ways that will permit him to maintain normal social relationships as long and as completely as possible. The place for institutional care should be carefully studied in terms of relatedness to an adequate system of non-institutional services.

In order to help define its social action objectives, the local church should take a close look at employment practices affecting older workers, pension and retirement plans, where the old people of the community live, what needs the public health service is providing for and what needs it is failing to meet, what the public welfare department is providing in the way of old age assistance, what the conditions are in local nursing homes, the admissions practices, programs and costs of the nearest institutions for the care of the aged, and other conditions which it may identify as being important to the welfare of older persons.

Because of the great need, many voluntary organizations are offering services designed for the aged. Some of these services are not very carefully planned, and often appear to be more an exploitation of need than an answer to it. For this reason, it is very important that the church be especially prudent in structuring the services which it provides, and that it work closely with community efforts to organize services on the most adequate and efficient basis possible.

In addition to the many voluntary organizations, government at almost every level is extensively involved in trying to provide for the needs of the aged. Because so many departments and agencies of the federal government were becoming engaged in such activities, the President, in April of 1956, established the Federal Council on Aging to co-ordinate their "policy development and planning and programming towards equitable employment opportunities, economic security, improved health, suitable living arrangements, and increased civil and social participation for older people." The Council also encourages "significant and co-operative programs and activities by State and local governments and the voluntary private organizations." It has formulated a statement of conviction that "in the efforts to serve older people, those measures should be favored which: protect the individual's freedom and responsibility; provide services through sources closest to him—family, employer, union, local voluntary and government organizations; and are consistent with the welfare of the whole population and the maintenance of a sound economy."

The address of the Federal Council on Aging is Washington 25, D.C. For 15 cents it will supply a bibliography of *Federal Publications on Aging,* which should be of much usefulness to individuals, groups, or communities interested in working in this field.

The principal specialized activities of the federal government on behalf of the aging are carried on in the Department of Health, Education, and Welfare, the Department of Labor, and the Federal

Housing Administration. The Department of Health, Education, and Welfare maintains a Special Staff on Aging. It publishes *Aging*, a monthly newsbulletin, subscription price $1 per year, which may be ordered from Superintendent of Documents, Government Printing Office, Washington 25, D.C. The Department of Labor carries on special activities in the Bureau of Employment Security. The Federal Housing Administration has a unit on Housing for the Elderly. (Address: 811 Vermont Avenue, N.W., Washington, D.C.)

Other important sources of information are:

Gerontological Society, Inc.
660 South Kingshighway Boulevard
St. Louis 10, Mo.

Senior Citizens of America
1129 Vermont Avenue, N.W.
Washington 5, D.C.

National Committee on the Aging of the N.S.W.A.
345 East 46th Street
New York 17, N.Y.

Urban Renewal and Housing[15]

While problems, needs, and services in urban renewal and housing are not identical, they are so closely related as to merit consideration together as an important area of the church's concern.

Urban Renewal

Today's broad and expanded urban renewal program may be traced back more than half a century to early philanthropic efforts to improve the housing of the poor. In 1937 the first United States Housing Act authorized the building of homes for families unable to purchase or rent on the private market. In 1953 an advisory committee on housing presented to the President of the United

---

[15] This section has been prepared by Professor Clifford Ham, the author's colleague in the Department of Sociology and Social Ethics at Wesley Theological Seminary. Professor Ham is developing a special emphasis at the seminary on the relationship of the church to problems of urban renewal.

States its conclusions, calling for an expanded outlook and a broader program of home-building and slum clearance in the cities of America. Said the committee:

> A piecemeal attack on slums simply will not work; occasional thrusts at slum pockets in one section of a city will only push slums to other sections unless an effective program exists for attacking the entire problem of urban decay. Programs for slum prevention, for rehabilitation of existing houses and neighborhoods and for demolition of worn-out structures and areas must advance along a broad unified front to accomplish the renewal of our towns and cities.[16]

Urban renewal generally includes: public housing; redevelopment or complete clearance; housing law enforcement; mortgage insurance; aid to relocated families and businesses; the requirement of a comprehensive, community-wide plan, as well as careful plans for the immediate renewal area; and citizen participation throughout. Urban renewal, one authority states, includes everything necessary to make the city a pleasant and desirable place in which to live, work, or play.[17]

Renewal may take the form of a "redevelopment project,"— which means the total clearing of a project area with replanning and rebuilding.

Renewal may also be a "rehabilitation project." Where the majority of buildings are still in adequate structural condition but have been allowed to deteriorate or to become overcrowded, the area can often be lifted to "minimum" standards by enforcement of housing codes along with civic and private expenditures.

A third type of renewal, appropriate in large areas in any community, is the "conservation project." This type of action requires existing housing in better than minimum condition, and involves efforts to prevent deteriorating and blighting influences.

Frequently, all three types of renewal action—redevelopment,

---

[16] The President's Advisory Committee on Government Housing Policies and Programs, *Recommendations on Government Housing Policies and Programs* (Washington, D.C.: U.S. Government Printing Office, 1953), p. 1.

[17] Paraphrased from Philadelphia Housing Association, *A Citizen's Guide to Housing and Urban Renewal in Philadelphia* (Philadelphia, April, 1959), p. 1.

rehabilitation, and conservation—are combined into one project.

In order to qualify for federal aid on a renewal project, a local government must show that the following provisions are present in its program:[18]

1. Housing and building codes to "assure minimum standards of health, sanitation, and safety."

2. A comprehensive plan for the development of the community, including a land-use plan, highways plan, community facilities plan, public improvements plan, and subdivision and zoning laws.

3. Neighborhood studies to determine the extent of blight.

4. An adequate administrative organization to carry out renewal programs.

5. An adequate financial program.

6. Housing available for relocated families and a program to aid those relocated.

7. Citizen participation.

These seven elements are called the "Fundamentals of a Workable Program."

The need for urban renewal is quite apparent. Deteriorated areas cost cities huge sums, yet bring in little tax revenue. More important, these areas may be breeding grounds for crime, delinquency, and other social and moral problems. They are always the cause of much personal distress. Moreover, it must be noted that it is not only residential areas that become "blighted." Industrial or commercial uses are frequently jumbled into a hodgepodge of inefficient, cramped, and costly quarters.

Large areas near the center of most cities either are slums or are failing to serve the city adequately and effectively.

To redevelop or rebuild in the city costs tremendous sums of money. Private investors, weighing the choice between tearing down and rebuilding in the central city or starting anew in the country, find city costs prohibitive. Land in the city is frequently divided into small lots that are too cramped and inadequate for modern building.

---

[18] Paraphrased from Housing and Home Finance Agency, *How Localities Can Develop a Workable Program for Urban Renewal* (Washington, D.C.: U.S. Government Printing Office, 1957), p. 12.

Renewal offers three incentives for builders. First, the government can use its powers of condemnation to assemble adequate sites. Second, with federal aid, the city can "write-down" the cost of city land to the equivalent of open land. Third, renewal allows for the complete replanning of the land use. Highways or streets can be provided, or eliminated, as necessary; open spaces can be left for light, air, or recreation; buildings can be planned with efficient relationships, adequate space, modern and safe construction.

Urban renewal requires citizen approval, and renewal programs should involve citizens at all levels and stages in the process. For example, there should be: a city-wide advisory committee on renewal; area-wide representative citizens' groups; neighborhood and block organizations; and special groups, such as a Ministers' Committee on Renewal, or an Interchurch Committee on Urban Renewal.

The focus of urban renewal should be upon people and their welfare. Renewal should mean better housing for all citizens. Slums should gradually be eliminated. Areas of good homes should be kept from becoming slums. Better housing should bring accompanying improvements in family and community life, health, safety, and the general welfare.

Urban renewal is encouraging re-examination of standards for city services. Schools are being viewed as perhaps the most crucial factor in neighborhoods. It is being recognized that police protection, sanitation services, street lighting, and traffic controls, must all be more than "minimum" if neighborhoods are to be upgraded.

But urban renewal programs, especially in the crowded inner-city areas, disturb large numbers of people. The uprooting of long-established families causes distress not only to those persons affected but also to all community, including all religious, institutions. In particular, renewal may bring special problems to the following: the aged or handicapped; persons dependent upon one building or a particular community for a livelihood; minorities, restricted in their search for new residences; small businessmen; large or unusual families; lower income families who seek low-rent dwellings.

Relocation of families is an essential element of renewal. Ade-

quate new or rental housing must be available to replace sub-
standard housing. Recognition must be given to the fact that some
families require more assistance than others.

Churches must become involved in the urban renewal process.
In order to do so, they must first become aware of renewal plans.
Awareness must then be accompanied by evaluation of all proposals in the light of human values. Where renewal or planning
agencies are truly desirous of citizen participation, the church and
church members, along with other citizens and organizations,
should seek a part in the formulation of plans. By their so doing,
an important contribution can be made.

Churches must be prepared to ask such questions as the following: Does renewal envision and work toward the type of community which churches also seek? Will churches and religious life
be encouraged in renewal areas? Are rights of minority groups protected? Are relocation and law enforcement procedures as humane
as possible? Are citizens represented in the planning and policy-
making processes? What individuals or groups will benefit from the
programs?

Other ways in which churches can participate are:

1. Each church must decide upon the role it will take in urban
renewal; it must define the goals it seeks, and outline its program
for the future.

2. Churches can educate members and constituents on renewal
plans, interpreting the role of government and the role of citizens
in renewal.

3. Church members can be motivated toward responsible Christian action.

4. Families disturbed by renewal activities can be counseled, directly aided, or referred to proper agencies.

5. Each church should maintain its own building in the best possible condition.

6. Churches should seek to maintain programs and services in
renewal areas, meeting needs wherever they exist.

7. Churches can aid in the relocation of families, even helping
to find suitable accommodations if this is necessary.

8. Through its members, ministers, and official delegates, the church should be involved in citizen organizations.

9. As churches participate in the formulation of plans, they can serve as "listening posts," relating the desires and needs of the citizens to the official agencies.

10. Each church can proclaim its willingness to accept all persons, regardless of race or background, into its fellowship and into the community. The dangers in segregated communities—the loss of human values—can be taught to members and constituents.

11. New families can be welcomed into the neighborhood, and where needed, they can be helped to acquire the new ways of life which the neighborhood expects of them.

12. Churches outside renewal areas can aid those involved in renewal, assisting with such matters as finances, leadership, and programs.

13. Churches can take direct "renewal" action, such as some have done—organizing communities for conservation, buying and rebuilding in slum areas, and encouraging community redevelopment efforts.

Housing

Miserable and disreputable housing conditions may do more than spread disease and crime and immorality. They may also suffocate the spirit by reducing the people who live there to the status of cattle. They may, indeed, make living an almost insufferable burden. They may also be an ugly sore, a blight on the community, which robs it of charm, which makes it a place from which men turn. The misery of housing may despoil a community as an open sewer may ruin a river.[19]

The church believes that the family is the foundation of human fellowship. Poor housing, which hampers wholesome family life, is as much a concern of the churches as those evil influences which destroy morals. Yet today, while the United States enjoys unprecedented wealth and prosperity, the supply of decent homes is in-

---

[19] From the opinion of Supreme Court Justice William O. Douglas in Berman V. Parker, 348 U.S. 26, 75 S. Ct. 98 (1954).

adequate, poorly distributed, often unavailable for minority groups, and largely inappropriate for conditions of modern living.

Of the approximately fifty million homes or dwelling units in the United States, one authority estimates that about fifteen million are sub-standard. In other words, almost one-third are dilapidated buildings, lack running water, have other serious deficiencies, or while being reasonably good structures are located in blocks where more than 50 per cent of the houses are sub-standard.[20]

Furthermore, the same authority estimates that population is increasing at such a rate that far more new housing is needed each year than is currently being produced.

New homes are constructed mainly for upper income families, and older housing is expected to "filter down" to middle and lower income families.

It is also a serious fact that new homes are constructed almost exclusively for white families. Non-white minority groups are seldom able either to purchase them or to choose a desirable area of residence. This automatically imposes racial segregation in churches, schools, and other community facilities. Segregation along lines of class and income is also fostered.

Public housing is an essential part of a national housing program. It serves that segment of the population which can neither purchase nor rent decent accommodations on the private market. Because of the stringent income restrictions placed upon occupants, and due to the fact that only a limited number of public housing units have been authorized and built, such housing has become a major source of homes for the most depressed minority groups. In consequence, such housing units are often racially, economically, and socially divorced from the rest of the community—a condition with many unwholesome overtones.

Housing needs of special groups, such as the aging, must be taken increasingly into consideration in the future. With keen awareness of the variety of special needs of individuals and fami-

---

20 William L. C. Wheaton, *American Housing Needs 1955–1970*, reprinted from *The Housing Yearbook 1954* (Washington, D.C.: National Housing Conference).

lies, churches should be in the forefront of a struggle for decent housing for all citizens.

Some churches are already at work in behalf of the right of all citizens to wider choice of homes—a choice not limited by race, national origin, or religion. Open-occupancy covenants signed by church members, and resolutions passed by church organizations, assert the Christian demand for social justice. An important example is the "Resolution on Non-Segregated Housing" adopted by the General Board of the National Council of Churches in 1959.

Churches may want to support a broadened public housing program to care for more families still unable to purchase or rent decent housing. They should also give attention to the fact that provisions governing public housing need amending to provide leeway for those tenants who increase their incomes and raise their standards of living. It should become a part of the burden of their concern that public housing be made more representative of the total community and become more fully integrated into the life of the community. Furthermore, churches should recognize the need for a more adequate ministry to all housing projects.

Federal legislation makes it possible for churches to participate in building homes for the aging. Similarly, churches can make use of the co-operative features of the Housing Act.

Churches should encourage more aid for the middle income families, who are caught in the squeeze between public housing on the one hand and high-priced, privately constructed dwellings on the other.

Ministers and laymen in many places serve on various official boards and agencies aiding in providing homes. Other committed Christian laymen work within community organizations for better housing. Both ministers and church members appear before zoning and planning boards, Housing Courts, or Health Departments, protesting violations of building, housing, or zoning laws, and seeking to improve housing in their communities.

Some special examples of churches involved in housing programs should be noted. In Philadelphia, the Quakers initiated a program of "self-help housing," helping to buy and renovate old homes for families willing to do part of the work. In Baltimore, Washington, and other cities the Church of the Brethren sponsors "pilot houses" to demonstrate and to aid rehabilitation work in urban renewal areas. "Neighbors, Inc.," a community organization in Washington, D.C., related to an integrated Methodist Church, seeks to maintain high community standards in housing for both the white and Negro residents. Ministers in Deerfield, Illinois, and elsewhere, are standing for "open-occupancy" in previously "closed" suburbs.

Resources for Information on Renewal and Housing

The best sources for information are local governmental agencies or private citizens' groups working in these fields. Examples are:

The local housing authority
The local department of city planning
The local renewal or redevelopment agency
The Council of Churches' Department of Planning or Research
Citizens' planning and housing organizations
Business groups, such as a Chamber of Commerce Committee on Renewal
Council of Social Agencies, or Community Chest
Professional groups: City Planners, Architects, Realtors, etc.
League of Women Voters, United Church Women, and similar groups

Nation-wide resources are also available through the following:

A.C.T.I.O.N., Inc. (American Council to Improve Our Neighborhoods), 2 West 46th Street, New York 36, N.Y.
American Institute of Planners, 2400 Sixteenth Street, N.W., Washington 9, D.C.
Department of Social Welfare (also Department of the Urban Church), National Council of Churches, 475 Riverside Drive, New York 27, N.Y. (Publishes *The City Church* magazine.)
Department of City Work, Division of National Missions, The Methodist Church, 1701 Arch Street, Philadelphia 3, Pa. (Similar departments in other denominations.)
Housing and Home Finance Agency, 1626 K Street, N.W., Washington 5, D.C.

National Housing Conference, 1025 Connecticut Ave., N.W., Washington 6, D.C.

National Association of Housing and Redevelopment Officials, 1313 East Sixtieth Street, Chicago 37, Ill. (Publishes the *Journal of Housing.*)

Sears, Roebuck and Company, 925 S. Homan Avenue, Chicago 7, Ill. (Has published *The A.B.C.'s of Urban Renewal* and *Citizens in Urban Renewal.* Single copies free upon request.)

Alcoholism

Though statistics concerning alcohol and alcoholism are highly unreliable, it appears that between 55 per cent and 65 per cent of the adult population of the United States drink alcoholic beverages. Of these some seventy million American drinkers, approximately five million are alcoholics; 750,000 are chronic alcoholics, and close to 15,000 are victims of alcoholic psychoses.

Consumption of alcoholic beverages for 1959 was approximately 222 million gallons, an increase of about 5 per cent over 1958. The alcoholic beverage industry spends considerably over $400 million annually for advertising.

Alcoholism has been identified as one of the nation's major public health problems, but it is more than this. Several million individuals and families are seriously affected by it. A very high per cent of automobile accidents and traffic deaths are caused by it. More than half of all arrests (57 per cent plus in 1,586 cities as reported by the F.B.I. for 1958) for law violations are related to alcohol. The cost of liquor-related crime and law enforcement is conservatively estimated to be at least three times as much as is collected in liquor taxes. And industry is suffering losses amounting to around $1 billion yearly from the use of alcohol by its employees.

Efforts at regulation and minimization have moved in the direction of restrictive legislation to control production, advertising, or distribution of alcoholic beverages, toward research and education to reduce the use of beverage alcohol, and toward increasing emphasis on therapeutic rehabilitation of the alcoholic and his family.

The most recent legislative efforts have been toward such matters as establishing a practical legal definition of drunkenness, restricting the advertising of alcoholic beverages, and prohibiting the sale of such beverages on commercial airlines.

Research and education are being extensively conducted, but on a piecemeal, unco-ordinated basis. Most of it is under the auspices of private groups and institutions, although the public schools are beginning to recognize the education need, and state and federal public health services are demonstrating a growing interest in both research and education.

The major current emphasis is on a humanitarian concern for the rehabilitation of the alcoholic. In the past, most alcoholics have been treated like criminals, and local governments are still spending more than $25 million a year on the maintenance of "drunk tanks" in city and county jails, which constitute the only type of institutional treatment that about 60 per cent of the nation's alcoholics still are receiving. Better arrangements are gradually being developed, however, for medical, psychiatric, and social casework treatment of alcoholism. The alcoholic is increasingly being looked upon as a sick person rather than as a criminal.

Since the beginning of the prohibition era the attention of most Protestant churches has been largely focused on restrictive legislation and the cultivation of supporting attitudes for such legislation and its effective implementation in law enforcement. While this emphasis, though somewhat abated, still continues, the churches are beginning to give much more attention to the victim of alcohol and to his need for humane, rehabilitative treatment. This, despite the importance of the broader social control efforts, represents a greatly needed re-focusing of the churches' vital concern.

By and large, the churches are using three somewhat different types of approach in their efforts to bring about the rehabilitation of alcoholics. These approaches have been designated (1) the evangelistic-authoritarian approach, (2) the psychologically oriented approach, and (3) the permissive, self-help approach.[21]

---

[21] Howard J. Clinebell, Jr., *Understanding and Counseling the Alcoholic* (Nashville: Abingdon Press, 1956).

Varying degrees of success are claimed for each of these approaches. Each seems to have values and limitations, and it is obvious that the church must find more effective ways of making use of the best features of all three.

Many local churches have, in addition to the usual social action temperance committee, a special committee or other type of group set up to identify and work with the most reliable therapy resources in the community. This organizational unit helps the pastor and staff contact and work with alcoholics and their families, does follow-up work with the alcoholic and his family after therapy has been administered or sobriety achieved, and keeps the congregation helpfully oriented. Though the old judgmental, authoritarian approaches can still be found, there is an ever greater likelihood that the local church will be sincerely trying to correlate its emphases with the most valid scientific insights and with the programs and purposes of the most helpful therapy resources in the community.

It is obvious that the church at the broadest levels of its influence must stay alert and must help keep society alert to the continuing need to approach the problem of alcoholism in terms of broad social planning and more effective methods of social control. It must help foster awareness that our whole social order needs to be reorganized in terms of its activity patterns, values, and philosophy so that demoralization such as alcoholism represents will not be the lot of so many individuals. The church must, also, increase its appreciation of the importance of collaboration with science, education, and government in the care and treatment of the demoralized, recognizing that it cannot alone solve the problems of alchoholism.

The church has a responsibility in the total community:

1. To correlate its functioning carefully with all other helping agencies and services which are equipped to assist in alcoholic rehabilitation.

2. To co-operate in seeking the establishment of more adequate community agencies and facilities for the prevention and treatment of alcoholism.

3. To help inspire co-operative community programs of a pioneering, experimental nature.

4. To help initiate and support legislation designed to provide more adequate publicly supported therapy services.

5. To help break down community indifference, harsh treatment practices, and negative attitudes toward the alcoholic.

6. To commit itself to strenuous educational and motivational efforts designed to help reduce the incidence of alcoholism.

7. To help correct the social conditions which contribute to alcoholism.

Most denominations maintain a board or other agency to promote the cause of temperance. Information, advice, printed materials, audio visual aids, and the like, are usually available from such sources. Special educational institutes and training programs are also conducted under these and interdenominational auspices.

The Yale Summer School of Alcohol Studies, 59 Hillhouse Avenue, New Haven, Conn., supplies special training opportunities for interested individuals, as well as highly reliable research data and other printed materials.

Information about the work of Alcoholics Anonymous or about the location of AA groups may be had by writing to AA Service Headquarters, Box 459, Grand Central Annex, New York 17, N.Y.

Information about self-help groups for families of alcoholics or for teen-agers with alcoholic parents may be obtained from Al-Anon Family Group Headquarters, P.O. Box 1475, Grand Central Annex, New York 17, N.Y.

Information on out-patient alcoholism clinics and on how to go about forming a local community committee on alcoholism may be secured from the National Council on Alcoholism, 2 East 103rd Street, New York 29, N.Y.

Helpful information can also be obtained from the local departments of public welfare, public health, mental health, and the vocational rehabilitation service. Where there are private clinics and social agencies working with alcoholics, they should be contacted. Since many industries are operating significant programs for the reduction of alcoholism among their employees, a survey of such practices in local industries may be rewarding.

Pornography

Modern media of mass communication lend themselves readily to the greedy purposes of individuals and groups who are willing to exploit morals for a monetary profit. It is not surprising, therefore, that the production and circulation of pornographic material is becoming a problem of alarming dimensions in American society.

Apart from the obscene and questionable which persistently appear in regular communication media, the traffic in specifically identifiable pornography is estimated to amount to as much as $1 billion per year.

Because postal regulations are fairly strict, much of the pornographic material is circulated through channels other than the regular mail service. Nevertheless, mail service is so extensively used for this purpose that the Post Office Department receives an average of 50,000 complaints annually from irate parents and other citizens concerning the circulation of such material. One of the most common complaints has to do with the receipt of unordered lewd material advertising the source of more of the same for a price. During the fiscal year 1958, Post Office Department investigations resulted in the arrest of 293 persons, which was 45 per cent above arrests for the previous year. All indications were that the number for 1959 would be even higher. Raids conducted in connection with the arrests netted from ten to seventeen tons of films, pictures, printed matter, and other materials, in each of several major cities.

These and many other facts were recently brought out in the report of a committee appointed by the House of Representatives of the United States Congress to look into postal operations. The committee statement went on to say:

> More than 1,200 magazines, including comics, are being regularly distributed among retailers who handle periodicals. Of these only 210 or so are magazines of healthy interest, acceptable to dis-

criminating readers. The rest are crime and love comics of low type
—fly-by-nights which usually fold after a few issues—and the
salacious girly magazines.[22]

Recommendations of the committee were:

1. That leaders in communities inaugurate organized crusades
against obscenity and watch newsstands and other distributors of
pictures and literature to prevent "careless dissemination" of
obscene material.

2. That national organizations encourage the formation of local
watch-dog panels to keep an eye out for the appearance of filth in
the literature and pictures that creep into materials invading their
neighborhoods.

3. That state governments adopt legislation to provide more effective and more uniform anti-obscenity statutes.

4. That state commissions be established to study the problems
created by the spread of pornography.

5. That local ordinances be adopted to strengthen the fight by
local groups in their crusades against receipt of "smut" materials by
youths as well as adults.

6. That various branches of the publications and movie industries
go in for self-policing of materials that overdramatize sex, as well as
cracking down on those segments that deliberately disseminate out-
right obscenity.

7. That the Post Office Department recommend necessary changes
in the law to prevent the mails from being abused by peddlers of
obscenity.[23]

The formation of a "Mayor's Committee for Good Literature
and Films" is taking place in many cities. A survey of the activities
of such committees show that they can:

A. ON THE LOCAL LEVEL

1. Determine what laws are available at the community, state,
and national levels.

---

[22] *A Report on Obscene Matter Sent Through the Mail* made to The
Committee on Postal Operations and Civil Service by the Subcommittee
on *Postal Operations,* Representative Kathryn E. Granahan, Chairman,
House of Representatives, September, 1959.

[23] As summarized in *Contact,* December 15, 1959.

2. Survey the community newsstands and entertainment media (assign persons in groups of two to work on the research), and study the publications and entertainment carefully to ascertain whether they do or do not violate community, state, or national laws.

3. Prepare and present a research report to the Committee.

4. Attempt to persuade newsdealers and entertainment managers to remove objectionable material voluntarily, pointing out the possibility of prosecution if they do not.

5. Present research briefs with findings to the proper local authorities.

6. Encourage local authorities to follow stricter enforcement procedures.

7. Rally public support for new and stricter legislation, enlisting press, radio, and television co-operation, including letters to the editor, special TV and newspaper reports, and editorials.

8. Determine which flagrant violations can best be faced with legal action, and take action in several communities at the same time if possible.

9. Publicize the healthy developments in the action against obscene materials and determine other essential laws necessary for the public welfare.

10. Urge newspapers to keep suggestive and obscene advertisements out of their movie pages.

11. Issue a list of co-operating dealers; providing a symbol for the dealers and managers to place in their newsstands and theaters.

12. Urge wholesome sex education in schools, churches and other youth-serving organizations.

13. Provide a speakers bureau for local groups; distribute films and printed materials.

14. Provide wholesome alternatives to pornography—educational, leisure time, and occupational, especially for youth; provide or recommend good reading and viewing materials and encourage the patronage of establishments and products upholding sound standards of decency and morality.

15. Remain vigilant.

B. AT THE STATE LEVEL

1. Determine laws available at state level.

2. Highlight legal precedents for effective action, and work with

bar association to obtain this action, including a legal definition of
pornography.

3. Have a lawyer draw up a brief covering the state situation on
pornography.

4. Consult competent lawyers on the effect Supreme Court decisions may have on the state laws.

5. Take steps for enactment of good laws—if the state does not
already have them—including laws prohibiting tie-in sales.

6. After local research, approach the Attorney General to get
an injunction sworn out prohibiting the sale and distribution of
objectionable material.

7. Stimulate stricter enforcement of good laws.

8. Publicize the campaign through state-wide media.

C. AT THE NATIONAL LEVEL

1. Urge congressmen and senators to support national legislation.

2. Write to the Postmaster General supporting and urging a continuing fight against pornography (address: Washington 25, D.C.).

3. Encourage such national organizations as PTA, Chamber of
Commerce, Service Clubs, etc., to join in the attack on the problem.

4. Join the Churchmen's Commission for Decent Publications.

5. Encourage the Council of State Governments to develop model
state legislation (address: 1313 East 60th Street, Chicago 37, Ill.).

6. Encourage publishers and the motion picture and television
industry to establish and follow codes of good conduct in dealing
with sex (two agencies to contact: National Association of Broad-
casters, 1771 N Street, N.W., Washington, D.C.; Motion Picture
Association of America, 1600 I Street, N.W., Washington, D.C.).

7. Encourage the U.S. House and Senate Post Office Committees
to maintain a continuing campaign to rid the mails of pornographic
materials.[24]

While the church must be careful to help safeguard the values
of freedom of speech and freedom of the press, and must not permit
itself to become stereotyped in the public mind as merely a moral-
izing negativist, it should be actively co-operating in all constructive
efforts to reduce the problem of pornography. It can do this through
the use of such means as: (1) taking part in the formation of a

---

[24] *Contact*, January 15, 1960.

"Mayor's Committee" and maintaining representation on it; (2) having its minister preach sermons related to the problem, especially sermons defining Christian attitudes toward sex; (3) participating in various types of social action programs aimed at producing better legislation, better law enforcement, or other improvement; (4) providing education in the church school on such matters as personality growth and Christian attitudes toward sex; (5) encouraging members to carry the fight against pornography into the community organizations to which they belong; (6) maintaining organized provision for giving its constituency guidance in determining where to place their patronage so as to uphold sound standards or morality and decency; and (7) strengthening the Christian fellowship, and deepening the moral commitments of church members.

In addition to denominational resources and information available through the offices of senators and congressmen, advice and assistance may be obtained from the following national organizations:

Citizens for Decent Literature
3901 Carew Tower
Cincinnati 2, Ohio

Churchmen's Commission for Decent Publications
601 Maryland Avenue, N.E.
Washington, D.C.

Juvenile Delinquency and Crime

The tragic facts and disturbing trends in connection with juvenile delinquency and crime in contemporary American society constitute a profound challenge to the church. Though the thrust of this challenge is felt at many points and in many ways, it is especially acute at the level of the church's concern for the worth of persons.

Juvenile Delinquency

Approximately two million children and youth under eighteen years of age come to the attention of the police in the United States each year for allegedly delinquent behavior. Of these about 600,000 are brought formally before juvenile courts.[25] The rate of juvenile delinquency seems to be increasing rather rapidly, as is suggested by the fact that while arrests of persons eighteen years of age and over have increased only 1 per cent each year for the past five years, arrests of persons under eighteen years of age have increased about 10 per cent per year. This is considerably more than the increase in the number of young people in the population.

While the causes of delinquency are quite varied and complex, they seem to be especially related to unstable conditions in family and community life resulting from rapid social change. A child or youth who is a delinquent is a symptom of something that is wrong in the structure of community relationships.

Children and youth who get in trouble often do not receive the kind of treatment that should be expected of an enlightened, wealthy, democratic society with great scientific skills and a widely proclaimed commitment to respect for the worth of the human individual. Though social and psychological techniques for therapy are known and available, punishment is still preferred for and practiced on young offenders in many quarters. Even where the punitive philosophy does not prevail, parsimoniousness prevents therapy programs from receiving sufficient financial support to enable them to function effectively.

There are two major patterns through which the handling of delinquent juveniles may proceed. The first consists of the un-official processes through which he and his family are given therapy and social casework assistance by one or more of the several agencies doing welfare work in the community. In this pattern the individual is never formally labeled a delinquent, but is looked upon as a person with problems. The purpose in working with him is to get at the root of his difficulty and help him become an adequate person who is able to function in an acceptable manner. The second pattern consists of the official processes through which the delinquent comes into the hands of the police, is sent to court and

---

[25] The number appearing before juvenile courts in 1957 was 603,000, a 16 per cent increase over the previous year. The number in 1958 was 700,000, an increase of 16.1 per cent, as compared with the youth population increase of 5.7 per cent.

labeled a delinquent, and is subjected to a court decision which usually either is intentionally punitive or fails to impress him with anything other than the expected punitive intent.

Juvenile courts have been established in most of the larger urban areas to try to minimize the damage done juveniles by the official treatment processes. They combine judicial procedures with social casework practice. Where they are adequately staffed and supported, and where they are linked to a network of specialized therapy institutions and other treatment resources, they can be very effective in salvaging young lives from crime and demoralization. Where they are not so equipped, they become only a deceptive front behind which bungling, frustration, and manipulative authoritarianism continue to punish and destroy the young. In the many places where there are no juvenile courts an enormous variety of procedures, most of them crude and damaging, prevails.

Churches should be concerned enough for children and youth to find out as much as possible about economic and social conditions in community life that may be affecting families and individual juveniles adversely, and to work for needed remedial measures. Especially should the church take interest in helping the community strengthen its resources for treating in a therapeutic and rehabilitative way the children and youth who have problems. Every church should know in clear detail what is happening to delinquents in its community. Are they being given rehabilitative social work treatment as much as possible? Are they being properly handled by police who have special training for the task? Are they being detained in a proper facility? Are they being processed through a juvenile court with sufficient personnel who are properly trained? Are too many being "dumped" in unspecialized institutions merely because the community wishes to be rid of them? Is probation failing to be truly rehabilitative because there are too few probation workers and too few enabling resources? Are the churches ministering effectively to the children and youth who bear the greatest "delinquency risk" or who already carry the labels and scars of official handling for delinquency?

Each church should familiarize itself with the workings of the police department, the local courts, the public schools, the guidance clinics, the casework social agencies, the recreational and other groupwork programs, and all other community resources that relate to juveniles. The manner in which each contributes therapeutically to the redemption of the delinquent should be carefully evaluated. Laws also need to be studied in terms of this perspective, and revised where necessary.

Crime

Of 2,340,004 persons arrested in the United States in 1958 in 1,586 cities of over 2,500 population, all but 284,215 were eighteen years of age or over. This throws light on the ratio of adult crime to juvenile delinquency, the percentages being 87.9 to 12.1. It also provides an index to the amount of crime per population unit, since the total population of these cities was 52,329,497.[26]

According to the Crime Index estimates of the Federal Bureau of Investigation, the over-all increase of crime in 1958 was 9.3 per cent above the 1957 level and five times as great as the population growth rate.[27] It is also conservatively estimated that approximately 6,000 major crimes are committed daily in the nation.[28]

Though no one knows the cost of crime, J. Edgar Hoover, Director of the FBI, has estimated it to be as high as $20 billion annually.

Increasing evidence of "hidden" and "white collar" crime makes it appear that not all types of offenders against the social welfare are equally liable to be apprehended. In fact, the weight of crime statistics falls heavily upon the poor, the uneducated, the youthful, and others disadvantaged in terms of power, influence, and status.

By and large, punishment is still considered to be the remedy for crime. From one end of the nation to the other, very little is being done that represents a serious effort to apply the best of scientific knowledge and social resources in a truly rehabilitative way to the treatment of offenders. Yet it has been demonstrated again and again that punishment cannot be counted on to reform,

---

[26] Federal Bureau of Investigation, *Uniform Crime Reports, 1958* (Washington, D.C.: Department of Justice, 1959), p. 94.

[27] *Ibid.*, pp. 1, 3.

[28] Robert G. Caldwell, *Criminology* (New York: The Ronald Press Company, 1956), pp. 91–92.

while it may almost certainly be counted upon to intensify anti-social attitudes and behavior.

One of the major dilemmas of our society is represented in the fact that our growing humanitarianism has robbed us of the capacity for the more overt forms of ruthless cruelty to offenders, while we still have psychological orientations to punishment which prevent our full commitment to the rehabilitative efforts that the logic of our humanitarianism requires. In many instances we have merely substituted more sophisticated, covert forms of psychological cruelty for the old, overt patterns of physical torture. In all probability the former are more damaging to the spiritual integrity of the individual.

Between two-thirds and three-fourths of our convicted offenders are sentenced to incarceration in some type of penal institution. At any given time there are, in state institutions, from 95 to 100 prisoners, and in federal institutions approximately 12 prisoners, for each 100,000 persons in the civilian population. Local jails and lock-ups contain a great number more, either convicted and serving short terms or awaiting disposition of their cases—a number estimated to total between 500,000 and 2,000,000 annually.[29]

Federal prisoners tend to receive the best treatment, and those in local jails the worst. Inadequate budgets, overcrowding, oppressively rigid discipline, insufficient trained personnel, and the like, are, except for a very few experimental situations, almost universally characteristic of the places of incarceration.

Yet 95 per cent of adult prisoners eventually return to the community—the great majority of them within two or three years.[30]

Probation, which substitutes the principle of casework supervision for punitive incarceration, is currently being used for a little more than one-fourth of all convicted offenders. It is far cheaper than imprisonment, and has the advantage of retaining the individual in regular social relationships while helping him to assume social responsibilities in a more acceptable manner. Most probation programs, however, are not given the support in terms of financial

---

[29] *Ibid.,* pp. 436, 490, 509.
[30] *Ibid.,* p. 436.

and therapy resources that would enable them to do as effectual corrective and rehabilitative work as they should.

It has often been pointed out that it makes little sense for us to keep throwing chronic offenders in jail for minor offenses without doing anything therapeutic to get at the root of their difficulty. Moreover, while fines are questionable because they fall more heavily on the poor than on the rich and can hardly be justified as a reformative influence, it is claimed that the English system of permitting installment payment of fines makes more sense than our requirement of cash or so many days in jail to "work it out." It may also make little sense for us to continue sending people to prison environments that are usually more limited and vicious than the environments that originally evoked their criminal responses, keeping them there only long enough to disrupt all their stabilizing social relationships, adding the stigma of a prison record to their overload of problems, and returning them to society with the expectation that they will be reformed.

Churches should pay close attention to the laws, the working of police forces and the courts, the probation program, and the institutions where offenders are held as prisoners. They should seek to make sure that at every point the inestimable worth of offenders as persons is kept clearly in view. They should carefully review the whole philosophy of punishment in terms of the imperatives of the Christian gospel.

It is very evident that social welfare and the logic of humanitarianism require that there be a more Christian application of scientific knowledge, social work skills, and all other social resources, in behalf of the human beings who are represented in our crime statistics.

Agencies and Resources

The following are important sources of information, advice, or other assistance on juvenile delinquency and crime:

The Federal Bureau of Investigation, United States Department of Justice, Washington 25, D.C., regularly issues *Uniform Crime Reports*.

The National Council on Crime and Delinquency, 1790 Broadway, New York 19, N.Y., offers a number of important services, among them being, upon invitation, partially subsidized studies of local juvenile courts and community programs of services to children and youth.

Information on probation and parole may also be obtained from Board of Parole, United States Department of Justice, Washington 25, D.C.

Other addresses that may be useful are:

American Bar Association
1155 East 60th Street
Chicago 37, Ill.

American Correctional Association, Inc.
135 East 15th Street
New York 3, N.Y.

National Legal Aid Association
American Bar Center
Chicago 37, Ill.

Bureau of Prisons
U.S. Department of Justice
Washington 25, D.C.

Summary and Conclusion

The reader is reminded that the purpose of this chapter has been to provide a brief summary of welfare needs and services in several areas that are of special interest to the church. The following areas have been surveyed: (1) Family and Child Welfare, (2) Unwed Mothers and Their Children, (3) Health and Medical Care, (4) The Handicapped, (5) The Aged, (6) Urban Renewal and Housing, (7) Alcoholism, (8) Pornography, and (9) Juvenile Delinquency and Crime.

Because of the limitations of space, many important areas have necessarily been omitted. Outstanding among these are: (1) racial and intergroup relations, (2) education, and (3) world order. These would have required much fuller treatment than could be given here, but should certainly command the church's serious attention.

What has been included should, despite its sketchiness, suggest the extent of need and opportunity for the church to become involved in the social process in the interest of human welfare. The summary should also provide insights and aids on how and where to begin when the church is ready to act.

QUESTIONS FOR DISCUSSION

1. What are the arguments for and against making public the names of individuals and families receiving assistance from the department of public welfare?

2. What further provisions should American society make for strengthening families and providing them with greater security?

3. Should public welfare grants be denied unwed mothers and their children? Why or why not?

4. What would be good and what would be bad about a program of compulsory national health insurance for the United States?

5. Why are the problems of the aged currently receiving so much attention in the United States?

6. In what practical ways can your church help with the problems and needs in the areas which have been discussed in this chapter?

FOLLOW-UP SUGGESTIONS

Individual

Pick the one of the problem areas discussed in this chapter about which you think you know the least. Resolve to learn everything you can about this area. Begin by studying the dimensions of the problem and the character of services related to it in your own city or county. After learning what the score is locally, move on to learn about the problem at the state and national levels. Use public library resources. Contact public and private social agencies for information. Request materials from your congressman, and from relevant divisions of government.

Group

Arrange a series of programs, discussions, or "public hearings," giving special emphasis to the needs and services in each of the areas of concern reviewed in this chapter (or to other areas that seem more important to the group). Feature the work of local agencies functioning in each area. Arrange exhibits; use appropriate audio-visuals; invite board and staff members of agencies; consider current legislative proposals.

VII: Social Welfare Policies
and Problems in Need
of the Church's Attention

Speaking at a recent Washington meeting of the American Public Welfare Association in observance of the twenty-fifth anniversary of the social security program in the United States, several social security experts made a number of predictions concerning developments that will probably take place in the next quarter of a century. These predictions are significant because they reveal present policies and point to continuing unmet needs in the social security program.

Expected soon, according to some of the speakers, were:

1. Expansion of the disability provisions of the old age and survivors' insurance part of social security beyond the present limitation of payments to disabled persons fifty years of age or older, to make provision for payments to all permanently disabled persons covered in the program, regardless of age.

2. The inclusion of medical and hospital care for the aged as a part of social security.

Other predictions concerning matters that may take a little more time, but that should take place in the next twenty-five years, were:

1. There will be at least a 50 per cent increase in social security pensions from the present maximum of $178 per month for a retired couple, and probably should be an arrangement developed for

automatically adjusting payments to changes in prices and living standards.

2. Medical and hospital care will be made available to all persons, regardless of ability to pay.

3. There will be an extension of unemployment benefits to provide higher rates and extend coverage beyond the present twenty-six weeks' limit.

4. The federal government will provide funds to move people from areas where there is not enough work to areas where workers are needed.

5. Social security benefits will be greatly increased, and rehabilitative re-training will be provided for persons temporarily as well as for those permanently disabled.

6. Every family not having a wage-earner will be aided by the government as a matter of right rather than as an object of charity.

7. Public assistance benefits will be made uniform throughout the United States.

8. Residence requirements as qualification for receiving public assistance will be eliminated.[1]

Regardless of the reliability of these predictions, to say that the church should maintain a deep interest in and concern for the unfinished business pertaining to social welfare which is implied in them is to put the matter altogether too mildly. Careful consideration of such items should be high on the agenda of any agency that has a concern for the welfare of persons and for the common good.

Much more, however, requires the church's attention in connection with welfare policies as they are and as they ought to be. Many other complex problems must not be overlooked. To list them all would be impossible, but some of those that seem to have special relevance to this discussion merit identification.

Policies

It should be noted that, in the predictions cited above, the following policies in current welfare practices were especially lifted up:

1. The policy of basing eligibility for public assistance on residence requirements.

---

[1] Based on a news report under the title "Cradle-to-Grave Security for All in Next 10 to 25 Years," *The Washington Post*, December 4, 1959.

2. The policy of permitting state and local administration of public assistance to produce great disparities and lack of uniformity throughout the nation.

3. The policy of restricting social security disability benefit payments to persons fifty years of age or over.

4. The policy of defining eligibility for public assistance in such a way that it manages, even in cases where there is no wage-earner in a family, to communicate the stigma of charity.

All of these are important. It certainly makes little sense, in this day of great mobility, when one family out of every five is changing residence every year, to withhold needed assistance from citizens of the nation simply because they have not been resident in a particular community for a sufficient length of time. A part of the problem is associated, of course, with the fact that public assistance is administered atomistically through local state and county units which have to protect themselves from being imposed upon by persons they do not know, especially in situations where one state makes better provisions than another by matching a larger proportion of available federal funds. There is need for greater equalization of benefits and for a much more broadly organized basis of identification for eligibility. It is obvious, too, that if a disabled person needs social security payments at fifty years of age, he may also need them at forty or thirty. Is he expected to starve or beg until he becomes fifty?

Establishing public assistance as a right rather than as an act óf charity is a more difficult matter, but the social security programs of unemployment insurance and old age and survivors insurance have been pointing the way. Families that are deprived of a wage earner surely have a right to survival assistance. It might also have been mentioned, however, that the present policy of refusing even the present grants of charity to those families in which there is an unemployed wage-earner is equally illogical in view of the fact that it invites the break-up of families through desertion where the wage-earner finds himself incapable of securing enough work to provide as well for his family as they could be provided for under public assistance. Furthermore, employment is not always easily available, and needs may be just as acute when the eligible worker is unemployed as if he were absent or not capable of working.

In informal as well as formal ways policy is also expressed in the following trends and practices:

1. The trend toward elimination of direct voluntary giving of money and services on the part of the individual.

Community Chests and United Givers' Funds strive to eliminate the risks of pure voluntarism in giving, as do taxation and the methods of collecting money for benevolences in many churches. All of these methods keep the giver far removed, too, from the recipient of his gifts. Moreover, the professional worker not only replaces the giver in the deliverance of his gifts but also takes his place in the rendering of personal services. While many values are being achieved in this trend, many liabilities are also inherent. The church, which has always stressed charitable giving of money and services on the part of every Christian, and which has always made much use of voluntary welfare workers, must strive to find new and better ways of involving individuals in service to one another. It must, furthermore, so interpret corporate needs and involvement as to help individuals achieve a sense of direct personal participation in the organized professional processes which their long-distance giving supports. At the same time, social work administrators are going to have to decide what place, if any, they will leave for voluntary workers in the field of organized services.

2. The trend toward extension of social work concerns, skills, and services into many additional facets of the organized life of society.

Social casework is being introduced into the public schools, into programs of medical care, into probation and rehabilitation services, and the like. Social group work is being made the core of recreational programs, delinquency prevention, and many educational efforts, as well as a means of marriage training, personal therapy, and improved economic production. Even the church is feeling the pressure to bring many of its traditional practices into line.

3. The trend toward insistence that responsibility for the administration of social welfare should rest primarily on states, coun-

ties, and cities, while at the same time the conviction increases that national standards and goals must be developed and that the federal government must provide funds for equalizing services on a basis of adequacy in all the states.[2]

How to keep the administration of social welfare local and community centered, and at the same time equitable and in line with national standards and goals, is one of the major problems for which creative solutions are urgently needed.

4. The trend toward increasing acceptance of public funds by church-related welfare agencies.

Church-related agencies of many kinds are increasingly seeking and receiving community funds, such as those raised by a community chest, and tax funds in the form of grants for new construction or of payments for services. This raises many questions and problems. Is it right for public money to be used for sectarian religious purposes? If the agencies are not to pursue sectarian religious objectives, what is their reason for existence? Could not public agencies do as good a job, or better, if the religious emphasis is to be bypassed? Will the use of public funds by church-related agencies impede or obstruct the development of needed public services? Will the acceptance of such funds cause dependency in the agencies and subject them to outside controls? Should public money be entrusted to sectarian agencies without controls and safeguards to insure its proper use in the interest of the general public?

The implications in terms of church-state relations are especially acute. In order to maintain as large a place as possible in the welfare field, Protestant churches seem to be accepting opportunities to use tax funds with an eagerness that suggests a possible careless disregard for their traditional convictions concerning separation of church and state. To say the least, there is great need for a careful study of this whole matter, so that the church may be sure of what it is doing, and so that its church-state emphases may rest on a foundation in practice that gives them the respectability of logical consistency.[3]

---

[2] Friedlander, *Introduction to Social Welfare,* p. 585.

[3] *Policy and Strategy* (*op. cit.*), pp. 42–44, contains a good summary-outline of this whole matter.

It should be added, too, that there seems to be a growing conviction among informed people that only public agencies should be entrusted with the administration of public money.[4] If this conviction continues to grow, the church may find involvement in the use of public funds a more and more serious embarrassment.

5. The trend toward careful planning of social services, rather than continuing to depend upon or permit their haphazard development.

With the increasing emphasis on careful planning at community, state, and national levels, there is less and less place for sporadic development of services based largely on factors of impulse and chance. This, of course, imposes obligations on the church not only to participate in co-operative planning but also to act responsibly and with great care in the matter of making decisions to establish new social services or to maintain or discontinue agencies and services it already has in operation.

6. The trend toward greater recognition that careful research and positive social action at the level of public policy formation are integral parts of social welfare efforts.

The church will do well to take cognizance of this growing concern for research and social action in the welfare field, and may find in these emphases some of its greatest opportunities for future usefulness to social welfare. In the meantime, if it is not careful, it can bring itself under judgment and condemnation for overlooking the need for a good research orientation in its welfare work and for being uncourageous or indifferent with respect to needed social action.

7. The trend toward elaboration of highly organized welfare services concerned primarily with providing economic and other material forms of security.

This trend, it has been strongly suggested, may only be adding to modern man's dilemma. Social action focuses on building larger and larger services at state and federal levels, gearing them principally to provision of economic security. At the same time, materialism and the impact of massive social organization on the spiritual integrity of man are, according to some experts, the basic social

---

[4] Friedlander, *Introduction to Social Welfare,* p. 585.

problems of this generation. Social work methods may be serving, therefore, as instruments for producing adjustment to a society sick with material acquisitiveness and over-organization. Neither organization, nor materialism, nor conformity, is to be condemned except as it becomes isolated from the broader spiritual perspectives in which these must necessarily be defined. It is of the greatest importance that social work be helped to maintain dynamic relevance to these perspectives.[5]

8. The trend toward standardization and uniformity of welfare services.

While this trend represents a needed corrective in the unorganized confusion of services resulting from the laissez faire processes of the past, it can become a hazardous liability. Standardized and uniform practices of error or of services that recognize only a segmental portion of total human need may produce disastrous consequences. Enough flexibility must be preserved for pioneering experimentation and for sufficient deviational differences in welfare practice to assure that there will always be a reliable yardstick for measuring the adequacy and effectiveness of all that is being done.

9. The trend toward substitution of therapy for punishment as a method of dealing with social delinquents.

The church should have a special interest in this trend because it reflects a growing concern for the integrity and worth of persons. Movement in this humanitarian direction is meeting many resistances, however, and is hampered by many practical difficulties and unresolved issues. It needs continuously consistent and enlightened encouragement, guidance, and stabilization.

10. The trend toward higher educational requirements for persons in professional welfare practice.

With this trend, too, the church should be sympathetic, since it represents the purpose to surround welfare practice with the highest possible safeguards for the protection of the persons being served. Higher requirements, however, make recruitment for the profession more difficult and impose additional hardships on individuals entering it. The church should help recruit and train persons

---

[5] See the discussion in Alfred J. Kahn (ed.), *Issues in American Social Work* (New York: Columbia University Press, 1959), pp. 212–213.

for the profession generally. Moreover, it should seek such adequacy of financial support for welfare services that salary inducements will provide better incentives for entering the profession.

11. The trend toward a policy of trying to protect the privacy of individuals who receive public welfare assistance and other services.

Back of this policy is the purpose to remove as much of the old punitive stigma as possible from the rendering of welfare services, and to protect the integrity and self-respect of the individual being served. At the same time, the public is due an accounting of its funds which are being used in welfare ministrations. The church can help interpret the situation so as not to minimize or violate the values in either of these areas of concern. It should adamantly resist any effort to make the receipt of welfare assistance an excuse for humiliating the recipient, even as it should resist those indiscriminate practices of welfare which demoralize rather than help individuals.

12. The trend toward better personnel practices in welfare administration.

Better pay, better working conditions, better retirement arrangements, better job security, and merit system advancement are receiving major attention in practically all branches of social work administration. It is a belated development which should receive the church's approval, since working conditions in the profession have been far from ideal. The church must recognize, however, that its own personnel practices must be brought into line. Its professional social workers are probably more overworked, underpaid, and insecure than most others. Christian motivations for service should not be made the excuse for unnecessary exploitation of conscientious workers.

In addition to the foregoing trends and practices, which reveal the manner in which policy is currently being expressed, it may be well to note a few of the directions in which there seems to be need for extensions of policy. The following will serve as suggestive examples:

1. The expansion of social policy and services to provide a fuller undergirding of security, assurance, and assistance to all members

of society—especially to the normal, who should be protected as much as possible from reasons for demoralization.

2. A re-structuring and re-definition of welfare services so as to remove all stigma and all excuses for stigma from those who receive them.

3. An integration of all branches of scientific knowledge, maximum economic potentials, and all valid religious insights and values in a comprehensive program of social services that ministers to the total needs of the whole man.

Problems

There are, of course, innumerable problems of which the church should be aware, and which it should do its utmost to help resolve in order that social welfare may make progressively better provision for human needs. The following, somewhat miscellaneous listing suggests their nature and extent:

1. How to build needed bureaucratic welfare structures and at the same time preserve democratic control.

2. How to encourage professionalization of welfare services without losing the values of voluntaryism.[6]

3. How to secure recognition of the need for a national system of recording and tabulating social statistics comparable to the system of collecting vital statistics.

4. How to overcome the difficulty of reconciling freedom and responsibility of the individual and his family with the national welfare and Christian concern for the worth of the person.

5. How to counteract negativisms in the folkways that persistently produce distorted evaluations of welfare services.

6. What to do about vested interests, particularly those in health services and services to children, which prevent society from making the more rational provisions needed for the common welfare.

7. How to put a more solid base of economic security under the

---

[6] The term "voluntaryism," suggested by the Rockefeller Foundation Study of Health and Welfare Programs, is deliberately used here, in the belief that it suggests the element of personal involvement more graphically than the word "voluntarism."

30 per cent of the nation's population who are still living on sub-marginal incomes.

8. How to deal with stubborn resistance to taxation for welfare purposes and to "bureaucratization" of welfare services on the part of people who prefer the satisfaction of more limited and direct giving to charity.

9. How to compensate for and what to do about the insufficiency, often the complete lack, of experimental work and research on a national scale with respect to most of the major problems.

10. What steps to take to correct the conditions reflected in the chronic shortage of trained personnel, and the relative ineffectiveness of recruitment efforts.

11. How to keep step with the changing nature of welfare needs due to dynamic processes which are constantly altering population characteristics, with respect to such matters as age composition, sex composition, marital status, place of residence, occupation, and the like.

12. What adjustments to make to the increasing introduction of automation in industry, especially with respect to worker displacement, planning for the use of increased leisure, and social action efforts aimed at maintaining equitable distribution of income.

13. How to define the responsibility of corporate society for the welfare of the individual in a complex economy, especially where the individual is capable of working but nevertheless arrives at a position of dependency.

14. What formula to use in determining how much security of what kind to provide.

15. How to overcome the negative implications in developments which permit people to buy their way rather than actually participate personally in deeds of charity.

16. What to do about the bureaucratic trend toward monopoly in welfare work, which increasingly threatens the elimination of small private agencies and groups.

17. How to keep social policy abreast of social work knowledge and skill.

18. How to conduct the search for security without losing the

values which motivate the search—without becoming so involved in programming, for instance, that persons are lost to sight, and without helping people so much or so crudely that they become pauperized and dependent.

19. How to balance the needs for better organization and co-ordination of services with adequate safeguards for the protection of the integrity of the individual—how to have effective social planning, for example, and still maintain freedom.

20. How to have adequate organizational integrity and retain, at the same time, the conditions required for the personal and social growth from which creativity must be drawn for continued maintenance of organizational integrity under conditions of rapid social change.

21. How to achieve adequate definition of community goals and keep them constantly reviewed and re-defined to fit changing conditions.

22. How to assure adequate support for welfare services through such indirect means of financing as taxation and united fund solicitations and still retain the degree of interest and understanding essential for the continued moral backing of agencies and programs.

23. How to evaluate and improve services without an adequate research program.

24. How to organize social work and the structure of society so as to minimize the deleterious effects of social organization on the individual.

25. How to achieve and maintain uniform standards where there are so many public and private agencies under so many auspices.

Summary and Conclusion

Examples have been cited, in this brief chapter, to indicate that many welfare policies and problems should receive the church's careful attention. Though the church should not expect to be able to resolve them alone, it should certainly not be uninformed concerning them and should understand that it has an important contribution to make toward their solution.

The church may go about giving its attention to these matters in many ways. It may begin by conducting research and making objective analyses in connection with its own welfare services from the local congregation to the denominational and interdenominational levels. It may encourage its representatives to participate continuously in exploratory conversations with social workers, legislators, and welfare administrators. It may carefully study legislative proposals, and the literature of welfare agencies and programs. It may establish procedures for systematic observation of the practices of social agencies and public welfare services. It may serve as a medium for distributing information and for stimulating creative discussion on problems and issues and on questions pertaining to policy and practice.

Most of all, the church must not become complacent or unduly critical and fail to recognize that social work and social welfare policy are in a peculiarly formative stage at the present moment in American history, and that they are in great need of all the spiritual undergirding and wise direction that the church is capable of giving. The church can unquestionably have a large part in helping to shape the welfare patterns of the future if it is willing to think and act in a frame of reference of sufficiently large dimensions. Nothing in the problems and policies which have been referred to suggests that the movements in social welfare are running counter to the fundamental concerns of the Christian gospel. Such difficulties as there are stem more from change, complexity, and inexperience than from lack of orientation to values which Christianity embraces. The church should rejoice that this is so, and instead of holding itself aloof from developments in the secular programs of social welfare, should identify with them as closely and as constructively as possible.

QUESTIONS FOR DISCUSSION

1. For what reasons should the church encourage or resist the trends toward professionalization and centralization of welfare services?

2. Why should the church accept or refuse public funds for the support of church-related welfare services?

3. How could provisions for welfare services be rearranged so as to remove all suggestions of stigma from persons who receive the benefits of the services?

4. What should be done about situations in which limited private services provided by the church or other sponsors seem to be doing just enough good to prevent more adequate public provisions from being made?

5. Is it more Christian to give money directly to people in need and to specific private charities of the giver's preference, or willingly to pay taxes sufficient to support a comprehensive program of public welfare services?

6. What provisions do you believe the United States should be making for social security and public welfare fifty years from now?

FOLLOW-UP SUGGESTIONS

Individual

Select for interviewing a number of persons in and outside your church. In as informal way as possible, ask these individuals how they feel about giving money to the Community Chest or United Givers' Fund as compared with how they feel about giving directly to needy persons or to particular preferred charity agencies. Analyze the impressions you gain from the sum of their replies. Do the responses of these individuals indicate attitudes or problems with which the church should be concerned?

Group

Appoint committees to make studies and bring in reports on the following topics:

1. Policies, problems, and trends in the operation of the local Community Chest or United Givers' Fund.

2. The amount of money the local church raises for benevolences, and how this money finally is distributed among what specific services.

3. Social action projects in which churches have participated in the local community during the past twelve months.

4. Current social action emphases of the denomination at the national and international levels.

VIII: The Church's Continuing Responsibilities in Social Welfare

It is imperative that the church maintain a vital sense of the infinite and the urgent in its relationship to social welfare in this formative age. Society's moral and organizational integrity may be presumed to be largely dependent upon an effective response to this imperative. The future effectiveness of the church as an agency of social influence may also be at stake.

Current developments are only the beginning of provisions American society must ultimately make for social welfare. The next hundred years will undoubtedly be both crucial and revolutionary. Expanding technology promises greater abundance, coupled with automation and increased leisure; the population "explosion" will necessitate further organization and interdependence; scientific knowledge and social work skills will be achieving added maturity; and there is every reason to assume that great growth will occur in the present trends toward scientifically minded social humanitarianism. As a matter of fact, the expanding pressure of social welfare needs and concerns is already so great that the next three or four decades may very well be pivotal for America's future.

In this situation, Protestant churches have almost immeasurable opportunities and responsibilities, despite trends that seem to have reduced their traditional welfare functions. In the main, these opportunities and responsibilities rest not only upon wise use of the continuing strength and influence of Protestantism in American life but also upon a forthright and unequivocal reclaiming of the central social welfare emphasis with which Protestantism began and for which it has always, when at its clearest-minded best, really stood.

This historic emphasis is on the responsibility of the total society to make responsible provision, primarily through agencies of government, for the security and welfare of all persons in community life. It is an emphasis on public responsibility exercised in sensitive responsiveness to the moral and ethical imperatives of the Christian gospel. Though it implies division of labor between church and state, it is predicated upon a mutuality of understanding and perspective which engenders close and continuous co-operation between the two.

There is nothing in the present situation which precludes the possibility of further rich and meaningful development in the direction of this emphasis, but there is much which, despite some very real obstacles, invites such development. In fact, there is every reason for Protestantism to rejoice over the prospect in this great nation that, at last in the long course of human events, material resources and ethical sensitivity make possible the dawning in society of the day for human welfare that the birth of ethical religion originally promised. Here, at last, free people with resources sufficient for the task, holding in their hands the power of government, are poised for whatever action the church may be able to inspire them to take.

Full appropriation of this opportunity will not be easy, however, for there are many countervaling influences. Government and all other responsible public agencies must be made to serve the purposes of maximum implementation of the good life for all men. But in order to render such services they must have the sympathetic counsel and complete support of moral and spiritual forces. Without such support, organized and unselfishly committed, government and public services will almost certainly be circumscribed by influences that focus on narrower interests than the common welfare.

The church must be operating on tiptoe, if it is to measure up to its opportunities in this respect. It must move boldly beyond protective consideration of vested sectarian interests in the welfare arrangements of a rapidly deteriorating status quo. The church must tear away the iron curtains of distinction between its own practical concerns for humanity and all those honest impulses for human welfare that are seeking expression in the so-called "secular" provisions of society which derive their support from public resources. It must courageously co-operate in every legitimate way to help the public process move toward the most value-filled welfare arrangements possible.

In short, the church must sincerely seek to articulate and implement, at all levels of vocational and political responsibility, the doctrinal conviction of the priesthood of all believers. Linked with this must be firm insistence on a continuing creative quest for social justice, and on the ethic of love as the only reliable foundation for an enduring society, in which justice and compassion may be adequately and freely expressed. What is more, the church must learn to define success in this broad phase of its task as taking precedence over consideration of its more narrowly institutional programs of welfare services.

One of the major purposes of this book has been to call Protestantism's attention to the great opportunities and continuing obligations of the church in the field of social welfare—opportunities and obligations which often appear to have become somewhat obscured in the confusion stirred up by the rapid movement of complex social change in the present era. Far from "losing out" in social welfare, the Protestant Church stands today in American society at the threshold of its greatest opportunity for social usefulness in behalf of needy humanity. Any irrelevance or rebuff which it experiences now or in the future must result from its choice or carelessness, rather than from necessity.

One may even venture to say that only Protestant Christianity stands in position to give the great secular programs of social welfare which are currently emerging the spiritual depth and perspective which they must have if they are to do the most good. It will be an irreparable loss to the whole society if Protestantism does not clearly see this opportunity, and hasten so to free itself from all impeding psychic and institutional entanglements as to be able to respond to the need in a manner in keeping with the loftiest insights of its great historical tradition and of its fundamental theological dynamic.

Among the church's continuing responsibilities in social welfare, as seen from the Protestant perspective, and in terms of the present urgency, the following are both significant and easily identified:

I. *The Responsibility to Clarify Its Relationship to Social Welfare*

The church must make up its mind not only as to the general direction of the welfare development it would like to see take place in society but also as to the specific role it would like to play in this development. Moreover, what it would like to do must be carefully geared to its capacities and resources. In particular, it must decide what value definition it will place upon public welfare services, how it will relate to these services, and to what extent it really wants "Protestant services." If it wants a broad program of social security and public welfare, it should say so unequivocally and should put the full force of its strength and influence back of public efforts to secure such a program. This should include a demonstrated willingness to help pioneer new programs which the public is not yet ready to provide, to bow out of the way when the public is prepared to assume responsibility in an area where it has been serving, and to continue working in a supportive and supplementary way in the same setting with the public services.

If there are services which only the church can or should provide, it should identify these services and put the full strength of its resources into them.

Opportunism, indecision, and petulance are marks of immaturity. The weighty decisions which society is having to make today concerning matters pertaining to the common welfare require the assistance of the church at the highest level of maturity of which it is capable.

One of the most encouraging and hopeful developments in Protestantism currently is in the increasing evidence that awareness of this responsibility to clarify its relationship to social welfare is coming ever more clearly into focus in the minds of leaders at denominational and interdenominational levels.

II. *The Responsibility to Clarify and Help Stabilize Religious Values*

Much confusion exists as to what constitutes religious values, particularly as these values relate to society and social relationships. Are there values that are specifically religious, and others that represent only humanistic concerns? If so, what is the distinction between them, and how, if at all, are they meaningfully related to one another? Does piety in the pursuit of values make them religious, or the absence of it make them non-religious? Are values more religious when they rest on the sanction of authoritarian tradition than when they are supported by rationalism and scientific humanism? Is there no Christian value in secularism?

It may be all right for the church to debate these matters, even quibble over them, if it wishes, in the academic discussions which take place in its theological schools, but great damage can be done when such discussions spill over into the decisional experiences of community life. There practical provision for meeting concrete human need may be dependent not so much on who wins the argument as upon the ability of the disputants to recognize their value-kinship and to work together in pursuit of their common concern for human welfare.

The church must seek to clarify Christian values in areas of social concern and, without compromising these values, must establish their identity with all that is spiritually valid in the social and behavioral sciences. It must stake Christ's claim on every honest impulse in humanism, rationalism, scientism, and secularism, and labor with these forces for the production of benefits for the meeting of the whole needs of all men.

In particular, the church must recognize that though the values in modern social work are essentially humanistic they are values embraced by Christian social concern, and make a significant contribution toward goals in line with the church's social and spiritual objectives. Indeed, in social work's use of its unique methodology the church may very well recognize one of its most valuable allies in the struggle to check the forces of barbarism in individuals and society. If social work merely helps men develop their capacities for constructive self-expression through participation in society, the church is aided thereby to contribute more largely to their welfare by leading them on in a search through the realm of values for that which is highest and best.[1]

The church has great responsibility for working closely with every agency and movement in society that seeks stabilization of values in the chaos of contemporary social change. Ultimately social welfare probably depends more on the fulfillment of this responsibility than upon any other condition that may be named.

III. *The Responsibility to Identify the Priorities of Concern which It Shares with Social Work*

Great need for a clearer and more emphatic affirmation of the overlapping concerns which the church shares with the profession of social work is apparent. Emphasis must be placed, not upon differences but upon the areas of overlap, for this is the way to needed improvement in understanding and co-operation. Frank recognition of the fact that, in the main, social work represents scientifically disciplined secular expression of many fundamental Christian value concerns would go a long way toward further strengthening relationships. It would at least clear the way for an honest mutual appraisal of the methods being used by the church and by social work in pursuit of their related objectives. As it is, defensiveness with respect to methodology, tied to rationalizations concerning presumed differences in objectives, often results in a breakdown in communication.

The best approach the church can make toward the correction of any faults it sees in social work is to confess its own sins in methodology and objectives at the point where its concerns co-incide with those of social work. Out of the sincerity of such a confession can arise an effective invitation to understanding and

---

[1] Most of these comments evoked by discussion in Kahn, *op. cit.*, pp. 204, 209, 212.

mutuality of effort in which both the church and social work can be better equipped to minister to men's needs.

It is especially important for the church to take cognizance of how far social work is moving beyond mere consideration of man's material welfare to involvement in efforts to strengthen his spiritual integrity. So strong is this tendency that social workers often sound like an echo of the voice of the church as they, while recognizing the importance of things material, deplore the problems which have followed in the wake of advances in material welfare.

IV. *The Responsibility to Join Forces with All Those Who Labor to Close the Gaps of Understanding between Current Interpretations of the Christian Religion and the Secular "Helping" Sciences*

While the major battles in the civil war between science and religion seem to have been fought, and an effective armistice seems to have been agreed upon, the antipathies and mistrust linger on with many serious consequences.

There can be no denying that the empire of science invaded and has absorbed much of the territory of the old-time guide and guardian of souls, but this does not mean that enmity and resentment should continue forever. Unmet needs called the scientific and secular revolution into existence. The problem now is one of how religion and science together can do the job of meeting the whole of human need that religion failed to do by itself and that both are incapable of while working separately. A new and vital rapprochement between religion and science is desperately needed. They must forget their differences of the past, be willing to learn from each other, and find effective ways of working together.

A good illustration of the manner in which the battle lines are still drawn may be found in the differences over the problem of guilt. Religion, which has traditionally regarded guilt as a personal problem of conscience curable by repentance and forgiveness, criticizes psychiatry and social work for failing to make conscience, moral values, and volitional responsibility an issue in treatment. Psychiatry and social work, on the other hand, accuse religion of being too authoritarian, too judgmental, and too inclined to unrealistic oversimplification with respect to the causes of guilt. Both positions obviously represent a degree of validity, but the more important fact is that neither emphasis is wholly valid without the other, and that inadequacy of approach to the predicament of the individual caught in the grip of guilt is inevitable so long as this gap of misunderstanding and difference continues to exist.[2]

"The churches," declared the 1957 National Conference on Policy and Strategy in Social Welfare sponsored by the National Council of Churches, "should initiate and encourage continuing conversations between the representatives of Christian theology and the philosophers in social work and the other helping professions."[3]

V. *The Responsibility for Social Education in Line with Christian Value Concerns*

One of the major responsibilities of the church is to help society understand what Christian values are and how they relate to the social process. Not only must God's judgment be proclaimed, and his redemptive mercy be revealed; there must also be careful and persistent labor to instruct in the ways of righteousness and to nurture the qualities of spirit that make for the kind of creative approach to social problems that is fundamentally and consciously Christian. Only by continuous and consecrated effort can there be developed and maintained the sensitivity of conscience and spirit in the general public that is capable of fostering and sustaining the will to make improvements in welfare services as needs and Christian concern require, and as resources make possible.

In a great nation such as this, almost plagued with abundance, it is a shame that there is still so much unmet physical and material need. In a society possessed of so many psychological and social skills it seems unthinkable that so many persons should be permitted to become demoralized and live out their lives in the shadows of despair without ever having access to the counseling and guidance services which might rescue them from such a plight. The church has something to say to society on these matters, and

---

[2] See discussion in John T. McNeill, *A History of the Cure of Souls* (New York: Harper & Brothers, 1951), p. 319.

[3] *Policy and Strategy* (*op. cit.*), p. 22.

it must say it emphatically, repeatedly, skillfully, and persuasively. It must instruct men in the social implications of brotherly love, and inspire them to desire obedience to Christ's command to love their neighbors as themselves.

As one spokesman has put it, the church must, while frankly recognizing its own sinful status, stand at the elbow of society and keep saying, "Not enough! Not enough!" with such sincerity and urgency that it comes to sound like the voice of God.[4]

Certainly one of the most practical means of Christian social education is through the witness of the church in its own social ministry. If it continuously and consistently expresses its faith through acts of love and service that encompass the well-being of the whole man and of the whole community of men, if it zealously espouses the cause of social justice, and if it produces members who are enthusiastic in their expression of Christian concern in political parties, economic affairs, and social movements, its impact on society cannot be other than effective. Men will give attention far more alertly to what the church is and does than they will to what it only says.

VI. *The Responsibility to Maintain Flexibility in Its Program of Social Services*

Adjustment to new responsibilities is essential in a rapidly changing society, and many of the programs which the church develops, and around which it is inclined to build traditions, may easily become outmoded. The repercussions on its influence are always tragic when the church persists in clinging to patterns of practice for which there is no longer support in the evolving consensus of the scientific and social work professions. Rigidity in such matters damages the church's influence. It also exposes the church to the risk of doing unnecessary injury to the persons whom it seeks, with all good intentions, to help.

It is just as important for the church to know when to liquidate a service that is outmoded or no longer needed as it is for it to be prepared to launch a new one when fresh need arises. To do so,

---

[4] Kenneth Scott Latourette, et al., *Church and Community* (Chicago: Willett, Clark & Company, 1938), Ch. 7.

however, requires greater alertness than the church has often shown to the hazards of letting individuals and agencies develop a vested interest in its program.

VII. *The Responsibility to Help Clarify the Values in Private Social Work Practice and to Continue Their Implementation*

With the increased development of public services which has accompanied government assumption of responsibility for public welfare, the place for the private agency has become increasingly vague and uncertain. Should such agencies simply cling to their vested interests in the status quo, struggling to maintain their functions against the rising tide of the public programs? Should they oppose the consolidation process of the public system and contend for private control of strategic functions within the public services framework? Should they maneuver for new footholds by exploiting opportunities to fill temporary vacuums created by the public program's somewhat haphazard development? Should they reconcile themselves to the necessity of constantly adjusting their functions so as to maintain a place on the periphery of public advance? Should they, even without a sense of a distinctive and appropriate role for themselves, insist, nevertheless, on sharing responsibilities with the public agencies for the basic pattern of welfare services?[5]

These are questions which the church must be willing to raise, and to which it must be sincerely committed to helping society find the wisest and best answers.

As one of the major sponsors of private agency services, the church has a great responsibility to help define the place for such services in the future of social welfare. Only as it conscientiously does so can it continue to participate in welfare work with a clear conscience. To implement the values in private practice will, however, be one of its increasingly significant privileges as the place for such practice becomes more clearly identified.

VIII. *The Responsibility to Help Preserve the Values in Voluntaryism*

---

[5] Questions based on discussion in Kahn, *op. cit.*, p. 225.

Closely related to the importance of helping evolve a new definition of the place for private agencies is the responsibility to help preserve the values of voluntaryism in social welfare work. This is a matter which should be close to the church's heart, since it long ago pioneered in the insistence that works of charity, rooted in love and including direct personal involvement, were the responsibility of every individual member of society.

While the church must not, of course, fail to recognize the evils which sprang from direct administration of charity, especially where pride and self-interest often displaced the spirit of genuine love, and must not minimize the necessity of organizing society so as to provide a broader base of assurance for welfare services than such direct administration would normally produce, it must not allow the values of voluntaryism to be lost entirely. Bureaucratically organized services, performed by professional workers, will no doubt be increasingly necessary, but there are obviously meanings in voluntary action which can never be achieved through such arrangements.

The church must help distinguish the goals for voluntary action. Without attempting to substitute the voluntary worker for the trained professional, or the direct gift of charity for the willing payment of taxes and generous contributions to community chest funds, it must nevertheless continue to find ways of involving the individual meaningfully in direct giving of services. He needs this, if he is to stand in a truly priestly relationship to God and his fellow man, and the testimony of human experience is that there is a quality of redemption which flows through warm, loving, human contact, freely given, for which there is no substitute in any other arrangement. The place for voluntaryism has become obscured, however, in the struggle to bring the values of scientific organization and specialization to social work. Fresh, creative effort is greatly needed to achieve a new orientation in which voluntaryism will have a distinct place in an integrated concept of social work. The church has a greater obligation than any other agency in society to help achieve this new orientation.

IX. *The Responsibility to Do Pioneering Work in the Development of Needed New Services*

If the church is to serve as the conscience of society, it must operate in advance of public opinion and must be the stimulator that provokes the public to take needed action. Since a vast bureaucratic program of welfare services cannot be expected to keep up with the advancing front of need in a dynamic society, there is likely always to be an important place for flexible and sensitive agencies such as the church is capable of providing. The responsibility of these agencies will be to probe beyond the lines of categoric public arrangements to reveal needs and techniques which public policy should consider embracing. Who can doubt that there will always be so many important new services which the church should be pioneering in providing, that there never need be a dissipation of its energy in competing with public services where they are ready to take over responsibility?

Society has a right to expect the church to support unpopular and difficult projects where neglected need exists. It should be encouraged, too, to look habitually and expectantly to the church for the most advanced and significant types of experimental and demonstration work. How better can the church continue to say, "Not enough! Not enough!"? How better can it demonstrate the quality of sensitivity and compassion which was revealed in Christ?

X. *The Responsibility to Demonstrate Good Stewardship in the Management of Its Social Resources and Obligations*

Because the church has an important commission to preach stewardship, it must be very careful to practice what it preaches. If a greedy, affluent, materialistic society is to be taught that it is under the judgment of God to make compassionate provision for all its members and to use all its resources to promote the maximum welfare of humanity, the church itself, as teacher, must take the lesson completely and convincingly to heart.

This should affect the manner in which the church structures priorities in its budget. What is spent on buildings, equipment, programs, and other symbols of prestige or means of self-satisfaction, should be carefully compared with what is unselfishly devoted to the promotion of human welfare beyond, as well as within, narrow congregational or sectarian boundaries.

The manner in which the church relates itself to people and areas representing extreme destitution and need should also be affected. The church that abandons the impoverished countryside or the demoralized transitional areas of the inner city in order to follow a select constituency to the more attractive residential suburbs is hardly demonstrating the quality of spirit that will inspire society to more compassionate provisions for all its unfortunate members. Neither, for that matter, is the church of wealth and prestige that functions in a community and insulates itself against genuinely empathetic contact with economic or racial groups of low prestige; or the church that happens to be fortunately situated in a neighborhood where there is little visible evidence of deprivation and degradation and that takes little responsible interest in other places where conditions are not so ideal. The church that truly practices Christian stewardship will make its ministry specifically relevant to the needs of all the people in its community, and it will be generously responsive to need that lies beyond its own immediate borders.

It may be well to note in this connection, that no major Protestant denomination has yet demonstrated either a capacity or a respectably serious intent to minister to the demoralized throngs that are crowding America's inner cities. Furthermore, not one has done a really admirable job of assimilating depressed minority racial groups, and hardly one can be found that is not gradually losing effective contact with the lower income, working classes. This is a terrible indictment that calls the church to repentance— an indictment that must be faced and dealt with sincerely if the church is to be qualified for its responsibilities in the realm of social welfare.

Finally, it is a part of the church's stewardship responsibility to use its prestige and its relatively universal organizational contacts to encourage and promote the development of comprehensive, integrated social services on a national, and ultimately, a world-wide, basis. The church is peculiarly qualified for this task, and can in this way make a major contribution toward eliminating many inequities in services and many isolated pockets of neglected need.

XI. *The Responsibility to Adhere to the Highest Standards in Its Own Social Work Practice*

So long as the church participates in social work it must either adhere meticulously to the highest standards of the profession or have excellent, rational, value-filled justifications for not doing so. As has been implied elsewhere in this discussion, for the church to do a careless, "sloppy" job in working with persons in need is to bring itself into disrepute.

Not only does this responsibility cover such matters as the use of properly trained personnel for professional tasks, commitment to the best administrative procedures, careful protection of the client's integrity, good arrangements with respect to pay, pensions, and work loads for staffs, and the like; it also involves respect for the values of research, a willingness to adapt procedures to conform to the new revelations of research, and a sharing of the responsibility to engage in research. The spirit of compassion in the church needs the solid grounding of research and scientific insight to safeguard it against the danger of being misspent.

XII. *The Responsibility to Keep Itself Socially Relevant*

Christianity is not a religion of escapism, and it is not a system of metaphysics. It is a practical religion that has much to say to the individual and to social groups about their everyday responsibilities to God and to one another. The church must both proclaim and exemplify this gospel. While it seeks to interpret the mysteries and immutabilities of life and the universe at the highest levels of men's questioning, it must not lose touch with the mundane realities that may be seen from its chancel windows. The church, no less than Jesus, must always be able to see and relate empathically to the blind, the leprous, the palsied, the sick, the socially outcast, the morally reprehensible, the demon-possessed, the bereaved, and the like. It must be capable of indignation at the blasphemy of greed and gain. It must be stirred to tears at the sight of the tragedy of cities. It must care enough about the grip of evil on the world to move beyond betrayals and the sweet fellowship of the upper room to the agony of its own Gethsemane and a bid for the victory that comes from God only by the way of the cross.

The church is in the world. It must stay in touch with the world. It is commissioned to deliver God's good news to the world.

In other words, the church must be THE CHURCH—that "genuine fellowship of believers and doers of God's will" that shares God's "being and beauty" in practical demonstration of His "outgoing love."[6]

XIII. *The Responsibility to Nurture a Keen Sensitivity to Needs*

The church cannot be socially relevant unless it is socially sensitive; and the kind of sensitivity that is necessary to support the quality of relevance needed in complex modern society has to be carefully cultivated.

"Social wounds," as one writer has put it, unlike the wounds of the man beside the Jericho road in Jesus' parable, "do not always bleed before our eyes." Instead, they are often "internal injuries, of the spirit as well as the body," and perception of them "becomes, like the rest of the modern task, more difficult."[7]

For this reason, the church has a great responsibility to keep dynamic, informed conversations constantly going on within its constituency on all matters of grave social import. This is especially true with reference to the so-called "controversial issues." The deeper and more complex a problem is, the greater is the likelihood that there will be controversy concerning it. Of all the agencies in society, the church should be the one most anxious for and most congenial to the careful exploration of controversy within a framework of concern for ultimate values.

One of the church's greatest and possibly one of its most neglected opportunities is represented in the current growth of interest in adult education. Through all educational and inspirational channels, however, it must be devoted to keeping people aware of the nature and dimensions of problems and of the bases of Christian concern with reference to them.

---

[6] Nels F. S. Ferre, *Christianity and Society* (New York: Harper & Brothers, 1950), pp. 5, 10.

[7] Clair M. Cook, *The Modern Samaritan* (Chicago: Board of Social and Economic Relations of the Methodist Church, 1956), p. 15.

XIV. *The Responsibility to Help Society Define Social Welfare Goals*

Involved in its efforts to function responsibly in society and to keep society sensitive to human needs and Christian values, is the church's added obligation to help clarify social welfare objectives.

This is not easy, for objectives, if they are to be meaningful, must be kept relevant to actualities in the social situation. Utopianisms must be transplanted into practicalities. The general must be made specific. The authoritative principle must be articulated in creative processes focused on intermediate goals that point toward the ultimate.

The truth of the matter is that modern American society is suffering from many value conflicts, and has made only halting progress toward defining the goals for the common welfare to which it is willing to commit itself. The crisis of confusion grows ever greater under the relentless impact of mounting social change. Despite commendable increases in humanitarianism, the problem of how to turn technology and organizational structure into happiness and meaningfulness becomes daily more acute.

The church seems to have a well-earned reputation for impracticality and authoritarian rigidity when it comes to defining social objectives. If it can, without abandoning basic principles, join the practical legislator and the creative social worker in trying to maintain an open mind "towards humanity's changing needs and the best methods or agencies for meeting them,"[8] the functional significance of its contribution can be greatly increased.

XV. *The Responsibility to Put the Full Weight of Its Influence Back of the Purpose to Insure Adequate Provision for Social Welfare*

Though the definition of specific intermediate goals requires continuous creative effort on the part of both society and the church, there is no need for the church to be hesitant about the general purpose to see that maximum provision is made for helping all

---

[8] James H. Tufts, *Education and Training for Social Work* (New York: Russell Sage Foundation, 1923), pp. 30–31, as quoted and discussed in Kahn, *op. cit.*, p. 38.

members of society get all their needs met. Since this is a purpose to which not all interests in secular society are committed, the church must keep its influence organized for the greatest possible effectiveness in this direction.

The logic of Protestant tradition requires that within the framework of American democracy, where church and state are separate, the state should carry major responsibility for the physical and material needs of all its citizens. The logic of democracy is that government is "a mechanism through which the people act together."[9] The logic of both Christianity and democracy is that government should be used by the people as a means of making maximum provision for the common welfare, not neglecting the needs of any and not allowing preventable injury to occur to any.

One of the finest contributions the church can make to the cause of social welfare in America is to let it be clearly and unequivocally known that it expects this affluent society to make completely adequate provision for the health and welfare of every one of its citizens.

To do this does not require that the church interfere with the prerogatives of the state, but it does require that the church fulfill its obligation to exercise its own prerogatives to the utmost to bring Christian precepts to bear upon the consciences of citizens and upon the policies and programs of government. Beyond carrying all the welfare load that it can appropriately manage, for example, the church can and must hold up to the light of public scrutiny and conscientious evaluation such facts as: that social security payments to a retired worker still average only $72.85 per month; that the average general public assistance allowance to a destitute family of three persons is only about $68,00; that out of a federal revenue budget totalling approximately $76 billion, less than $2 billion goes to the public assistance program; and that public expenditures from federal, state, and local sources for child welfare services specifically amount to considerably less than $200

---

[9] From "What the Community Expects of the Church in Health and Welfare," an address by John A. Perkins, U.S. Under-Secretary of Health, Education, and Welfare, given at the National Conference on Policy and Strategy in Social Welfare, 1957. (Mimeographed.)

million annually while the federal government alone spends $15 million for an Atlas missile and $3.5 billion annually on its missile program.

XVI. *The Responsibility to Co-operate Fully in Positive Preventive Efforts*

The purpose to insure adequate public provision for social welfare must be supplemented by forthright attack on identifiable conditions which contribute to the creation of social problems. Society must not only devote itself to mitigating the results of bad social conditions and to ministering to the victims; it must also sincerely labor at correcting the bad social conditions themselves.[10]

The church must help foster awareness that the social order needs much reorganization in terms of its activity patterns, values, and philosophy, so that neuroses, maladjustment, physical suffering, and demoralization will not be the lot of so many individuals. It must heartily embrace the conviction that full collaboration with science, social work, economics, education, and government, in prevention as well as in the care and treatment of unfortunate victimized individuals, is a matter of the greatest importance.

Because the church by itself cannot do the job of prevention, even as no other single agency can, it must help encourage concerted attacks on problems by all the institutions and agencies of society.

Many people in this great society are still experiencing desperate needs of numerous kinds. We have a long way yet to go if we are to bring together our vast resources of science, religion, economic affluence, and organizational genius for the most effective meeting of these needs at the level either of mitigation or of prevention. There must be careful research, extensive experimentation, broad social planning, and more effective methods of social control. The church and all other institutions and agencies must stay alert at this point and be determined to relate to one another in increasingly efficient ways.

It is, of course, axiomatic that it makes little sense to treat the

---

[10] Watson, *op. cit.*, p. 201.

victims of social illness without taking intelligent steps to get at the sources of infection.

Even so, the best prevention is positive rather than negative. As one of America's leading sociologists has said: "Real welfare is fair wages, shorter hours of labor, a larger voice in management, better conditions of working and living, more certainty of work, and more guarantees against old age dependency."[11] Whether or not this is an adequate cataloguing of welfare guarantees, it is a good reminder that preventive concern must give full recognition to the importance of such broad general items as a sound and prosperous economy, a stable government, and an integrated system of moral and spiritual values.

XVII. *The Responsibility to Be Organized for and Committed to Social Action*

It is obvious that the church cannot discharge many of the responsibilities which have been mentioned without being organized for and committed to social action.

Admittedly, this is a dimension of its responsibility which is hazardous for the church. Social action on its part is dangerous without the stabilizing influence of an adequate spiritual preparation and perspective. But not to take action or not to be prepared to act with the greatest possible effectiveness, may involve even greater risks. In a society governed by the weight of organized interests—which seems to be a necessary pattern for democracy at the mass level—the church must either exercise good stewardship of its position and influence, through taking effective action, or fail in its stewardship through organizational impotence.

The church is not a spiritualized abstraction of theological values and precepts; it is a concrete social institution. And as such it has real obligations and concrete relatedness in the social order of which it is a part. For it to fail to act responsibly as a unit of society, is for it to yield its strength by default to forces that move in other directions.

The real test of the American Protestant churches is increasingly

---

[11] Emory S. Bogardus, *Sociology* (3rd ed.; New York: The Macmillan Company, 1949), p. 423.

shaping up around the issue of whether or not they can develop enough muscle and enough unity of purpose to perform their civic duties in the society as a whole.

To say this is not, of course, to suggest that Protestant churches should be engaging in political and social action for the promotion of narrowly dogmatic or sectarian emphases. Such emphases are always not only inimical to the best interests of democracy but also a betrayal of the fundamental Protestant ethic. It is to say, however, that the churches must be prepared to help implement Christian values in the organized functioning of the social process.

"The churches," declared the 1957 Conference on Policy and Strategy in Social Welfare, "ought to seek to assist in the creation of the best possible type of society in which every person has an opportunity to develop to the fullest capacity of his God-given endowment and to make his maximum contribution to the whole community."[12] This means, the Conference went on to add, that they "should be vitally related to all aspects of social welfare," including "social justice"—even to the point of taking "corporate action, often political action for the improvement of . . . institutions and structures."[13]

So important is social action to the future of social work that it is rapidly becoming a recognized phase of the professional discipline of social work. Without it, social workers realize that they will be reduced from the stature of those who strive for the highest welfare to the status of technicians promoting adjustment to and patching up the victims of the status quo.

Social work is, however, still without the status it needs to be sufficiently influential in social action.[14] This is all the more reason why the church, blessed with an abundance of prestige, and social work, equipped with insights and skills, should seek a closer teamwork relationship. A full and harmonious commitment of their combined strength in concrete action for social welfare can have a telling effect.

XVIII. *The Responsibility to Inspire People to Social Service*

---

[12] *Policy and Strategy (op. cit.)*, p. 10.
[13] *Ibid.*, p. 19.
[14] See discussion in Kahn, *op. cit.*, p. 191.

What has been said about the importance of corporate social
action should not divert attention from the church's very great responsibility to inspire in individuals the highest motives of social
service. The Christian doctrines relating to vocation need clearer
and more emphatic enunciation. People throughout society need to
be challenged to devote their lives to the promotion of the common
welfare in the spirit of co-operative service. The narrowly selfish
individual pursuit of private gain or satisfaction must have its
shabbiness exposed under the bright light of the Christian social
imperative.

"Salvation," Walter Rauschenbusch once declared, "is the voluntary socializing of the soul."

Unless the church is able to inspire people to commit themselves
voluntarily to co-operation in the spirit of mutual helpfulness, some
form of totalitarianism will almost certainly arise to force them
into a crude facsimile of such co-operation. Highly organized
mutual aid is the only reasonable avenue of hope for the rapidly
growing masses of humanity under the conditions of an increasingly
complex technological way of life.

XIX. *The Responsibility to Help Recruit and Train Personnel
for Work in the Welfare Professions*

The church has a unique opportunity to help relieve the acute
shortage of trained workers in the social work and other welfare
professions. It has channels of communication and psychological
access to people in the realm of their motivations. And it should be
using these not only to inspire everyone to service that does "all
to the glory of God" in worthwhile vocations of every sort, but
also to lift up with particular emphasis the needs and opportunities in these very special "helping" professions.

"The churches should," to quote again from the National Conference on Policy and Strategy in Social Welfare, "recruit and
train workers for a social ministry. This includes both full-time
workers and volunteers, those who serve in professional and in
non-professional categories. Moreover, it should see that these
workers are provided with Christian understanding and motivation
and the best possible training and skill available for their areas of

service. No one of these is a substitute for any other. While the focus of their recruitment efforts may be for their own institutions and agencies, the churches should also assist in recruiting workers for other health and welfare agencies in the communities."[15]

XX. *The Responsibility to Clarify Its Philosophy of Church and State Relations, and to Bring Its Practices into Line with Such Clarification*

As the discussion in an earlier chapter indicated, this is one of the most pressing needs with which Protestantism is presently confronted. All Protestant efforts to relate meaningfully to the field of social welfare are affected by it. Continued procrastination at this point may well be an open invitation both to demoralization of Protestant churches in terms of their welfare functions and to bankruptcy of their influence in the decisional processes by which the future course of welfare developments in the nation will be set.

XXI. *The Responsibility to Maintain and Emphasize a World View*

Humanity is a single community, after all, and no agency in society should be more aware of this than the church. Because social welfare can never be adequately provided for on any basis of parochialism that excludes or limits the world view, the church must forever be lifting up the claims of humanity as a whole. This aspect of its mission looms ever larger as technology daily shrinks the world toward the dimensions of a small neighborhood.

The kinship bonds of interdependence grow stronger around the world; they must be made the bonds of genuine brotherhood. No nation or people or individual is adequate or secure as long as any languishes in untended need.

The church must be ardently committed to helping keep attention focused on world need and to seeking ways of expanding welfare concern into effective arrangements for meeting the needs of the whole human community. It is under the same obligation to foster a co-operative approach at this level as it is to participate in such an approach at the level of the local community.

---

[15] *Policy and Strategy* (*op. cit.*), pp. 10–11.

Summary and Conclusion

This concluding chapter in the discussion of the relationship of Protestant churches to social welfare has been devoted to a summary of the church's continuing responsibilities in the welfare field.

Twenty-one of the most significant and easily identified responsibilities have been briefly discussed. While many more could be added, it may be that they all boil down to the one all-inclusive responsibility of so proclaiming the good news in Christ that it results in the building of the Christian community.

It is authentic Christian love that the world needs—love that, in glad response to the grace of God, expresses itself in open, inclusive, compassionate, organized fellowship.

In the building of this fellowship the church must move beyond all institutional boundaries to identify with the whole of humanity and with the total social order. It must maintain the grace of humility and a willingness to learn and to co-operate, without losing the zeal of its divine commission. It must welcome as allies every person, every agency, and every skill honestly devoted to promoting the general welfare. It must help the fumbling processes of corporate society lay hold of a practical vision of the Kingdom of God.

The Protestant churches of America have an unprecedented opportunity to demonstrate how the power and grace of God can be permitted to work through free men and a free church to bring into the framework of a free society the concrete expressions of love that the human spirit is crying for throughout the world.

QUESTIONS FOR DISCUSSION

1. What will be the place of the church in welfare work of the future?

2. Should the church encourage expanded public programs of welfare services when such programs threaten elimination of agencies the church has been sponsoring?

3. What new patterns of relationship are needed between the church and the rapidly expanding programs of public welfare?

4. What are the church's most unique opportunities at the present time in the field of social work?

5. To what extent should the church become involved in efforts to recruit persons for the social work profession?

6. How can the church best preserve the values of voluntaryism and direct personal involvement in this age when massively organized charitable programs seem increasingly necessary?

FOLLOW-UP SUGGESTIONS

Individual

Visit a number of local social agencies or institutions and ask how you and your church can be most helpful to them in their work.

Write the National Association of Social Workers, Inc., 95 Madison Avenue, New York 16, N.Y., for information on needs and opportunities in the social work profession. Request information, also, from your denominational headquarters concerning the church's need for trained social workers. Using this information, counsel with young people you know about the opportunities for meaningful service in the field of social work.

Group

Plan and conduct a public forum on the future of the church in the welfare field. Use as leaders representatives of church-sponsored social agencies or institutions, as well as persons representing public agencies and government.

Make a survey of local opportunities and needs for the services of voluntary, untrained workers in connection with the operation of professional welfare services.

Sponsor a Christian Vocations Conference for youth, giving special emphasis to vocational opportunities in the field of social work and public welfare.

Begin a scholarship fund to help students in training to become professional social workers.

Index